A WORLD BANK COUNTRY STUDY

Slovak Republic —Joining the EU

A Development Policy Review

THE WORLD BANK
Washington, D.C.

ISBN: 0-8213-5510-4
eISBN: 0-8213-5511-2
ISSN: 0253-2123

Library of Congress Cataloging-in-Publication Data

Slovak Republic--joining the EU: a development policy review.
    p. cm. -- (World Bank country study)
  Includes bibliographical references.
  ISBN 0-8213-5510-4
  1. Slovakia--Economic conditions--1923- 2. Slovakia--Economic policy--1923- 3.
European Union--Slovakia. 4. Economic forecastng--Slovakia. I. World Bank. II. Series.

HC240.25.S56S56 2003
330.94373--dc21

                                           2003050062

CONTENTS

Acknowledgments ix

Abbreviations and Acronyms xi

Executive Summary xiii

Overview 1

    The Strategic Setting 1

    Challenges and Objectives 7

    Trade, Finance, and Enterprise Reform 7

    Fiscal Consolidation 14

    Labor Market Reform 25

    Governance 25

    Macroeconomic Outlook and Welfare Impact 28

    Conclusions 29

1. **Strategic Setting** 31

    Role of Structural Reforms 33

    Sources and Impact of Domestic Demand 34

    External Environment 40

    External Financing 41

    Strategic Challenges and Objectives 42

    Conclusions 47

2. **Structural Transformation** 49

    Enterprise Restructuring 50

    Financial Sector Reform 54

    Trade Integration 60

    Agriculture 74

    Energy 79

    Conclusions 82

3. **Regional Dimensions** 85

    Level and Sources of Regional Disparities 86

    Impact of EU Accession 92

    Outline of a Regional Development Strategy 93

    Conclusions 96

4. **Expenditure Strategies** 97

    Agriculture 100

    Transport 102

    Social Protection Programs 107

    Health 128

    Education 140

    Conclusions 150

5. **Governance** **153**

   Public Expenditure Management 154

   Consolidating Local and Regional Governments 160

   Judiciary Reform 165

   Conclusions 167

Annex **169**

Statistical Appendix **171**

LIST OF TABLES

Table 1:   Slovak Republic—Key Economic Indicators, 1995–2001 2

Table 2:   Demand and Output, 1995–2002 (percent) 3

Table 3:   Public Sector Deficit and Debt Outcomes—Two Scenarios, 2001–09
             (percent of GDP) 4

Table 4:   Labor Force Indicators in Selected Countries, 2001 (percent) 5

Table 5:   Factor Intensity of Slovak Trade with the EU, 1995–2000 (percent) 6

Table 6:   Perceived Quality of Governance in the CEECs, 1997/98–2000/01 8

Table 7:   Trends in Goods and Passenger Transport (ton-km or passenger-km billions) 9

Table 8:   Ratio of Residential to Industrial Prices for Energy, 1993–2001 12

Table 9:   Selected Indicators of Financial Soundness for the Banking Sector,
             1997–2001 (percent) 13

Table 10:   Bankruptcy and Settlements, 1993–2000 (number of firms) 14

Table 11:   Expenditure of Consolidated General Government (percent of GDP) 16

Table 1.1:   Key Economic Indicators, 1995–2001 32

Table 1.2:   Demand and Output, 1995–2002 (percent) 34

Table 1.3:   Sustainable Primary Balances (percent) 38

Table 1.4:   Selected Labor Market Indicators, 1994–2002 39

Table 1.5:   Unemployment Rates by Education Levels (percent) 40

Table 1.6:   Labor Force Indicators in Selected Countries, 2001 (percent) 41

Table 1.7:   Public Sector Deficit and Debt Outcomes—Two Scenarios, 2001–09
             (percentage of GDP) 44

Table 2.1:   Evolution of Enterprise of Profitability, 1998–2002 (percent of GDP) 50

Table 2.2:   Enterprise Ownership Structure (percent) 51

Table 2.3:   Average Profit Margins by Ownership type, 1996–2001 (percent) 52

Table 2.4:   Evolution of Profit Margins by Sector, 1998–2001 (percent) 53

Table 2.5:   Average Firm Size by Sector and by Form of Ownership, 1996–2001 54

Table 2.6:   Financial Soundness Indicators for the Banking Sector, 1997–2001 (percent) ...56

Table 2.7:   Bankruptcy and Settlements (number of firms) 59

Table 2.8:   Evolution of Exports and Imports Volumes, 1993–2000 (percent change) 61

Table 2.9:   Geographic Distribution of Slovak Foreign Trade, 1994–2000 61

Table 2.10: Share of "Free Trade" Partners in Foreign Trade 62

Table 2.11:   Foreign Direct Investment, 1998–2002 63

Table 2.12:   Share of Foreign Investment Enterprise in Foreign Trade, 2000–01 63

Table 2.13:   EU Imports from CEEC-10, 1993–2000 (millions of US dollars) 64

Table 2.14:   Share of Slovak Exports in Total EU Imports, 1993–2000 64

Table 2.15:   Export Specialization Indices of Selected Product Categories, 1994–2000 65

Table 2.16:   "Sunrise" Sectors in EU-Destined Slovak Exports, 2000 65

Table 2.17:   Participation in EU-Based Network Trade (millions of US Dollars) 66

Table 2.18:   Specialization and Factor Intensity of Slovak Trade with the EU, 1995–2000 . . .69

Table 2.19:   Share of the Slovak and Czech Republics in their Respective Trade,
              1993–2000 (percent) 70

Table 2.20:   Factor Intensity of Slovak Trade with the Czech Republic, 1995–2000 71

Table 2.21:   End-User Prices for Electricity and Natural Gas 81

Table 2.22:   Ratio of Household Prices to Industrial Prices for Energy 82

Table 3.1:   Regional GDP per Capita at PPS, 1996–99 (percent) 86

Table 3.2:   Regional Differences in Productivity and Employment .86

Table 3.3:   Regional Distribution of Small and Medium Enterprises, 2001 (percent) 88

Table 3.4:   Gross Fixed Capital Formation by Region, 1996–99 (percent of GDP) 88

Table 3.5:   Foreign Direct Investment by Region, 1999–2001 89

Table 3.6:   Share of University Graduates among the Unemployed and in the Economically
              Active Population, 2001 (percent) 89

Table 3.7:   Relative Level of GDP Per Capita in Selected Capital Regions, 1999
              (percent of national average) 90

Table 3.8:   Gross and Net Money Income per Person Month, 2000
              (percent of national average) 91

Table 3.9:   Regional Differences in Productivity and Wages (percent of national average) . . .91

Table 3.10:   Regional Unemployment Rate, 1997–2001 92

Table 3.11:   Potential Utilization from Cohesion and Structural Funds, 2004–06 96

Table 4.1:   Expenditures of the Consolidated General Government (percent of GDP) 98

Table 4.2:   Structure of Budget Expenditure on Agriculture and Food, 2000–01 102

Table 4.3:   Trends in Goods and Passenger Transport
              (billions of ton-km or passenger-km) 103

Table 4.4:   Transport Basic Indicators, 1996–2000 103

Table 4.5:   Central Government Funds to and Expenditures in the
              Transport Sector, 2001 (millions of US Dollars) 104

Table 4.6:   Public Expenditure on Social Protection Programs, 1995–2001 108

Table 4.7:   State Social Benefits (SKK billions) 122

Table 4.8:   Social Assistance and Social Care (SKK Billions) 123

Table 4.9:   School Enrollment Trends, 1990–2000 (number of students) 142

Table 5.1:   Perceived Quality of Governance in the CEECs, 1997/98–2000/01 154

Table 5.2:   Expenditures to be Transferred to Regional and Local Governments
              (1999 execution & 2000 budget, SKK thousands) 161

Table 5.3:   Regional Offices Expenditures (SKK billions) 162
Table 5.4:   Budgets of Municipalities, 1999–2000 (SKK millions) 162

Annex 1
Table 1:   Key Demographic Assumptions for Pension Projections 169

Statistical Appendix
Table 1:   Slovak Republic—Gross Domestic Expenditure and Product 170
Table 1A: Slovak Republic—Gross Domestic Expenditure and Product (current prices) ..171
Table 2:   Slovak Republic—Annual growth rates of National Income and Product
              at constant prices (percentages) 172
Table 2A: Slovak Republic—Gross Domestic Product by Expenditure,
              National Income and Savings 173
Table 3:   Slovak Republic—Prices 174
Table 4:   Slovak Republic—Consolidated Public Sector Finance 175
Table 5:   Slovak Republic—Monetary Survey and Interest Rates 176
Table 6:   Slovak Republic—Balance of Payments 177
Table 7:   Slovak Republic—Trade 178
Table 8:   Slovak Republic—External Debt and Debt Service 179
Table 9:   Slovak Republic—Financial Sector Indicators 179
Table 10:   Slovak Republic—Vulnerability Indicators 180
Table 11:   Slovak Republic—Investment Climate 181
Table 12:   Slovak Republic—Millennium Development Goals Indicators 182

LIST OF FIGURES

Figure 1:   Education Spending by Level 18
Figure 2:   Public Spending on Health 20
Figure 3:   Balance of PAYGO System, Three Mono-Pillar Reform Scenarios 22
Figure 1.1:   Real Effective Exchange Rate, 1995–2002 35
Figure 2.1:   Enterprise Past Due Receivables 52
Figure 2.2:   Number of Profitable/Loss-Making Firms by Sector, 1998–2001
              (percent change) 53
Figure 2.3:   GDP and Agriculture Value Added 75
Figure 2.4:   Terms of Trade of the Agriculture and Food Sector 75
Figure 2.5:   Level of Agricultural Support 77
Figure 2.6:   Relative Productivity of Individual and Corporate Farms 77
Figure 3.1:   Regional Value Added and Employment by Sector, 1999 87
Figure 4.1:   Structure of Budget Support to Agriculture 2001 100
Figure 4.2:   Balance of PAYGO System, No Reform, Alternative Demographic Scenarios ..111
Figure 4.3a: Balance of PAYGO System, May-2002 Reform Scenario 112
Figure 4.3b: Old Formula and New Formula Pensions 112
Figure 4.4:   Balance of PAYGO System, Three Mono-Pillar Reform Scenarios 113

Figure 4.5a: Average Entry Replacement Rates, "Current" Transition Plan 115

Figure 4.5b: Balance of PAYGO System, "Current" Transition Plan 116

Figure 4.6a: Balance of PAYGO System, Three Transition Scenarios 117

Figure 4.6b: Average Entry Replacement Rates, Three Transition Scenarios 117

Figure 4.7:   Total Health Expenditure 130

Figure 4.8:   Public Spending on Health 130

Figure 4.9:   Total Health Spending by Source 131

Figure 4.10:   HIC Spending and Revenues 131

Figure 4.11:   Inpatient Costs as % of Total HIC Spending 133

Figure 4.12:   Trends in Infant Mortality Rates 137

Figure 4.13:   Public Spending on Education 142

Figure 4.14:   Shares in State Education Budget by level 143

LIST OF BOXES

Box 1.1:   Fiscal Sustainability 38

Box 1.2:   Current Account Deficits Consistent with Stable Net Debt to GDP Ratios 43

Box 2.1:   Overview of the Financial System 57

Box 2.2:   Integration into International Production Networks .68

Box 2.3:   Tax Incentives for Investment 73

Box 4.1:   Current Public Pension System 110

Box 4.2:   Main Features of the May 2002 Pension Reforms 111

Box 5.1:   Definition of Responsibilities in the Decentralized System of Primary and
           Secondary Education 163

ACKNOWLEDGMENTS

This report was prepared by a core team comprising Bernard Funck (main author), Marcelo Bisogno, James Harrison, and Anton Marcincin, based primarily on specific contributions and background papers by Bartek Kaminski and Beata Smarzynska (trade integration); Emily Andrews and Patrick Wiese (social protection); Martin Bruncko (regional development); Lubomira Zimanova Beardsley and Alexey Proskuryakov (judiciary reform); Marie Renee Bakker (financial sector); Csaba Csaki and his team (agriculture); and Roland Clarke (public expenditure management).

The team also drew upon the work of Mukesh Chawla (health), Mary Canning and Halil Dundar (education), Jean Jacques Dethier (public expenditure management), Istvan Dobozi and Laszlo Lovei (energy), Ana Revenga and her team (poverty), Dena Ringold (Roma); and Lodovico Pizzati (fiscal sustainability).

The team gratefully acknowledges its indebtedness to the analytical work of the IMF, the OECD (particularly its latest country survey focusing on labor markets), and the European Commission.

The team is also grateful to Roger Grawe, Kyle Peters, Ingrid Brockova, Milan Brahmbatt, and Roberto Rocha for their support and advice.

The production of this report would not have bee possible, however, without Mismake Galatis, Anita Correa and Emily Evershed's excellent support in respectively processing and editing the manuscript. Oana Maria Croitoru also helped put together the statistical data.

ABBREVIATIONS AND ACRONYMS

ALMP	Active Labor Market Policies
CAP	Common Agricultural Policy
CC-11	EU Candidate Countries Minus Malta and Turkey
CEEC	Central and Eastern European Countries
CET	Common External Tariff
CIT	Corporate Income Tax
CJSR	Council of Judges of the Slovak Republic
CMEA	Council of Mutual Economic Assistance
COFOG	Classification of the Functions of Government
CSU	Czech–Slovak Customs Union
EU	European Union
EU-15	European Union's Actual 15 Members
FMA	Financial Markets Authority
GDP	Gross Domestic Product
GHIC	General Health Insurance Corporation
GP	General Practitioner
HEI	Higher Education Institutions
HIC	Health Insurance Company
IAS	International Accounting Standards
IFP	Institute for Financial Policy
IIPE	Institute of Information and Prognoses on Education
IMF	International Monetary Fund
IMR	Infant Mortality Rate
INEKO	Institute for Economic and Social Reforms
LDB	Live Database
MNC	Multinational Corporations
MoE	Ministry of Education
MoF	Ministry of Finance
MoH	Ministry of Health
MoJ	Ministry of Justice
MoLSAF	Ministry of Labor, Social Affairs, and Family
MSL	Minimum Subsistence Level
MTBF	Medium-Term Budgetary Framework
MTPC	Ministry of Transport, Posts and Communications
NBS	National Bank of Slovakia
NDC	Notional Defined Contribution
NUTS-3	Nomenclature of Territorial Units for Statistics (Regional Level 3)
NKU	Supreme Audit Office
NLO	National Labor Office
NPF	National Property Fund
NPL	Non-Performing Loans
OECD	Organization for Economic Co-operation and Development
OPT	Outward Processing Trade
PAYGO	Pay-As-You-Go
PEP	Pre-Accession Economic Program
PIT	Personal Income Tax

PPA	Public Procurement Act
PPS	Purchasing Power Standard
PSO	Public Service Obligations
RONI	Regulatory Office for Networks Industries
SBRA	Social Benefits Reform Administration
SE	Slovenske Elektrane
SGI	Slovak Governance Institute
SI	Sickness Insurance
SIA	Social Insurance Agency
SITC	Standard International Trade Classification
SKA	Slovak Consolidation Agency
SME	Small-Medium Enterprises
SOP	Sectoral Operational Programs
SPP	Slovak Gas Utility
SRA	Slovak Road Administration
TEN	Trans-European Network
TINA	Telecommunications/Informatics Infrastructure New Assistance Products Program
UI	Unemployment Insurance
ULC	Unit Labor Cost
UVO	Public Procurement Office
VAT	Value Added Tax
WTO	World Trade Organization
ZS	Zeleznicna Spolocnost; Railway Company
ZSR	Zeleznice Slovenskej Republiky; Railways of the Slovak Republic

EXECUTIVE SUMMARY

The Slovak Republic's external current account and fiscal deficits (net of privatization receipts) are unsustainably high (at about 8 percent of GDP in 2002), despite some recent declines. With a capital account surplus of perhaps 20 percent of GDP this year, the Slovak Republic may not find it particularly difficult to finance these deficits, but this favorable situation will not last. Furthermore, through its impact on the real exchange rate, this policy mix is undermining the employability of large segments of the population (particularly those with low skill levels) and will ultimately choke growth (projected at 4 percent for 2002). While much policy attention has gone to stimulating investment, future growth will also depend on raising the employment rate, currently one of the lowest among the CEECs at 50 percent of the working age population.

The year and a half that separates the Slovak Republic from EU accession offers a window of opportunity to act on these key issues. The new government will be well advised to take advantage of this opportunity to deliver the following *immediate 11-point agenda:*

(i) Curtail *enterprise (current and capital) subsidies and other guarantee payments* (currently the highest among the CEECs at about 6 percent of GDP), including by pruning down all non-CAP compliant agricultural support and sharply reducing transfers to railways.

(ii) Redirect, rather than expand, existing expenditure programs to meet the eligibility criteria for *structural funds* financing (including to facilitate the maturation of a growth pole around Bratislava).

(iii) Further increase the *retirement* age to 65 for all to put public pensions on a sustainable footing and avoid the massive fiscal deficits the demographic transition is bringing.

(iv) Postpone the *revenue* reduction planned under the pre-Accession economic program (from 38 percent of GDP in 2000 to a projected 35 percent of GDP in 2002, to a target of 33 percent of GDP in 2004) until such time as the expected cutback in expenditure has actually materialized.

(v) Rebalance the tax burden away from payroll taxes (starting with health and sickness contributions) and toward other tax bases (e.g., by streamlining VAT refunds, by taxing away windfall gas profits, by trimming down tax incentives for investment to EU-compatible levels, and by subjecting all personal income—including child allowances, if they remain universal—to the personal income tax).

(vi) Bring forward the planned increases in *electricity and natural gas tariffs* (with targeted lifeline blocks for low-income consumers, if necessary).

(vii) Use privatization receipts from abroad to retire *foreign rather than domestic debt* (to avoid further stimulating domestic demand).

(viii) Start to privatize *power generation* (nuclear and thermal separately) as well as "unclaimed" *land*.

(ix) Reduce *labor market* rigidities (which are among the highest in the CEECs), including by again revising the recently adopted labor code, by reforming the minimum wage, by decentralizing collective bargaining, and by redesigning Social Assistance benefits.

(x) Remove bottlenecks in *debt resolution* procedures with a view to facilitating a second round of ownership transfer on those assets questionably acquired under the Meciar government and removing a critical obstacle to bank lending to SMEs.

(xi) Bring down the *internal trade border* within the Czech-Slovak Customs Union ahead of EU accession.

Parallel with these immediate actions, the new government should also act now to set in motion *longer haul* efforts to reform major spending programs, including the following actions:

(i) In social protection, after initiating an increase in the retirement age to put the first pillar on a sustainable footing, *shift gradually towards a mandatory fully-funded second pillar* to raise pension replacement rates, the timing being phased to ensure that the regulatory institutions are in place to supervise the second and third pillars, and to take advantage of the country's incipient access to the EU's integrated capital markets, or better, to the euro zone; and *curb the rising cash social assistance payments* and correct the disincentives that prevent recipients from working their way off the welfare rolls, by *adjusting benefits* to more appropriate levels, *reducing the rate of withdrawal of benefits* as recipients earn income, and improving, and strictly enforcing, *activity tests*.

(ii) In health, *contain excess demand for health care* (through more narrowly defined benefits and greater cost sharing); *make the financing mechanism more efficient and equitable* (by merging health insurance companies, integrating collections with other social contributions, improving compliance, and broadening the revenue base); *increase provider efficiency* (through better-designed payment mechanisms, a provider network rationalization plan that reduces overstaffing and excess hospital beds, a strong mechanism to hold providers accountable to quality and service delivery standards, and the development of management skills at the facility level); *ensure* adequate *support and focus for public health functions;* and *protect access to health services for all, especially the Roma*.

(iii) In education, *consolidate facilities and staff at the primary and secondary levels* (particularly by intensifying and expanding the ongoing "rationalization program") with the support of *a new funding mechanism* based mainly on capitation payments; *reorient secondary education* to better meet labor market demands (by increasing both general academic enrollments and the general academic content of vocational streams); and use the cost savings from consolidation and reorientation *to improve quality at all levels* and *fund (along with tuition payments) gradual expansion at the tertiary level;* establish stronger *mechanisms, including systems of national student assessments and university accreditation, to hold schools and higher education institutions accountable;* and *ensure equal education opportunities for the Roma*.

The success of this strategy is predicated on enhancing the country's governance framework. This would involve:

(i)   Transforming the medium-term budgeting and program budgeting frameworks into effective fiscal planning tools, improving the quality of underlying financial and performance information, and enhancing the systems' integrity. This should include establishing a well-designed, periodic household budget survey as a key tool for policy analysis and design.

(ii) Consolidating the recent decentralization to ensure that capacities and accountability mechanisms are in place before moving to the next phase of devolution.

(iii) Launching a major reform of the justice sector in particular to professionalize court management; to step up the investigation and prosecution of corrupt judges; and to strengthen the regulation bodies of legal professions, including enhancing client protection.

OVERVIEW

The Strategic Setting

The Slovak economy has in 2002 experienced its best growth performance since it pulled out from the financial crisis of 1998. The economy is now on a recovery path, with output and private sector employment growth expected to reach 4 percent and 2 percent, respectively, in 2002 year (see Table 1). However, no sooner did recovery get under way and begin to generate jobs, then macro-economic imbalances resurfaced: the fiscal and external current account deficits hover around 8 percent of GDP, while more than 18 percent of the labor force remains unemployed.

The current situation differs, however, from the pre-1999 period in at least four respects: the main drivers of growth, the sources of domestic demand expansion, the nature of the international environment, and the forms of external financing have all changed.

Growth through Structural Reform

First, *growth is underpinned by structural reforms rather than over-investment.* The most striking manifestation of this change has been the turnaround in enterprise profits, which rose by about 10 percentage points of GDP between 1998 and 2002. *Most of the improvement can be attributed to the sharp drop in the number of loss-making firms.* Banking sector reforms succeeded in breaking up the old-boys' club mentality that used to tie together banks and their corporate borrowers. Enterprises in turn proved more reluctant to extend credit to their clients, forcing enterprises to restructure or to go out of business. Furthermore, the government managed to privatize or close down about 40 percent of those enterprises that remained in state hands as of 1998. Better still, the quality of privatization improved, attracting reputable strategic investors. While the average domestically owned firm is still working out the stress of restructuring, those foreign-owned firms are now expanding.

Furthermore, while the number of profitable firms increased somewhat between 1998 and 2002, their *profit margins remained essentially unchanged,* reflecting the growing degree of competition associated with the near elimination of import tariffs with the EU and other preferred trade partners.

TABLE 1: SLOVAK REPUBLIC—KEY ECONOMIC INDICATORS, 1995–2001

	1995	1996	1997	1998	1999	2000	2001
Real Economy							
Real GDP (growth rate)	5.8	5.6	4.0	1.3	2.2	3.3	4.0
Unemployment rate	13.1	11.3	11.8	12.5	16.2	18.9	19.4
Inflation (CPI, period average %)	9.8	5.8	6.1	6.7	10.6	12.0	7.3
Private Consumption/GDP	50.5	52.3	52.2	53.4	55.4	55.3	55.8
Gross National Savings/GDP	28.6	25.2	25.9	25.1	23.4	22.8	22.9
Gross Domestic Investment/GDP	26.5	35.6	35.2	34.7	28.2	26.4	31.9
Balance of Payments							
Trade Balance/GDP	−1.2	−11.2	−9.9	−10.7	−5.4	−4.5	−10.4
Exports of Goods and Services (growth rate in US$)	...	−0.5	8.3	10.2	−5.6	15.2	6.8
Imports of Goods and Services (growth rate in US$)	...	26.3	5.4	11.6	−13.4	13.2	15.3
Current Account Balance/GDP	2.0	−10.2	−9.3	−9.7	−4.9	−3.5	−8.6
Capital and Financial Account/GDP	7.2	12.0	8.6	8.3	7.6	7.5	9.1
Gross Official Reserves (US$ billion, end-year)	3.4	3.4	3.3	2.9	3.4	4.1	4.2
Reserve Cover (months of imports of G&S)	...	3.2	2.9	2.3	3.1	3.4	3.0
Gross External Debt/GDP	...	...	47.4	55.2	53.0	55.7	56.3
External Debt Service (% of exports of G.S.I. & T.)	...	...	...	13.3	15.5	17.1	10.5
Public Finances							
General Government Balance/GDP	...	−3.2	−4.8	−5.1	−4.3	−9.1	−8.5
Idem, excluding extraordinary items	...	−1.4	−4.3	−4.7	−4.5	−6.0	−6.6
Public Debt/GDP (%)	...	26.4	28.8	28.8	40.1	44.1	43.0
Interest Rates							
Average nominal lending rate (in percent)	16.9	13.9	18.7	21.2	21.1	14.9	11.2
Average real lending rate (deflated by CPI, in percent)	...	7.7	11.8	13.6	9.5	2.6	3.7
Average nominal deposit rate (in percent)	9.0	9.3	13.4	16.3	14.4	8.5	6.4
Average real deposit rate (deflated by CPI, in percent)	...	3.3	6.9	9.0	3.4	−3.2	−0.8
Money and Credit							
Money (annual growth)	...	15.8	−4.4	−11.4	4.2	21.5	21.3
Quasi-Money (annual growth)	...	16.4	18.3	14.6	15.0	12.5	7.7
Credit to Enterprises and Households (% growth)	...	6.0	42.7	34.9	9.2	20.9	25.2
Labor and Wages							
Nominal gross wage growth (%, period average)	14.3	13.3	13.1	8.4	7.2	6.5	8.2
Real gross wage growth (%, period average)	4.1	7.1	6.6	1.6	−3.0	−4.9	0.8
Exchange Rates							
Nominal Exchange Rate (SKK per US$, average)	29.7	30.7	33.6	35.2	41.4	46.0	48.4
Nominal Exchange Rate (SKK per Euros, average)	40.6	39.9	38.0	39.2	44.1	42.6	43.3
Nominal Effective Exchange Rate (1995=100)	100	100.7	105.8	103.6	93.4	94.5	93.2
Real Effective Exchange Rate (CPI, 1995=100)	100	100.3	106.3	106.5	104.2	116.5	116.7
Real Effective Exchange Rate (ULC, 1995=100)	100	108.6	120.0	115.6	110.6	111.0	109.8
Memo Items							
Gross Domestic Product (current SKK billion)	568.9	628.6	708.7	775.0	835.7	908.7	989.3
Gross Domestic Product (current US$ billion)	19.1	20.5	21.1	22.0	20.2	19.7	20.5
Per Capita Income (US$)	3,569.7	3,816.0	3,916.3	4,080.5	3,744.9	3,654.2	3,783.4

Source: World Bank calculaions based on Ministry of Finance, National Bank of Slovakia and Statistical Office of the Slovak Republic.

Sources and Impact of Domestic Expansion

Second, where domestic demand used to be driven by (state sponsored) financial laxity among enterprises, it is now being fueled by greenfield investment—which is good—and fiscal expansion—which is not (see Table 2). Both phenomena are in part linked to the surge in foreign direct investment from about 1 percent of GDP annually in the 1990s to an expected 17 percent of GDP this year. Driven by greenfield investment, capital accumulation rebounded strongly in 2000 from a brief contraction in 1999–2000. Alongside greenfield FDI, however, a sizable portion of the incoming privatization receipts was also allowed to enter the domestic economy, further inflating domestic demand. This made it possible to finance (i) a gaping fiscal deficit (widening from 4.3 to 8.5 percent of GDP between 1999 and 2001); and (ii) a range of other expansionary measures (such as the redemption of National Property Fund bonds in 2001, and the retirement of domestic public debt this year) without crowding out private demand. Interest rates actually declined throughout the whole 1999–2002 period.

The recent fiscal deterioration reflects primarily the impact of policy-driven revenue losses, unmatched by corresponding spending retrenchment. To the general tariff reduction in the context of the Europe Agreement and the Uruguay Round, and the elimination of the import surcharges imposed in 1999, the government of the Slovak Republic added a range of fiscal measures aimed at making the country more competitive and attractive to investors. These included corporate income tax (CIT) rate cuts from 40 to 25 percent and generous tax holiday schemes. Similar cuts were implemented in the personal income tax (PIT) with the marginal tax rate dropping from 40 percent to 38 percent at the highest end of the income distribution and from 15 to 10 percent at the lowest end, combined with a significant increase in the basic deduction. As a result, the ratio of general government tax revenues to GDP fell by some 7.5 percentage points of GDP between 1996 and 2001.

The corresponding alleviation of the tax burden is in itself welcome as it should help fuel growth. The expenditure retrenchment on which it was predicated unfortunately never materialized. General government expenditure (excluding net lending) actually rose by close to 2 percentage points of GDP between 1999 and 2001. Worse, recent spending measures taken in the pre-electoral phase are threatening to expand spending in areas that are primary targets for retrenchment. These measures included a 17 percent increase in civil service wages, a 5 percent hike in pensions, a ban on tuition for "external" university students, and the universalization of previously income-tested child allowances.

TABLE 2: DEMAND AND OUTPUT, 1995–2002
(percent)

	1995–98	1999–00	2001–02
	Percent change		
Private consumption	6.9	0.6	4.5
Government consumption	6.9	−2.6	5.3
Gross capital formation	20.5	−10.5	10.4
Total domestic demand	9.7	−3.6	6.2
Exports	8.9	9.5	4.5
Imports	15.5	1.9	7.6
Gross domestic product	5.5	1.8	3.5
	Contribution to growth		
Gross capital formation	5.2	−3.6	4.4
Total domestic demand	9.8	−3.9	7.5
Net exports	−4.3	5.2	−4.0

Source: World Bank calculations based on Statistical Office of the Slovak Republic.

The resulting fiscal deficits are not sustainable. Left unattended, the current fiscal deficits would unleash explosive public debt dynamics. After starting from an almost debt-free situation at independence less than 10 years ago, the country would breach the Maastricht criteria on public debt of 60 percent of GDP as early as 2007 (see Table 3). Budget deficits are not the only risk involved. Other risks arise also from (i) the significant amount of government guarantees that the Slovak Republic has accumulated (equivalent to 18 percent of GDP as of end-2001), mainly to ensure the continued financing of troubled state-owned enterprises, such as the railway and power companies; (ii) the recurrent pressure to bailout critical sectors (such as health) after they have run up unbearably high payment arrears; and (iii) unexpected banking troubles (until such time as the deposit insurance scheme is recapitalized). Moreover, even after the reforms of May 2002, the pension system's deficits are projected to rise over the long run, further darkening the fiscal outlook.

Misguided incomes policies and a rigid labor market have stifled the supply response to domestic demand expansion, exacerbating the impact of the fiscal deficit on macro balances. Indicators of labor market rigidity abound (see Table 4). Even before the labor code was recently tightened, the country's employment protection legislation was more restrictive than in the average OECD country. Under the influence of a centralized wage bargaining system, wages differ less across the country than underlying productivity. According to labor survey data, fewer than 9 percent of those who have a job are self-employed or family workers, whereas these types of working arrangements reach almost 19 percent of the employed in the rest of the Visegrad countries and 16 percent in the EU. Similarly, at 2.4 percent of total employment, part-time work is at the very bottom among the Visegrad countries (averaging 6.4 percent) and is far below the average for the EU (18 percent). Furthermore, due in part to Social Assistance benefits that are high relative to the average wage (particularly in the poorer parts of the country), labor force participation is among the lowest observed in Visegrad countries.

To make matters worse, *a deliberate policy of rapid minimum wage increases* (by 86 percent between 1998 and October 2002) *resulted in a sharp compression at the bottom of the wage distribu-*

TABLE 3: PUBLIC SECTOR DEFICIT AND DEBT OUTCOMES—TWO SCENARIOS, 2001–09
(Percent of GDP)

	2001	2002	2003	2004	2005	2006	2007	2008	2009
Reform Scenario									
1. Gross debt level	43.0	42.0	43.1	44.3	44.1	43.3	43.0	42.8	42.8
2. Gross assets	30.2	34.7	33.4	31.3	27.4	27.4	27.4	27.4	27.4
3. Net debt	12.8	7.3	9.7	13.0	16.6	15.9	15.6	15.4	15.4
4. Primary deficit	4.5	3.6	2.6	1.5	0.5	−0.5	−0.5	−0.5	−0.5
5. Interest	3.9	3.9	3.2	3.2	3.1	3.0	3.0	3.1	3.1
6. Overall deficit	8.4	7.5	5.8	4.8	3.6	2.5	2.5	2.6	2.6
No Reform Scenario									
1. Gross debt level	43.0	42.9	45.9	50.0	53.8	58.2	63.3	68.7	74.3
2. Gross assets	30.2	34.7	33.4	31.3	27.4	27.4	27.4	27.4	27.4
3. Net debt	12.8	8.2	12.5	18.7	26.4	30.7	35.9	41.2	46.8
4. Primary deficit	4.5	4.5	4.5	4.5	4.5	4.5	4.5	4.5	4.5
5. Interest	3.9	3.9	3.3	3.5	3.5	3.9	4.4	5.0	5.6
6. Overall deficit	8.4	8.4	7.8	8.0	8.0	8.4	8.9	9.5	10.1
Common Assumptions									
7. Nominal GDP growth	8.9	7.2	8.9	9.1	9.3	8.0	7.0	7.0	7.0
8. Privatization receipts for debt repayment	0.0	5.6	1.3	0.0	0.0	0.0	0.0	0.0	0.0

Source: World Bank estimates.

TABLE 4: LABOR FORCE INDICATORS IN SELECTED COUNTRIES, 2001 (percent)	Slovak Republic	Poland	Czech Republic	Hungary	Slovenia	EU Candidates	EU-15
Employment							
Employment rate							
15–24 years	27.7	21.4	34.4	31.4	30.3	27.0	40.4
25–54 years	74.6	69.5	82.0	73.1	83.8	73.8	77.0
55–64 years	22.5	30.5	36.9	23.7	23.4	34.6	38.2
15–64 years	56.7	53.8	65.0	56.3	63.6	57.8	63.9
Self-employed & family workers	8.6	28.0	15.3	14.6	17.1	27.1	15.7
Contract of limited duration	5.0	11.9	8.1	7.5	13.1	8.0	13.4
Unemployment							
Unemployment rate							
−15–24 years	38.9	41.5	16.3	10.5	15.7	28.8	14.0
−25–64 years	15.9	15.6	6.9	5.0	4.6	11.3	6.5
−15 + years	19.4	18.4	8.0	5.7	5.7	13.0	7.3
Unemployment-12 months and more	58.3	50.1	52.9	44.8	63.3	52.4	44.0

Source: EUROSTAT, Statistics in Focus, Population and Social Conditions, Theme 3-20/2002, staff calculations.

tion: the ratio of the minimum to the average wage rose by close to 35 percent over the period. High payroll tax rates, which at 50.8 percent of gross wages are currently at the very top among regional economies, further contributed to pricing less qualified workers out of the market. Unsurprisingly, the risk of unemployment for a worker with an apprenticeship degree is now four times higher (compared to three times in 1994) than that for a worker with a college degree.

With expanding demand running against supply-side rigidities, *the CPI-based real effective exchange rate*, which had initially depreciated in the wake of the floating of the currency in 1998, *promptly swung back up*. It appreciated by 16 percent between January 1999 and April 2002 (see Table 1). The comparatively greater stability of the unit-labor cost-based real exchange rate reflects *the exit or downsizing of less productive firms under the pressure of competition*. While some fast-restructuring enterprises were able to generate sufficient productivity gains to offset wage increases, other large segments of the economy struggled to compete, causing heavy job losses and soaring unemployment, particularly among low-skilled workers.

This rise in unemployment has no doubt had an adverse impact on living standards. An analysis of poverty in the Slovak Republic[1] found a *close link between unemployment and poverty:* a household headed by an unemployed person was five times more likely to be living in poverty than a household headed by an employed person. This finding was based on an analysis of 1996 data when unemployment was only 11 percent, and suggests that, with unemployment over 18 percent now, there would have been a very sharp rise in poverty in recent years. However, it is likely that the social assistance program has played a critical role in limiting the increase in poverty following the rise in unemployment and its persistence at a high level. As unemployment rose after 1995, social assistance rolls expanded by about 80 percent (to cover a total of about 12 percent of the population, including dependants). Without this program, poverty levels would certainly be much higher (by how much is unknown, since there has been no adequate survey of household income and spending since 1996).

---

1. *Slovak Republic: Living Standards, Employment, and Labor Market Study*, World Bank, 2002.

But now, with the economy growing and unemployment receding only very slowly, there is a growing concern that this *well-intentioned program may contain elements of a "poverty trap"* that could leave the beneficiaries with little incentive to move from the welfare roles into productive jobs (especially at the lower end of the wage spectrum), and thus may hinder employment growth. This concern results because benefits are high relative to average wages (especially for larger families) and because benefits are withdrawn on a one-to-one basis as recipients earn income from a job. The implications of this program, and other labor market rigidities, will need to be carefully considered as part of a strategy to broaden the growth of productive job opportunities and thus reduce unemployment and poverty.

Role of the International Environment

The return to rapid domestic demand expansion has been taking place in a less supportive external environment than during the mid- to late 1990s. Reflecting the country's growing integration into the global production networks of European multinational corporations, Slovak exports managed to resume their penetration of the EU market in 2001–02. But growth in that market has decelerated in 2001–02 to about half the rate observed in the 1994–98 period, dampening exports accordingly. Furthermore, trade with the Czech Republic continued to contract, as it had throughout the 1990s. With imports soaring under the pressure of domestic demand, the contribution of net exports to GDP growth turned negative again in 2001–02 (as in 1995–98). Consequently, by 2001 the current account balance fell back to deficit levels of about 8.6 percent of GDP, and it is estimated to remain at a similar level this year.

In parallel, *the country's pattern of trade specialization shifted away from unskilled labor-intensive products* (see Table 5). While it might be desirable for the Slovak Republic to move up in the value chain over time, one could wonder whether the overall policy framework is not inducing a faster "graduation" than would be desirable, threatening to leave large segments of the population by the wayside.

Forms of External Financing

The country has to date been fortunate enough to be able to finance its widening current account deficit through privatization receipts, instead of through international borrowing as was the case in the mid-1990s; this is the fourth key difference with the past. The large FDI inflows contributed to stabilizing gross foreign debt to GDP ratios, which remain today below the 1998 levels (at about 53 percent of

TABLE 5: FACTOR INTENSITY OF SLOVAK TRADE WITH THE EU, 1995–2000
(percent)

Factor Intensity	1995	1996	1997	1998	1999	2000
	Composition of Exports to the EU					
Natural Resources	19.2	20.3	17.9	12.6	13.8	10.8
Unskilled Labor	21.8	21.0	22.5	19.3	18.3	17.9
Capital Intensive	23.8	25.8	24.9	23.1	24.5	25.0
Skilled Labor	35.2	32.9	34.6	45.0	43.4	46.3
	Composition of Imports from the EU					
Natural Resources	15.5	17.2	17.9	15.0	10.5	11.0
Unskilled Labor	7.4	9.4	14.5	16.2	11.3	14.3
Capital Intensive	53.5	60.9	58.1	54.4	38.9	47.0
Skilled Labor	24.4	36.5	38.4	42.0	27.1	35.1

Source: World Bank calculations.

GDP). With record high FDI inflows this year (on the order of 17–18 percent of GDP), *net foreign debt* should drop to around 18 percent of GDP by the end of the year.

Challenges and Objectives

This situation of easy external financing will unfortunately not last. With the bulk of assets already privatized, privatization receipts are already shrinking. Unless the fiscal deficit is brought under control, the resulting interest rate hike would be sure to choke recovery, bringing unemployment even higher.

Under the circumstances, the incoming government will need to chart a feasible course in the direction of three objectives: (i) invigorating the recovery of GDP growth and (ii) broadening the incipient employment growth, while (iii) securing external stability.

Achieving all three objectives will require a combination of the following three instruments:

(a) *Continued trade, finance, and enterprise reform*
(b) *Fiscal consolidation*
(c) *Labor market reform*

The next year and a half that separates the Slovak Republic from EU Accession offers a window of opportunity to act on these key issues. The drive to meet the obligations of membership should provide the framework and impetus for much of the needed policy actions. This is true in such diverse areas as agriculture, trade, financial sector development, energy, regional development, and government financial control. As the prospect of membership becomes closer, the country will also be called on more pressingly to live up to the commitments made in its Pre-Accession Economic Program (PEP), as a prelude to the discipline of the European Monetary Union. Beyond that, the decision by the Slovak Republic (like the other candidate countries) to espouse the so-called "Lisbon Strategy" for turning the enlarged EU into "the most competitive economy in the world with social cohesion and full employment of 70 percent of the adult population" (compared to 49 percent at present in the Slovak Republic) is expanding the policy agenda from merely clearing the formal hurdle for EU membership to actively contributing to the overall goals of the EU.

The benefits of those policies will arise from *their actual implementation, not from pro forma legislation,* as will be seen below. Only if the government has the institutional capacity to carry these policies out will the expected benefits materialize. The results of a recent perception survey (reported in Table 6) indicate that the Slovak Republic has come a long way in improving the effectiveness of its administration and the quality of the governance framework more generally. That being said, the country still rates among the lowest on most counts among acceding countries, indicating the urgent need to step up efforts.

Trade, Finance, and Enterprise Reform

A first set of priorities revolves around the need to amplify the domestic supply response and to boost net exports through continued reform on the supply-side. While much has been accomplished, certain critical issues remain, which the new government will now need to tackle, including the following: (i) performance has been lagging behind in the agriculture sector, owing in part to a government policy to pursue food self-sufficiency and to support inefficient large corporate farming with large subsidies; (ii) the internal border within the Czech-Slovak Customs Union (CSU) is hindering trade expansion and has allowed the country to fall behind in aligning its trade regime with EU requirements; (iii) energy sector privatization is as yet incomplete and energy tariffs, particularly for gas, remain heavily distorted in favor of residential users; (iv) biases against small business in the business framework have arisen from the preferential tax treatment provided to large (and largely foreign) investors and from the absence of actionable debt resolution procedures. Partly as a result, Slovak banks are reluctant to lend to small business.

TABLE 6: PERCEIVED QUALITY OF GOVERNANCE IN THE CEECs, 1997/98–2000/01

	Government Effectiveness		Regulatory Quality		Rule of Law		Control of Corruption	
	1997/98	2000/01	1997/98	2000/01	1997/98	2000/01	1997/98	2000/01
Acceding countries								
Czech Republic	0.59	0.58	0.57	0.54	0.54	0.64	0.38	0.31
Estonia	0.26	0.86	0.74	1.09	0.51	0.78	0.59	0.73
Hungary	0.61	0.60	0.85	0.88	0.71	0.76	0.61	0.65
Lithuania	0.13	0.26	0.09	0.30	0.18	0.29	0.03	0.20
Latvia	0.07	0.22	0.51	0.30	0.15	0.36	−0.26	−0.03
Poland	0.67	0.27	0.56	0.41	0.54	0.55	0.49	0.43
Slovak Republic	−0.03	0.23	0.17	0.27	0.13	0.36	0.03	0.23
Slovenia	0.57	0.70	0.53	0.52	0.83	0.89	1.02	1.09
Other EU candidates								
Bulgaria	−0.81	−0.26	0.52	0.16	−0.15	0.01	−0.56	−0.16
Romania	−0.57	−0.54	0.20	−0.28	−0.09	−0.02	−0.46	−0.51

Note: The range is between −1.5 (worst) to +1.5 (best).
Source: World Development Indicators.

Agriculture

The restructuring of the agriculture sector has lagged behind that of the rest of the economy. In response to the output collapse of the early 1990s, the emphasis of agricultural policies shifted from privatization and market reforms to food self-sufficiency. This objective was to be championed by the large corporate farms that emerged from the former collective farms, and to be backed by a complete battery of policy interventions targeted to them. Furthermore, corporate farms have enjoyed the use of the state land "unclaimed" in the land restitution process.

The policy proved misguided and the hopes placed in corporate farms proved disappointing. Indeed, individual farms—commercial and subsistence operations combined—currently achieve a level of productivity four times higher than corporate farms do, producing 30 percent of the agricultural output on 7 percent of the agricultural land. Similarly, while individual commercial farms showed a small aggregate profit as a subsector, corporate farms reported aggregate losses until 2000.

There are indications that corporate farms are beginning to face harder budget constraints. For the first time in recent history, agricultural enterprises, taken as a whole, reported a small aggregate profit in 2001, reflecting a sharp drop in the number of loss-making agricultural enterprises (from about 725 in 1999 to about 400 in 2001), as credit conditions tightened following bank privatization.

The adoption of the Common Agricultural Policy (CAP) upon EU accession is expected to give sectoral profitability a further boost (even in the absence of direct payments, the higher CAP-prices would boost farmers' income by an estimated 18 percent). The country would benefit most, however, if it joined the CAP with a farming sector already restructured. Otherwise, there is a danger that the large subsidies associated with EU agricultural policies will serve to mask enduring inefficiencies in the sector rather than to modernize it, leaving the sector as a constant drag on overall economic performance. While policy instruments should be aligned with CAP requirements, the levels of support offered should be adjusted to EU levels only after the accession and with EU funding. In the meantime, policies should focus on the following:

(a) *Completing land privatization.* A strict deadline should be set for the identification and resolution of "unclaimed" land ownership. Beyond that deadline, much of the State Land

Fund should be expeditiously privatized through auctions. If at all possible, the 2005 deadline for filing restitution claims should be brought forward (and late claimants given financial compensation instead).

(b) *Redirecting support policies towards the CAP.* First, the government support program needs to be redirected towards preparing farms and food industries to compete in EU-wide markets, rather than subsidizing them (see also below). For this purpose, it is indispensable that food legislation and the associated regulatory agencies be made fully compatible with the EU directives on food hygiene, inspection, and certification, and with the legal responsibilities of producers. Substantial work and educational efforts are still required to implement the relevant *acquis* (including those related to animal registers, meat testing and inspection, and the certification of food processing industries).

(c) *Further tightening budget constraints.* Following the privatization of banks and major energy utilities, and with reduced subsidies, arrears on tax payments and social security contributions remain the main loopholes to close.

Transport

The transport sector in the Slovak Republic faces fundamental challenges in the coming years. The sector needs to adapt and respond to long-term changes in the underlying patterns of demand and correct years of misallocation of resources that have left the basic sector infrastructure under-maintained. In addition, the supply response needs now to make room for additional demands arising from the upcoming integration with the EU. The sector needs to address the following key problems/demands: (i) the sweeping transition-induced shifts in demand across transport modes, with rail freight dropping by over 25 percent, while road freight grew by about 70 percent (1993–2000, see Table 7); (ii) large operating losses and mounting debts and arrears in railways; (iii) the build-up of a large backlog of maintenance in roads, railways and public transport; and (iv) a major program of new transport investments, mainly for the Trans-European Network (TEN) corridors.

TABLE 7: TRENDS IN GOODS AND PASSENGER TRANSPORT
(ton-km or passenger-km billions)

	1993	2000	% change
Goods Transport			
Rail	14.17	11.23	−26
Road	16.80	28.58	+70
Inland Water	1.60	1.38	−15
Air	0.057	0.022	−59
Oil Pipeline	−	2.08	−
Total	32.63	43.29	+32
Passenger Transport			
Rail	4.57	2.87	−59
Automobile	14.36	24.41	+69
Bus	12.34	8.68	−42
Inland Water	0.006	0.004	−50
Air	4.46	2.51	−77
Total	35.74	38.47	+8
(Thousand passengers/year)			
Urban Public Transport	649	405	−60

Source: Statistical Yearbooks of the Slovak Republic

In addition to resolving these issues, the policy response should: (a) make room for an increased participation of the private sector in transport activities through privatization and commercialization of existing transport activities; (b) reduce Public Service Obligations (PSOs) and reconsider their use as a vehicle for social policy in light of the leaks to non-targeted population and the price distortions they impose; and (c) make a more intensive use of cost recovery options such as electronic tolls to contribute to the financing of new investment and maintenance.

The supply response remains biased towards: (i) new motorway construction (accounting for 82 percent of total road expenditures) and (ii) excessive rail services. The bias towards new motorway construction diverts funds for road maintenance and the necessary upgrading of the existing road network to EU standards. The oversupply of rail services, on the other hand, contributes to increase losses in the sector and results in periodical assistance to the sector from the Central Government. They all combine to put extra pressures to the already strained fiscal situation in Slovakia. In dealing with these expenditure pressures, the Slovak Republic will need to concentrate scarce public resources exclusively on those activities where the private sector cannot operate and/or invest effectively. It needs to reallocate public funding progressively away from decaying subsectors (railways) into the most dynamic ones (roads) with due consideration of environmental and social issues as well as balancing carefully the urgent needs for repair and maintenance against proposals for new investment in the area of road infrastructure. The sector needs also to complete the commercialization and restructuring of transport activities (especially in railways).

Road Infrastructure

Demands for maintenance and capacity increase to EU standards should be carried out minimizing the demands for budget funding. This would require a combination of new cost recovery alternatives and EU funding. To correct the backlog in maintenance and to increase capacity in both basic and high standard road network would require a 2.3 fold increase in funding. However, by no means this should translate into a corresponding increase in state budget allocations. A number of alternative source of funding are available. They include the use of structural and cohesion funds which are becoming increasingly available to the Slovak Republic. These sources could cover up to 75 percent of individual Slovakia TINA (Telecommunications/Informatics Infrastructure New Assistance) projects. Alternatively, the financing of motorways and expressways could recur to the use of electronic tolls and quite generally, to various public-private partnerships (PPPs).

The use of electronic toll systems would allow the conversion of the motorway system into an open toll road network Along this lines, a Motorway Company (MC) would be able to securitize revenue from the existing toll network for the issuing of bonds to finance its expansion. While initially state owned, the MC could be later concessioned or sold to a private company. Revenues from tolls could provide sufficient funds for the construction of about 100km of motorway per year, allowing the completion of the remaining 356 km of the planned 648 km network within about 4 years after the existing debt was paid off.

The imminent decentralization of government functions will bring about a radical change in the way roads are administered. This will become a window opportunity to implement key changes in the sector. Current plans contemplate the decentralization of about three-quarters of the road network to the eight new regional governments and the remaining roads to the municipalities by 2005. However, these plans need to be complemented by the transferring of revenues and technical expertise to regional governments.

Railways

The current situation in railways is financially unsustainable with the railways resorting to expensive short term borrowing. The rail surface coverage is currently too large, contributing to increase losses; while operation of uneconomic lines due to low traffic gives the railways companies the excuse/justification not to decrease staffing. Not surprisingly, ZSR's (Zeleznice Slovenskej Republiky) staff productivity has declined over the past five years and currently compares unfavorably with railways systems of similar network size and traffic density.

Restructuring. The reduction of the government's control of ZSR through the creation of a separate operating company (ZS) at the time of the decentralization of responsibility for funding the PSO for passenger services provides an excellent opportunity to reorient the railway. While size considerations renders uneconomic the division of de railways infrastructure company (ZSR) into separate regional railways; the large difference between its principal businesses—freight, long distance passenger, and local passenger services—suggests that a separation along these lines would be desirable. The present restructuring plan for the railways remains too modest. In terms of staff reductions, it would fall short of improving efficiency to the level of private railways. Once stripped of non-essential activities, the freight, intercity and regional passengers railway businesses should be able to operate with combined labor force of no more than 25,000 employees. Even this number, could be further reduced if the new regional governments decide they cannot support local passenger services. In parallel, the railways infrastructure company—ŽSR—could reduce staffing by about 10,000 employees some four years ahead of the seven years indicated in the current restructuring plan, provided a source of funding is available to cover redundancy costs.

As the size of the country is more appropriate to motorway-based bus services than to express passenger trains; the long distance passenger company would have an uncertain future. Few EU countries can maintain a profitable inter-urban passenger service and most depend on subsidies. Therefore, the chosen scheme, which combines the existing passenger railway assets–provided by the state at a nominal value- with private operation of an strategic operator into a joint venture is commendable. This scheme could attract existing passenger operators in EU countries with close connections to Slovakia. On the other hand, the freight operations of ZS could be a prime candidate for privatization.

PSO need to be reduced. In light of the ongoing decentralization, it would be desirable to have a stable system of PSO payment by multiple regional governments in place—one that will not have to be changed within a few years—to accommodate the new institutional structure of the railway. However, the overall envelope for PSO needs to be revisited and likely reduced. Its use as a vehicle for social policy should be examined in light of the leaks to non-targeted population and the price distortions they impose.

Energy

In contrast, restructuring is well advanced in the energy sector. The Slovak Republic has (i) unbundled the power and gas sectors and proceeded in 2002 to privatize the gas utility (SPP) and power distribution assets to strategic investors; (ii) begun to adjust tariffs toward cost-recovery levels (although that process came to a halt in the last 18 months); and (iii) established an independent Regulatory Office for Networks Industries (RONI). The key next steps will involve the following:

(a) *Privatizing power generation.* The best option from the point of view of speed, flexibility, and privatization revenue would be to sell nuclear and non-nuclear generation facilities separately, rather than as a single corporate entity. The main reason for this is that there is no precedent for the sale of nuclear plants in the region (or indeed outside of the United Kingdom and the United States).

(b) *Proceeding with the opening up of the electricity and gas markets to competition.* Under the current schedule, electricity markets should gradually be opened by reducing the eligibility threshold for access to the wholesale market from an annual consumption of 100 GWh in 2002 to 9 GWh in 2005, and by opening up the Slovak market to foreign suppliers in 2003. Foreign access will initially be subject to a cap of 5 percent of domestic consumption. As the Slovak Republic reaches agreements on a reciprocal basis (as it should seek to do), the number of actors in the electricity market will gradually expand.

The gas market has similarly begun to open up (up to 20 percent of the market, as of January 1, 2002). Access should gradually expand, first to all power and heat plants and for consumers of more than 20 million m³/year, and later to all non-household consumers.

(c) *Adjusting residential tariffs for gas and electricity so as to eliminate the* corresponding *cross-subsidies ahead of EU Accession.* Although cross-subsidization has been reduced, the ratio of residential to industrial tariffs in 2000 remained at about two-thirds of the OECD-Europe level for electricity and about one-quarter of the OECD-Europe for gas (see Table 8). Bringing tariffs in line with EU directives may now require residential tariff increases in the range of 40 percent in the case of electricity and more than 100 percent in the case of gas. The pattern adopted for electricity is to raise residential tariffs at four times the rate of inflation until the target rate is reached. No such schedule exists as yet for gas. With the expected date of EU Accession fast approaching, and with the urgent need for fiscal adjustment, there is now little scope for gradualism in phasing in the new gas tariffs. Rather, the government would be well advised to advance the process as much as possible, even into 2002. It should also consider introducing in parallel a special levy to tax away the windfall gas transmission rent that would otherwise accrue to the privatized SPP.

Because of the delays incurred, the *required price adjustments will be more abruptly painful for households, particularly at the lower end of the income scale, than they might have been.* Rather than that delaying the process, it would be preferable to consider introducing, on a temporary basis, a targeted lifeline tariff for the first block of basic electricity consumption or a targeted subsidy for basic heat (and hot water) consumption. These temporary subsidies could be phased out over time, as the increased cost of energy is reflected in revised Social Assistance benefits (based on new household budget survey data).

An important side-benefit of those price adjustments would be to relieve some of the current pressure on the balance of payments, either directly through substitution effects or indirectly through their income effect.

Trade Integration
Eliminating the internal border within the Czech-Slovak Customs Union (CSU) ahead of EU accession would not only reinvigorate trade with a country that remains the Slovak Republic's second largest trading partner, but would also help the Slovak Republic catch up with EU requirements

TABLE 8: RATIO OF RESIDENTIAL TO INDUSTRIAL PRICES FOR ENERGY, 1993–2001

	1993	2000	2001
Electricity			
Slovak Republic	0.60	1.19	1.43
Czech Republic	0.56	1.26	1.33
Hungary	0.81	1.33	1.33
Poland	1.40	1.76	1.68
OECD Europe	1.80	2.00	n.a
Natural Gas			
Slovak Republic	0.62	1.07	1.10
Czech Republic	0.73	1.45	1.44
Hungary	0.91	1.33	1.16
Poland	1.33	1.86	n.a
OECD Europe	2.67	3.98	n.a

Source: International Energy Agency: Energy Prices and Taxes, OECD.

"by osmosis." The CSU has so far failed to deliver one of the two major advantages of a customs union over a free trade area. The arrangement has allowed the two countries to avoid very costly rules of origin among members, as all products entering the Customs Union are subject to a low common external tariff. But trade between the two countries has remained subject to customs controls. The internal border has allowed considerable discretion in decisions affecting imports, such as the temporary imposition of import surcharges (on the Slovak side) or import deposits (on the Czech side), and the introduction of other technical barriers to trade. Behind that internal border, also the Slovak Republic has allowed itself to fall behind in terms of adjustment to the EU trade regime.

Aligning Slovak standards with EU standards together with the application of the principle of mutual recognition would help make up the lost ground and provide an extra boost to the integration of domestic firms into international *supply chains* spread out over several countries, as common standards reinforce linkages between component manufacturers, assembly operations, and distributors in the final product markets. This should not be problematic, as both countries have special arrangements for mutual recognition of certificates and test results. Both countries will have a common objective: to implement the EU requirements on standardization. Both have been moving in that direction, but at a different pace. Furthermore, the proposed enhanced regulatory cooperation within the CSU and the elimination of internal economic borders could yield rapid and substantial improvement in the overall business environment and would avoid the need to attract FDI through costly tax incentives (see below).

Financial Sector Development

As already noted, the turnaround in enterprise performance owes much to the major restructuring of the banking sector that the government undertook in 1999–2001. Building on these stronger foundations, banking sector growth is likely to be fueled in the future by expansion into consumer finance, leasing, housing finance, and small business sector lending. In contrast, several factors will encourage larger companies to raise capital abroad—foreign ownership, EU integration, and deeper, more liquid, more reliable and cheaper markets. This would leave domestic banks to focus mainly on household and small business needs.

Two risks are involved in this scenario, however. One is that banks, now highly liquid (see Table 9), will seek to branch out too rashly into new, high-risk business activities in a bid to boost their currently low profits. Hence, there is a need to step up banking regulation and supervision, including (i) by mandating the use of international accounting standards (IAS) first by banks, and then by other corporations, and (ii) by not allowing the creation of an integrated financial sector regulator to distract from the efforts to enhance the supervisory capacity of the exiting regulatory bodies, the National Bank of Slovakia (NBS) and the Financial Markets Authority (FMA).

TABLE 9: SELECTED INDICATORS OF FINANCIAL SOUNDNESS FOR THE BANKING SECTOR, 1997–2001
(percent)

	Dec-97	Dec-98	Dec-99	Dec-00	Dec-01
Regulatory capital to risk-weighted assets	8.0	6.6	12.7	13.1	19.7
NPLs to gross loans	27.2	31.6	23.7	15.3	14.0
NPLs net of provisions to capital	22.5	25.2	15.7	6.9	7.9
Liquid assets to total assets	13.5	9.7	12.1	18.1	27.5
Operating profit	1.4	1.4	−0.1	0.1	−0.1
Return on Equity	2.8	−13.4	−36.5	25.2	25.3

Source: National Bank of Slovakia.

The second risk is that bank lending might be guided more by the degree of enforceability of creditors' rights in different business segments, than by the economics of the underlying business propositions. In the absence of an effective bankruptcy framework (witness the mounting backlog of unprocessed bankruptcy cases in Table 10), banking may thus remain atrophied in the small business segment. Key steps needed include: (i) modern legislation, providing for, among other features, an effective reorganization mechanism (rather than only liquidation) when the enterprise is potentially viable, and greater creditor initiative and participation; (ii) more limited scope for debtors, land registry offices, and other parties involved in bankruptcy cases to delay proceedings; and (iii) more resources for bankruptcy courts, better training of judges, and stronger regulation of trustees with a view to reducing the current backlog and making proceedings more foolproof. In addition to removing a critical obstacle to bank lending to SMEs, de-bottlenecking debt resolution procedures could also facilitate a second round transfer of ownership of assets questionably acquired during the Meciar years (including through a resolution of the bad debt portfolio of the Slovak Consolidation Agency (SKA) and their return into more productive hands).

Fiscal Consolidation

Fiscal consolidation, the second fundamental leg of government's medium term strategy, is now required both in its own right (to arrest potentially explosive public debt dynamics) and to relieve current pressures on the balance of payments. The report suggests that (i) the *external current account deficit would need to be cut back from 8.6 percent to about 4.8 percent of GDP* to keep the ratio of net foreign debt to GDP ratio at end-2002 levels throughout the next five years, and further reduced thereafter; and that (ii) to achieve this target would require *bringing down the overall fiscal deficit from the current 8 percent of GDP to about 2.5 percent of GDP* over the next four years.

This adjustment will be facilitated by the expected expansion in EU transfers to the Slovak Republic. With *net* transfers from the EU projected to increase by 2 percentage points of GDP, the size of the purely *domestic fiscal effort would be around 3.5 percent of GDP* by 2006 (under the proviso that structural funds are not applied to finance new spending over and above existing levels, see below). Such deficit levels would stabilize both the ratio of (gross) government debt to GDP and the ratio of net foreign debt to GDP at end-of-2002 levels. Furthermore, this strategy would set the Slovak Republic on track toward meeting the Maastricht criteria for joining the euro-zone at an appropriate time.

TABLE 10: BANKRUPTCY AND SETTLEMENTS, 1993–2000
(number of firms)

	1993	1994	1995	1996	1997	1998	1999	2000
Bankruptcy proceedings initiated of which:	538	1,115	1,530	1,321	1,755	1,831	2,161	2,008
Processed:	169	466	591	672	488	702	1289	1547
Petition withdrawal	20	104	113	—	—	—	—	—
Cessation of proceedings	85	267	388	272	275	279	451	514
Cases handed over to locally authorized bodies	57	69	64	—	—	—	—	—
Rejection due to lack of assets	7	26	26	66	100	219	425	574
Other	—	—	—	334	113	204	413	415
Declaration of bankruptcy	11	32	74	198	427	654	665	638
Non-processed	369	649	939	2,663	3,896	5,025	5,897	6,358

Source: Ministry of Justice.

Consistent with the experience of successful fiscal adjustment in other OECD countries, the government would be well-advised to base its fiscal consolidation strategy on the following three principles:

(a) *The bulk of adjustment should be achieved through expenditure retrenchment,* primarily in subsidies and transfers and in the government's wage bill.
(b) *While this should remain a medium-term goal, the revenue reduction proposed under the country's pre-*accession *economic program* (from 38 percent of GDP in 2000 to a projected 35 percent of GDP in 2002, and to a target of 33 percent of GDP in 2004) *should be postponed* until the time that the expected cutback in expenditure has actually materialized.
(c) *Both revenue and* expenditure *should be redirected toward growth and employment objectives.*

Expenditure Restructuring
A comparison of spending patterns in the Slovak Republic (see Table 11) with those of the other CEECs brings out useful indications of where there is scope to restructure expenditure. Compared to the other CEECs, the Slovak Republic spends very high levels on:

(a) Transfers to non-financial enterprises (6 percent of GDP in 2001, 40 percent higher than the CEEC average), largely on account of continued large subsidies to agriculture, railways, and hospitals
(b) Public sector wages and salaries (8.6 percent of GDP, nearly 20 percent above the CEEC average), reflecting in particular the burden of disproportionately large workforces in health and education (reaching 5.6 percent of the population as compared to 3.8 percent in the other CEECs).

In addition, with high unemployment and the prospect of a rapid aging of the population, pressures are building up in the area of social protection. EU accession, and the access to EU structural funds that goes with it, will also create a push for additional spending on regional development.

To illustrate the scope for expenditure restructuring, the report examines public spending programs and issues in agriculture, regional development, social protection, health, and education, spending areas that, combined with enterprise subsidies, accounted for over two-thirds of public spending in 2001. While the report proposes both short-term and medium-term recommendations in the areas discussed below, it does not pretend to provide a fully detailed, comprehensive reform blueprint. Instead, it seeks to illustrate the difficult issues that need to be confronted. In each sector, the discussion focuses not on across-the-board cuts, but rather on reform options that can help to reduce or contain spending while improving its effectiveness in supporting the strategic goals of growth, employment, and stability.

Agricultural Support
The Slovak Republic currently spends excessive amounts to support an agricultural policy that is condemned to disappear with the imminent accession to the CAP. The level of support provided to corporate farms may have declined over the years, but the underlying policy direction has remained in favor of self-sufficiency in food production, a concept diametrically opposed to that of the CAP. Even at the current reduced level, the Slovak Republic spends twice as much (as a percent of GDP) on agricultural support as the average CEEC (2.4 percent of GDP compared to 1.2 percent in 2000, respectively).

It is now time *to prune down and reformat the support programs so that they conform to CAP requirements.* First, government support programs need to terminate all programs that do not comply with the CAP (including most credit subsidies, support for modernization and restructuring to agro-processors, and tax refunds on diesel fuel used for farming purposes). This would reduce agricultural spending by about 15–20 percent. Second, other support programs need to be

TABLE 11: EXPENDITURE OF THE CONSOLIDATED GENERAL GOVERNMENT
(percent of GDP)

	1996	1997	1998	1999	2000	2001	Other CEECs 2000
ECONOMIC CLASSIFICATION							
Total Revenue and Grants	**43.5**	**40.1**	**37.8**	**39.8**	**37.9**	**35.7**	**38.0**
Total Expenditure and Net Lending	**46.7**	**45.0**	**42.9**	**44.0**	**47.0**	**44.2**	**39.6**
Total Expenditure	**45.5**	**43.9**	**41.9**	**40.3**	**43.1**	**42.1**	**40.5**
Current Expenditure	39.0	37.2	36.6	36.4	37.5	36.6	36.3
Exp. on Goods and Services	17.3	17.7	16.4	15.9	15.8	15.9	16.6
Wages and Salaries	10.1	9.8	9.7	9.4	9.1	8.6	7.1
Other Goods and Services	7.2	7.9	6.7	6.5	6.8	7.3	9.6
Interest Payments	2.1	1.9	2.8	3.2	3.2	4.0	2.6
Subsidies and Other Curr. Transf.	19.6	17.5	17.4	17.3	18.4	16.7	17.0
Capital Expenditure	6.5	6.7	5.3	3.9	5.7	5.5	4.2
Investment.	4.4	5.4	3.9	3.2	3.2	3.2	2.7
Capital Transfers	2.1	1.4	1.4	0.7	2.4	2.3	1.4
Lending minus Repayment	1.2	1.1	0.9	3.8	3.9	2.1	−0.9
Overall Deficit/Surplus	**−3.2**	**−4.8**	**−5.1**	**−4.3**	**−9.1**	**−8.5**	**−2.5**
memo item							
Transfers to Enterprises	8.0	5.3	5.1	4.2	7.3	6.0	4.3
FUNCTIONAL CLASSIFICATION							
Total Expenditure	**45.5**	**43.9**	**41.9**	**40.3**	43.1	**42.1**	**40.5**
General Public Services	3.7	3.7	3.1	3.0	3.3	3.7	2.9
Defense	2.3	2.1	1.9	1.7	1.8	1.6	1.5
Public Order and Safety	2.3	2.3	2.2	1.6	1.6	1.7	2.0
Education	4.4	4.2	4.0	3.9	3.8	3.7	5.2
Health	6.3	6.0	5.5	5.5	5.7	5.7	4.6
Social Security and Welfare	13.7	13.6	13.6	13.8	13.6	13.1	14.2
Housing and Communal Services	2.3	1.8	2.1	2.1	1.9	1.7	1.9
Recreation and Culture	1.1	1.0	1.0	0.8	0.9	0.9	1.1
Economic Services	7.4	8.0	6.5	5.3	8.3	6.6	4.5
Fuel and Energy	0.8	0.7	0.5	0.2	0.0	0.1	0.1
Agriculture	2.5	2.4	2.0	1.5	2.4	1.8	1.1
Nonfuel Mining and Mineral	0.7	0.5	0.5	0.2	0.6	0.4	0.2
Transport and Communication	1.6	1.4	1.1	0.6	1.9	1.6	2.4
Other Economic Services	1.8	3.0	2.5	2.9	3.5	2.7	0.8
Interest Payments	2.1	1.9	2.8	3.2	3.2	4.0	2.6
Miscellaneous	−0.1	−0.7	−0.8	−0.7	−1.1	−0.6	−0.1

Source: World Bank calculations based on Ministry of Finance.

refitted to CAP requirements, including by adjusting *market support systems* to incorporate the potential use of quotas and to reform the current intervention scheme from an ex ante system (based on short-term forecasts on production and consumption) to an ex post system (based on the observed evolution of EU market prices); and by shifting the intervention point from the farm-gate to the wholesale level for most products. *Direct payments and other current structural support measures* should also be adapted to the EU format. Upon accession, much of the remaining charges should be transferred to the EU budget, relieving the Slovak budget accordingly of this uncommonly high burden.

Regional Development
This is another expenditure policy issue that is gaining prominence as EU accession is approaches. The magnitude of the EU funding potentially involved is considerable (up to 4 percent of GDP in EU transfers plus counterpart funds) and could conceivably help fuel the country's convergence toward EU standards. In the absence of a carefully thought out strategy, however, this potential could easily be squandered.

The observation that significant regional differences exist in the Slovak Republic in terms of output per capita should not lead to the wrong policy conclusions. First, these differences reflect similarly large productivity differentials. Second, they have only a limited impact on household income and living standards. Indeed, it is the attempt to equalize living standards (through labor market and social polices) irrespective of productivity differentials that is at the core of the most worrisome form of regional disparity: the wide differences that persist in regional unemployment rates. Unsurprisingly, it is in those regions where wages are most attractive in relation to productivity (particularly Bratislava) that employment growth concentrates.

The experience of the Cohesion countries (Greece, Ireland, Portugal, and Spain) suggests that, to achieve the most rapid overall convergence possible, the government should target public investment to those areas in which such investment generates higher growth, even if that involves an initial widening of regional GDP differences. In the case of the Slovak Republic, some of the most promising investments in the context of EU accession may well be in and around Bratislava. Rather than to direct EU structural funds away from that region in the name of equity, the appropriate strategy would be to maximize its growth potential while facilitating the diffusion of the convergence process to other regions. This will be first of all the role of labor markets and social welfare reforms. Improving transport access between Bratislava and the east would help firms move out of this initial growth pole as wage costs begin to rise and toward those regions that manage to establish or maintain wage competitiveness.

To be viable, *the utilization of structural funds will need to fit within a declining overall expenditure envelope.* The implication of the figures presented in the country's pre-accession economic program (PEP) in this respect is that, by 2006, *more than one-quarter of the monies spent on government consumption and* investment *will need to come from EU structural funds.* To make this possible, the Slovak government should avoid the temptation of creating new spending programs for the purpose of using EU funding. On the contrary, what is required is *a massive redirection of existing government programs to meet the eligibility criteria for EU funding* (including the so-called "additionality" criteria).

Education
The sweeping changes brought about by the transition are having a major impact on the demand for education, but *the supply side has not adapted fast enough or far enough in response.* This is partly because the shifts in funding needed to reorient the system have been sluggish at best (see Figure 1), continuing to generate more excess capacity in terms of teaching staff and facilities, especially where it is least needed, and suggesting the need for a new funding mechanism. For example, while enrollments in state vocational and technical schools fell by 16 percent between 1990 and 2000, the number of teachers rose by nearly 20 percent and the number of schools by over 44 percent. *The system still needs to be refocused* to provide the more general, higher-level skills that the economy needs (and students demand) by reorienting secondary education, by expanding access to tertiary education, and by raising quality at all levels. There are good reasons to believe that this can be done while keeping public spending on education at its current level of under 4 percent of GDP for some time to come, by taking advantage of the sharp drop in the school age population, the substantial potential for efficiency gains in the present system, the increasing role of private

FIGURE 1: EDUCATION SPENDING BY LEVEL

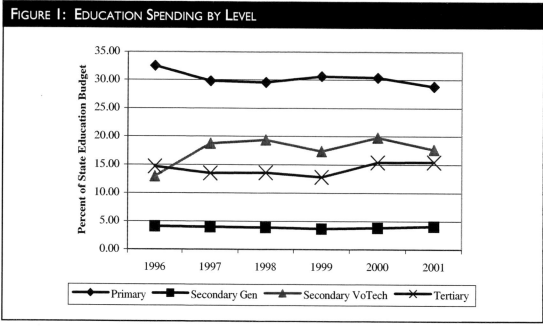

Source: IIPE & Statistical Yearbook, 2001

providers, and the scope for generating additional resources from tuition at the tertiary level. The challenge of decentralization also suggests the need for new, more transparent mechanisms for funding and accountability.

The key proposals to reorient the education system include the following:

(a) *Consolidation of the excessive numbers of primary and secondary schools and teachers,* capitalizing on the sharp drop in the school age population, through an expanded and intensified "rationalization program," and the reallocation of the savings to raise quality at all levels and help fund gradual, demand-driven expansion, as well as a system of need-based scholarships, at the tertiary level.

(b) *Reorientation of the secondary level,* so that most students acquire the general academic skills needed for lifetime learning, by expanding enrollment in general secondary schools, and by reforming the technical and vocational school curriculum to increase the general academic content. These reforms should be developed in preparation for EU Accession and should be designed to facilitate access to the EU Social Fund. These measures should be coordinated with reforms at the primary level to ensure that students are well prepared for these changes. Cost savings should be reallocated to raise quality.

(c) *Introduction of tuition at the tertiary level,* both to contain excess demand and to finance the needed expansion of enrollment and quality improvements at existing institutions.

(d) *Introduction of new funding mechanisms in which "money follows the student,"* based mainly on capitation payments and numbers of students enrolled. Parallel reforms would be needed to grant schools and higher education institutions greater autonomy in using these funds (and the skills and tools to use them well), while increasing their accountability. These measures could greatly increase the incentives to consolidate and reorient the schools, and help increase efficiency, transparency, quality, and equity across different regions of the Slovak Republic.

(e) *Strengthening of the accountability mechanisms,* including *establishing a system of national student assessments* and gearing up the school inspection system, so that schools are held accountable for achieving agreed outcomes and service standards within a hard budget constraint, with the results publicly available, especially to parents and school managers. Similar strengthening of accountability mechanisms, including in the accreditation process, would also be needed at the tertiary level. Improved accountability mechanisms, combined with the proposed funding mechanism, would be a powerful tool for ensuring that decentralization reinforces national education goals, and that disparities across districts in education funding and achievement are monitored and corrective action is taken.

(f) *Intensified efforts to ensure equal opportunities,* especially for Roma children at the primary and secondary levels and for all students at the tertiary level. These efforts could include *using opportunities within the school consolidation program to provide Roma children with* greater *access to education in an integrated setting,* head-start pre-school programs, and other interventions specifically targeted for the Roma. For all students, greater equity could be achieved by *correcting the apparent wide geographical disparities in educational spending, as well as reforming the process and content of testing and admissions* at the secondary and tertiary levels. Student loans and need-based scholarships will become increasingly important at the tertiary level as the use of tuition expands.

The above agenda outlines steps to increase the relevance and quality of the education system, as well as its efficiency and equity, within tight resource constraints, mainly by refocusing resources that are already being used. The consolidation and reorientation at the primary and secondary level would free up resources for quality improvements, as would tuition at the tertiary level. The proposed funding mechanisms, combined with appropriate school-level autonomy, would give schools more flexibility to use resources to raise quality, and to adjust to changing needs, while the stronger accountability mechanisms proposed would ensure that this autonomy is used effectively to support the country's objectives in education. *By containing the overall use of public resources, and achieving a better link between the education system and the country's skill needs, the proposed reforms would contribute to the country's strategic objectives of growth, employment, and macroeconomic stability.* Such reforms, however, cannot be carried out by the stroke of a pen. Careful analysis and design work will be required to develop specific reform strategies and policies, to strengthen the institutions needed to implement them, and to build a consensus behind them. Consequently, *a critical early step in the reform process would be to designate a highly qualified team to take the lead in this effort.*

Health

Despite more than a decade of frequent and continuing reforms, and despite some improvements in the Slovak Republic's health indicators, health care remains beset by serious problems. *First, the health care system does not appear to be financially sustainable.* Demands on the system have risen rapidly (see Figure 2), bringing public spending to levels that are high compared to other CEECs and to the country's income level. The payroll tax rate for health (14 percent) is the highest in the region, yet the system runs persistent deficits, reflecting a very broad benefit package, unconstrained demands, inadequate revenue growth, and inefficiencies in the provision of care. For example, between 1990 and 1999, hospital admission rates rose by 18 percent, and per capita outpatient visits by 20 percent. Efforts to contain public spending have resulted in widespread formal and informal private payments, as well as in recurrent, large payment arrears throughout the system. Substantial infusions of extrabudgetary privatization revenues have been used to reduce the levels of debt from time to time, but the underlying imbalances that caused them remain, with system-wide arrears approaching 2 percent of GDP by March 2002. The country's multiple health insurance companies may only add to the problems by increasing administrative costs and fragmentation.

Second, *the existing health infrastructure continues to rely heavily on relatively costly, input-intensive approaches,* with too much emphasis on costly in-patient care and specialist physicians. Little progress has been made in realizing the substantial scope for improved effectiveness and

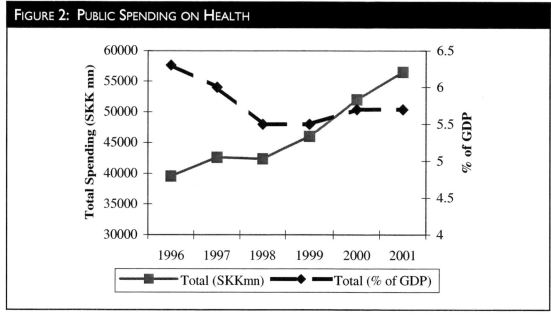

FIGURE 2: PUBLIC SPENDING ON HEALTH

Source: MoF

efficiency through less intensive input use and a shift toward more cost-effective preventive and outpatient approaches. The incentives in the system do not appear adequate to reduce overstaffing and excess numbers of hospital beds and facilities. *Unsurprisingly, there appears to be widespread dissatisfaction with the health care system both among patients and among health care providers,* with concerns ranging from declining quality, denial of service, and rising informal payments, to low salaries for medical personnel. Surveys have shown that *more than half of households and public officials viewed the health care system as having "very widespread" corruption,* the highest level of perceived corruption of any public sector activity.

Without substantial reform, these problems are only likely to get worse: demands on the system will rise as incomes rise, yet resources will become more constrained as the numbers of employees, the system's main contributors, decline relative to the elderly, whose health care costs are much (some 2.5 times) higher than those of the rest of the population. Over time, these problems are likely to compromise the quality of health care, particularly in the vitally important and cost-effective areas of disease prevention and health promotion, and to result in an erosion of the health of the population. While there are no ready-made solutions, the most productive areas for short- and medium-term action and reforms include the following:

(a) *Containing the excess demand inherent in the system* by narrowing the scope of the benefit package, tightening the link between contributions and benefits, and increasing cost sharing by consumers, with safeguards for those with low incomes.
(b) *Reforming the health financing mechanism,* to make it more efficient, to improve collection compliance, and to broaden its revenue base. This would include *consolidation of the health insurance companies into a single payer system, integrating collection of health insurance payments with other social contributions,* improving collection compliance, and shifting responsibility for funding a larger share of the non-contributing participants from the payroll tax to general taxation.
(c) *Increasing the efficiency of the provider network, reducing overstaffing and excess hospital beds.* A provider network rationalization plan should be designed and implemented to

reduce overstaffing and excess capacity. *Improving provider payment mechanisms and other health system incentives could further help.* A range of mixed provider payment systems could be considered, preferably *incorporating a "money follows the patient" approach.* In parallel with these measures, and a tighter accountability mechanism discussed below, providers will need the autonomy and the management tools and skills to respond effectively to changes in the incentive structure.

(d) *Ensuring that the system has adequate incentives and funding for essential public health* functions, including cost effective programs to prevent sickness and promote good health practices.

(e) *Protecting access and equity* for all groups in the country, but with particular emphasis on meeting the needs of the Roma. This community has greater health problems than the general population, and less access to health care.

(f) *Strengthening the institutional framework* both to design and implement a systematic reform program and to better manage the health system. This would include: professional and technical capacities for policy and program analysis; the necessary information systems; and the mechanisms for holding a more decentralized, autonomous system of providers accountable for quality standards and cost-effectiveness.

Reforms in the areas outlined above should serve to make the health care system more effective in meeting the needs of the people while containing its cost. Such reforms would contribute directly to the government's strategic objective of macroeconomic stability by reducing the pressure of rising expenditure. However, while many countries share the symptoms afflicting the health system, worldwide experience suggests that this does not make these symptoms easier to diagnose and cure. *A first priority therefore would be to establish a team to lead this reform effort* and develop and give direction to the institutional framework discussed above.

Social Protection
The Slovak Republic's spending on social protection programs has been fairly stable as a share of GDP in recent years, and (at 13.1 percent of GDP or nearly one-third of public spending) is around the CEEC average. But these aggregate numbers mask serious underlying problems, as well as some unrealized opportunities to stimulate growth and employment. First, despite significant reforms enacted in May 2002, *the PAYGO pension system faces unsustainable deficits as the demographic shift already under way inexorably reduces the numbers of contributors while increasing the numbers of pensioners.* A deeper reform of the pension system is therefore a high priority, not only to secure macroeconomic stability, but also to ensure adequate pensions for future generations, as well as opening some possibility for reducing the payroll tax.

Second, among *Social Assistance programs, cash assistance for the unemployed and support for the disabled have grown exceptionally rapidly* in recent years and need to be carefully reviewed. While the cash assistance program, in concert with other components of social protection, has helped the country reduce poverty and deal with rising unemployment, *the level and structure of benefits generate major work disincentives and risk creating a "poverty trap."* Third, the surplus now being generated in the sickness insurance fund provides an opportunity to reduce the payroll tax, especially if combined with tighter spending control. Fourth, several other features of the social protection system, some of them relatively new, should be carefully reassessed to identify ways to ensure that they are cost-effective and well targeted to assist the poor. These features include the active labor market programs (ALMPs) administered by the National Labor Office, the child allowances recently made available to all parents regardless of income, the subsidies for spa care, and the recently established housing allowance.

The Slovak Republic's social protection system is comprehensive and complex. It not only uses a large share of the country's public resources, but also plays a vital role in reducing poverty and securing the welfare of the people. In considering improvements to such a system, *it is important that reforms be based on sound technical analysis within a holistic view of the relationships among the programs* and *their impact on the people, especially the poor.* A starting point in developing such a reform strategy would be to *designate a highly qualified team responsible for coordinating the technical analysis and consensus building needed to design the reform program* and to strengthen the institutions to manage it subsequently. This report cannot substitute for the detailed design work such a reform requires; rather, it points to what appear to be the main problem areas and options for significant reforms, as summarized below.

In **pensions,** *the most critical reform needed to secure the system's long-run financial viability is an increase in the retirement age to 65* (see "CPI, 65" line in Figure 3, compared to the "2002 Reforms only" line). Careful consideration should also be given to further tightening the link between benefits and contributions by further modifications of the benefit formula, which is still quite redistributive, even after the recent reform. This could include either a modification of the current Defined Benefit formula, or the adoption of a Notional Defined Contribution approach which would generate more stable fiscal outcomes as well as a tighter link between benefits and contributions (the "NDC, 63" line in Figure 3). Other desirable reforms of the PAYGO system include measures to improve contribution compliance, especially from the self-employed; transparent accounting, rigorous assessment, and possible phasing out, of some of the "non-system" benefits (such as accrual of pension rights by university students), and full state budget funding of those "non-system" benefits that remain; and removal of the recent provision allowing parents to reduce their pension contribution by 0.5 percent per child. Any savings to the pension fund arising from these reforms could be passed on to participants as lower payroll taxes.

While these reforms to the first pillar (the PAYGO system) are being launched, *the technical work for a mandatory, fully funded second pillar should be completed.* If the first pillar is financially sound, introducing a second pillar offers scope for gradual increases in benefits (as a percent of gross wages) over time. However, *if the first pillar is not sound, the transition costs involved in introducing the second pillar will only make the pension system less sustainable.* This is why it is critically important to secure adequate reforms of the first pillar. In designing the second pillar, options regarding its size, phase-in period, and switching age should be considered, and *the timing phased*

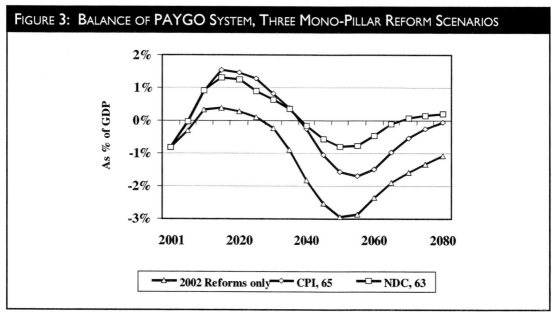

FIGURE 3: BALANCE OF PAYGO SYSTEM, THREE MONO-PILLAR REFORM SCENARIOS

Source: World Bank calculations.

to take advantage of the Slovak Republic's incipient access to the EU's increasingly integrated capital markets, or even better to the euro-zone. At the same time, institutional and administrative arrangements should be put in place to manage the reformed system, including the regulatory and legal framework for the existing private, voluntary third pillar, as well as the mandatory second pillar.

In *Social Assistance,* there is a need to *contain the growth of spending on cash assistance for the unemployed and to reduce its work disincentives.* This can be done through: (i) *reductions in the benefit levels* (to widen the gap between benefits and average wages) by adjusting benefits to reflect regional cost of living differentials (or calculating them excluding Bratislava) and/or reducing the per child allotment as the number of children rises; combined with (ii) adjustments in the benefit structure to *"make employment pay"* (mainly by reducing the rate of withdrawal of benefits as recipients earn income, strictly enforcing activity tests, and developing more effective ones, possibly linked to ALMPs). Strengthening the capacity of Social Assistance staff to conduct activity testing and to work effectively with the Roma could also be important. In addition, the programs to assist the disabled should be examined to determine if the recent rapid increase in spending is justified.

In *sickness insurance,* there is an opportunity to return the surplus currently being generated to participants by *reducing the payroll tax (possibly by as much as 2 percent),* and to contain future pressure on spending by having employers (instead of the fund) pay for the first few days of sick leave. In addition, given the potential for fraud and abuse, consideration should be given to ending the participation of the self-employed in sickness insurance. For *unemployment insurance, active labor market programs should be kept under close review and rigorously assessed to ensure their cost-effectiveness* and to identify ways in which they can *work in tandem with Social Assistance* to move people off the welfare rolls.

For *other state social benefits,* consideration should be given to *reversing the recent changes in the child allowance* by subjecting recipients again to an income test. Various options for modifying the level and structure of the benefit could also be considered. If the universal child allowance is retained for parents of all income levels, it should be subject to the income tax. Spending to subsidize *spa care* could be reassessed to determine if there are not more effective uses of funds to improve social protection (e.g., to fund tapering of the withdrawal of social assistance benefits as recipients earn income).

For *housing subsidies,* consideration should be given to *terminating the program,* relying on Social Assistance to meet the needs of the poor in this area. If needed as a transition, measures such as targeted lifeline tariffs for low-income customers should be considered.

Revenue Rebalancing and Consolidation

On the revenue side, given the steep tax reduction implemented in the last four years, the time has come to place top priority on fiscal consolidation and to postpone any further *reduction in total revenue until* fiscal *consolidation objectives are accomplished.* There is, however, a broad scope for important changes in the structure of revenues.

Most significantly, the expenditure reform strategies discussed above would open up opportunities for *rebalancing the revenue base by significantly reducing reliance on the payroll tax. The largest opportunity lies in health insurance,* where the 14 percent payroll tax paid by employees generates some 70 percent of health insurance revenues, while the government payments for the 60 percent of the population that does not contribute provide less than 30 percent of revenues. The employed workers therefore heavily cross-subsidize the rest of the population, and the link between their insurance contribution and their benefits is correspondingly weakened. This could be corrected by shifting more of the burden of funding the non-contributors from the payroll tax to general taxation. Rough calculations indicate a payroll tax on the order of 7 percent would generate enough revenue to cover the insurance costs for the participant.

Reforming sickness insurance opens another opportunity to reduce the payroll tax: here, a 4.8 percent payroll tax has been generating a surplus equivalent to 2 percent of payroll. Tightening control on spending of this fund by having employers take on the burden of financing the first few days of sick leave would help contain spending levels and lock in the surplus. The payroll tax could then be safely reduced by as much as 2 percent.

Finally, *some of the pension reforms proposed may provide some scope for further reducing payroll taxes.* In particular the transparent assessment of the full costs of "non-system benefits" (primarily accrual of pension rights by students and those on maternity leave, and pension increments to top up pensions to a socially acceptable minimum), phasing out those not justified, and shifting the full cost of the rest to the budget, could result in savings to the pension fund that could be passed on as payroll tax deductions.

The reduction of labor taxes should be *offset by an expansion of the tax base of both the CIT and the PIT.* On the CIT side, the proposed improvements in the business climate could pave the way for *scaling back the currently excessive tax incentives provided to investors,* as a result of the destructive tax competition waged by Visegrad countries. In the Slovak case, the process started in 1998 when the government offered a tax credit allowing exemptions from corporate income tax for particular activities. Subsequently, the incentive package was amended several times, with the last changes being introduced in December 2001. The most recent innovation has been the almost indiscriminate promotion of industrial parks (the state covers 70 percent of the development of industrial parks by the municipalities).

The prospect of EU Accession offers a golden opportunity to break the vicious circle. The Slovak authorities would be well advised *to support any initiative taken in the context of the negotiations of the competition chapter of the accession treaties to* harmonize *tax incentives at the lowest possible level.* Furthermore, without denying the advantages that industrial zones can provide, it would be in the country's own interest to *subject any incentive for the creation of such zone to two market tests: (i) the demonstrated commitment of an interested investor; and (ii) the presence of a majority private sector stake in the industrial zone itself.*

Similarly, *those categories of income currently exempted from PIT should be brought into the tax base.* This concerns in particular pensions (which would need to be appropriately rebased), and child allowances, if they continue to be available to all parents. *Some indirect taxes could also be raised.* Increasing excises for beer and tobacco and unifying VAT tax rates at the current top level would be the most relevant measures in this area. *There is finally room to expand non-tax revenues,* particularly those linked to revenues from government participation in gas and electricity companies (including the special levy proposed above), as the planned increase in regulated prices would produce profit windfalls.

Finally, current and future inflows of privatization receipts from abroad should be used to retire *foreign rather than domestic debt.* Not only is this needed to keep such inflows from spilling over into excessive domestic demand; such an approach would also be consistent with a strategy to optimize the currency structure of public debt and to deepen the domestic debt market. At present 52 percent of public debt is in foreign currency, which is relatively high, and about one-third of that foreign debt is in currencies other than the euro, which may be unduly risky given the country's prospect of joining ERM-2 in the not too distant future. On the other hand, the domestic debt market is under-developed, and lacks predictability and transparency: there is, for instance, no firm issuance program, making it difficult for market participants in turn to plan and manage their own cash flows. To overcome this deficiency, the government would be well advised to undertake the following:

(a) Integrate cash and debt management within the Ministry of Finance (international experience would seem to advise against delegating that task to a separate debt management agency in circumstances where oversight capacities are weak).

(b) Rely primarily on regular, non-discretionary debt issuances designed to create liquid benchmarks spread along the yield curve.

(c) Develop an asset/liability management strategy in line with best practices among EU members and develop the attendant risk management systems.

Labor Market Reform

Reducing unemployment is perhaps the clearest mandate emanating from the recent elections and is consequently a priority for the new government. The recent OECD country report lays out a comprehensive agenda in this regard; this one can therefore be brief.

Some of the labor demand-side measures have already been mentioned. In particular, the discussion above highlighted the substantial scope *to reduce labor costs by reducing payroll taxes.* This in turn would require the parallel transfer of the costs of the social welfare components of pensions and health insurance from the social insurance system to general taxation.

Increased flexibility in labor relations and wage setting mechanisms are a second way to boost labor demand. In this regard, it is strongly recommended to put an end to the deliberate policy of raising the minimum wages more rapidly than other wages, as part of *a broader policy to discard the minimum wage as an instrument of incomes policy* (while continuing to see it as an instrument for worker protection). As presented in the PEP, the current approach intends to "gradually increase the proportion of the minimum to the average wage level." While this policy may encourage some extra workers to participate, it is also sure to reduce labor demand, particularly at the low end of the wage scale. It would also be desirable to limit the extension of regional or sectoral collective bargaining agreements only to those firms that participated in the negotiations. The extension to firms not involved may result in wage awards that are not in line with improvements in productivity. Along these lines, the *decentralization of wage bargaining will enable wage agreements to reflect more closely productivity conditions at the firm level.*

Furthermore, the easing of many of the restrictive regulations currently embedded in the new labor code could facilitate job creation and the reallocation of the labor force following the structural changes in the enterprise sector. This would include increasing the flexibility of regulations limiting working hours, and protecting employment in general, and reducing the labor unions' role in the management of personnel issues. Instead, regulations should be modified so as to improve flexibility, reform provisions for part time employment, reduce red tape for the creation of SMEs, and soften some of the most protective employment provisions of the labor code for SMEs.

On the supply side of the labor market, it will also be necessary, as discussed above, to encourage labor force participation by revising the social assistance benefit levels and structure, to widen the gap with average wages and to increase incentives to move from welfare to work. Labor force participation would benefit from making the activity tests for Social Assistance more effective and tapering the withdrawal of benefits as recipients find gainful employment. In the longer term, efforts should be aimed at adapting the supply of human capital to the new market requirements. Promoting general as opposed to vocational secondary education and gradually expanding enrollment at the tertiary level, as recommended above, would contribute to this end.

Governance

The government's success in designing and implementing a reform program on the lines discussed in this report will depend fundamentally on its capacity to strengthen the institutional framework in which those policies are conceived, decided upon, and executed. While there are many critical issues and areas for action for improving the institutions of governance, this report focuses primarily on *public sector management* issues, the implications for *the decentralization process* currently under way, and *reforms of the justice sector,* three areas where stronger institutions are strategically critical if the public and private sectors are to operate with efficiency and integrity.

Public Sector Management

How successful the government will be in its fiscal consolidation efforts, and in its broader efforts to reform the economy to prepare for EU accession, will depend critically on progress in building the institutions and capacities needed to design reforms and manage them, and in improving the tools of fiscal management and program assessment. While there are a number of important measures that can and should be taken in the short term (especially reducing enterprise subsidies and starting to raise the retirement age), most of the important measures for containing expenditures in a sustainable way, based on sound program reforms, will require a thorough, comprehensive review of the overall expenditure program. This should not be a one-shot exercise, but should be a continuous process to identify reforms of the main expenditure programs, including a careful assessment (and subsequent monitoring) of the impact of the reforms on the poor, especially the Roma. The process will also require a parallel strengthening of institutions to manage programs following their reform. This process will involve choices over time about what the public sector should do, how much it should do, and how it can do it most effectively. Many of these choices will be politically sensitive, and thus an important part of the effort would be to develop an understanding of and a political consensus for the need for such reforms.

Public Expenditure Management. Transforming the medium term budgeting and program budgeting frameworks into effective fiscal planning tools, improving the quality of underlying financial and performance information, and enhancing systems integrity are thus all important goals. It is especially important to ensure that the basic fiscal accounts are accurate and timely, and are maintained in ways that are consistent and well understood across line and core agencies. Furthermore, it will be important to *consolidate the recent decentralization to ensure that capacities and accountability mechanisms are in place before moving to the next phase of devolution.* Finally, in responding to this challenge, the country needs to *avoid the temptation of paper reforms.* Not only are they pointless, but reforms that exist only on paper are also potentially dangerous: they create the illusion that problems are being corrected, while pushing actual practices into a legal and administrative limbo where they become harder to regulate.

This report emphasizes the critical need for the Slovak Republic to develop the institutions, capacities, and processes that will generate the objective assessments of program performance and reforms needed for continuous improvements in effectiveness and efficiency. This would call for the development of analytical capacities in core and line agencies alike, including continued improvements in the measurement and comprehensiveness of budget accounts, the development of a more formal and systematic medium-term approach to fiscal programming in both the Ministry of Finance and the line ministries, and a move toward greater performance orientation in budgeting, as well as the establishment of periodic, representative household budget surveys. It would also call for the designation of highly qualified teams to coordinate the detailed design work needed to translate ideas for reform into workable strategies for implementation.

Medium Term Budget Framework. To assist in their efforts towards fiscal consolidation, a growing number of governments are finding it *useful to bind themselves to medium-term budget rules.* The Slovak Republic has also made a formal commitment to medium-term budgeting (most recently in the new Act on Budgetary Rules), but the actual move toward multi-year budget frameworks has hardly begun. Three-year projections of aggregate revenues and expenditures are now being produced (including those used as a basis for the annual pre-accession economic program that the country presents to the EU). In practice these forecasts have remained a peripheral activity to budget preparation and execution. One illustration of this phenomenon is the wide gap between the target presented in the 2001 PEP for general government expenditure in 2002 and the current official projection (37 percent of GDP versus 40.6 percent of GDP). Perhaps the best way to institutionalize a medium term budgeting framework would be to elevate it to a formal political commitment binding the government to the general public.

Program Budgeting. Expenditure rationalization would also be easier if the budget process generated a better sense not only of where public monies are spent but also of what is being delivered and achieved with these monies. The introduction of program budgeting, with that objective in mind, appears to be proceeding in a well-structured manner. Nevertheless, concerns have been raised as to whether units in the line ministries fully understand the changes implied by program budgeting, or whether they simply see it as a set of forms and information requirements imposed from outside. Program budgeting will successfully assist resource allocation only where *its goals* are well understood, so that government operations can be assessed (or at least challenged) in terms of their cost as well as their conformity with stated policies and objectives; and where *its procedures* are seen to facilitate the running of the line agencies themselves. One of the implications of this is that progress in budget methodologies needs to rest firmly on the strengthening of analytical capacities within line ministries.

At the same time, *capacities and instruments to assess program impact and effectiveness* need to be put in place, *including a well-designed system of periodic household income and expenditure surveys.* This can be a key tool in assessing the impact of a broad range of programs and policies, especially their impact on the poor.

Performance and Financial Information. The possibility of making such productive use of the program budgeting framework will therefore *depend critically on the quality and reliability of the underlying financial and information systems.* Unfortunately, the lack of an integrated financial information system to bring together the Ministry of Finance, the line ministries, the spending units, the National Bank of Slovakia (NBS) and the NKU creates problems of untimely, unshared, and inaccurate information. *The main justification and focus of the proposed Treasury reform ought to be to remedy these deficiencies.* The reasons for wanting to transfer payment functions away from the Central Bank as envisaged in the Treasury Act are less clear, and prima facie, less urgent with regard to the fiscal consolidation priorities outlined above. Worse, this initiative is proceeding on an unrealistic implementation plan, threatening to leave that critical function in the same legal and administrative limbo that now surrounds debt management operations (following a similarly hasty reform). There is therefore an urgent need to (i) recalibrate and prioritize Treasury reform objectives to serve the requirements of the government's overall fiscal strategy; and (ii) clarify the responsibilities (transitional responsibilities, if need be) so that debt management and Treasury operations do not proceed in a legal vacuum.

Systems Integrity. *The integrity of budget execution systems appears to have been compromised more often by weaknesses in procurement and audit* than by problems with Treasury operations per se. Weak points in the public financial accountability system are: (i) defective procurement practices; (ii) weak follow-up and remedial action on significant audit findings; (iii) weak accountability arrangements for local government units; and (iv) an administrative culture that tolerates corrupt acts.

A blueprint was recently submitted to the government *on how to improve the transparency and efficiency of procurement.* Key next steps should include: (i) establishing permanent procurement committees within contracting authorities that are responsible for decision making and for providing oversight and evaluation committees to deal with the bidding process; (ii) developing a formal code of ethics for government employees to improve their accountability in procurement; and (iii) completing procurement guidelines to cover non-public tendering procedures as well as procurement of consultants and updating of standard bidding documents. It is also recommended that the role of the NKU in conducting procurement audits of contracting authorities at regular intervals be enhanced and its reports made public.

At present, the *existing audit* (carried out by the NKU and the Ministry of Finance) *is essentially external in nature* and directed primarily at fault-finding rather than at assessing the adequacy of systems. Modern concepts of financial control, which have not made much headway in the Slovak public sector, locate the prime responsibility for financial control with the management of the entity concerned. If the country wishes to achieve strong public financial management, it has to locate the essential controls (and accountability) at the entity level. NKU's external audit could then focus on whether the internal control systems established by management are adequate and are working properly. That function would be more effectively discharged if the Ministry of Finance were mandated to follow up with line ministries on defects identified at audit and to report to the legislature on the status of remedial actions taken.

Decentralization
The ongoing decentralization may potentially complicate the task of putting public finances on a sound footing. All in all, about 4.5 percent of GDP in new responsibilities is to be transferred to the existing 2,886 municipalities and to eight newly created regions. Unless measures are taken to consolidate the

process, the risk is that the resulting greater fragmentation of public services might make it all the more difficult to realize the existing potentials for economies of scale, while further bloating the bureaucracy by duplication and fragmentation. There is indeed little empirical evidence that fledgling decentralized authorities would have the needed administrative capacity or political mettle, or that they would operate in an accountability framework that would maximize the public good. In the face of hard budget constraints, what is more likely to be weakened is the quality and accessibility of services for large segments of the population (especially those with little clout, like the Roma).

For the immediate future therefore, the priority is to *consolidate the present phase of decentralization*—before planning (or executing) new advances—by:

(a) *Clarifying the respective roles and responsibilities* (including in terms of assets and liabilities) of the regional and district levels of the national government on the one hand and of the municipalities and newly created regions on the other.

(b) *Actually creating regional administrations.* This essential piece of the institutional framework exists only on paper. To facilitate transitions and avoid duplications, it would be preferable to keep the new self-government services, and the remnants of the regional office of the national government under one single, integrated administrative structure.

(c) *Overcoming the disadvantages of municipal fragmentation.* As long as this fragmentation persists, the district offices will have a critical role to play in stimulating intermunicipal cooperation and overseeing and backstopping weaker and smaller municipalities. That capacity should be maintained.

(d) *Funding newly transferred* responsibilities *through itemized, tied decentralization subsidies.* This current arrangement is appropriate to a situation in which administrative capacities and accountability mechanisms are either weak (municipalities) or, at best, untested (regions). Only over time will it be safe to move towards untied grants as local implementation and fiscal capacities strengthen and the need for central oversight lessens accordingly.

Justice Sector Reform
Modernizing the justice sector is critical for accelerating and maintaining economic growth, ensuring equitable access for vulnerable groups, and increasing social cohesion and stability. For example, the formal bankruptcy procedures that are so important for efficient enterprise restructuring may not become truly dependable until the structural deficiencies in the judiciary system have been corrected. Unfortunately, despite initial reforms over the last decade, the judiciary has earned a reputation for being slow, expensive, and corrupt. Indeed, surveys indicate that the judiciary comes second only to health care in terms of perceived corruption.

To remedy this situation, the country should give priority to (i) refocusing the Supreme Court on its core mandate; (ii) strengthening the management and policy capacity in the Ministry of Justice; (iii) creating a body of professional court administrators; (iv) rolling out the modernized case management system throughout the judiciary; (v) stepping up the investigation and prosecution of corrupt judges; (vi) strengthening the regulatory bodies of the legal profession and separating this role from that of advocacy; and (vii) enhancing client protection.

Macroeconomic Outlook and Welfare Impact
The proposed policy package should help the economy converge towards EU-levels of income and reduce unemployment. In itself, the prospect of a now imminent EU accession unquestionably improves the economy's outlook. While training their sights on that target, it will be important for all to keep in mind that it is *the implementation of EU policies,* more than *membership per se,* that will determine the pace of the hoped-for convergence. With the measures proposed above to invigorate the supply side, output growth should continue to outpace average EU growth, expanding at a rate of 3.5–4 percent in 2003 and accelerating to an average 4.7 percent over the next four years.

Action will also be needed on the demand side for such a scenario to materialize. Timely fiscal consolidation will be central if private sector demand is to continue to expand apace when privatization inflows subside—without threatening external stability. Bringing down the fiscal deficit to 2.5 percent of GDP over the medium term will help that scenario come about. This would allow combining robust private investment with a steady lowering of the external current account deficit, in a first phase below 5 percent of GDP by 2007. With demand under control, inflation would bounce back only briefly to some 7 percent in 2003 due to adjustments in utility prices before settling back down towards 3–4 percent.

The measures proposed in this report to secure sustained growth and broader-based employment, especially in the lower-wage, lower-skill end of the job spectrum, should also set the economy on a path to reduce poverty. Of particular importance for poverty reduction will be:

- Measures to ensure the expansion of a diverse and efficient enterprise sector, able to compete in world markets and generate productive jobs
- Labor market reforms that would reduce rigidities, especially those that tend to price low-wage labor out of the market
- Reforms in social assistance and other components of the social protection system that will ease the transition of recipients from welfare to work, as well as make the system more sustainable
- Reductions in payroll taxes to reduce their impact on discouraging growth and employment
- Implementation of decentralization with a view to securing equal access to quality basic health and education services for all
- Reforms in education that will ensure that those entering the labor market have the skills needed to function effectively in a dynamic labor market
- Pension reforms that will help ensure more secure and more adequate benefits for future generations of retirees
- Improvements in the capacities and instruments for the analysis of program and policy impacts in general, and poverty in particular.

On the other hand, some of the policies discussed above may unfortunately hurt the lower income group of the population. This would be the case particularly with the adoption of the EU's Common Agricultural Policy (through its impact on food prices), and with the necessary adjustment of energy tariffs. A key element in mitigating such negative effects would be to adjust social assistance benefits at regular intervals in the light of well-designed, periodic household budget and expenditure surveys.

Conclusions

The Slovak Republic's external current account and fiscal deficits (net of privatization receipts) are unsustainably high (at about 8 percent of GDP in 2002), despite some recent declines. With a capital account surplus of perhaps 20 percent of GDP this year, the Slovak Republic may not find it particularly difficult to finance these deficits, but this favorable situation will not last. Furthermore, through its impact on the real exchange rate, this policy mix is undermining the employability of large segments of the population (particularly those with low skill levels) and will ultimately choke growth (projected at 4 percent for 2002). While much policy attention has gone to stimulating investment, future growth will also depend on raising the employment rate, currently one of the lowest among the CEECs.

This report lays out the broad thrust of a policy strategy to bolster the recovery and bring the economy towards convergence with the EU. This strategy consists of three key elements:

(a) *Continued trade, finance, and enterprise reform* to complete the structural transformation of the economy and align it with the EU framework

(b) *Fiscal consolidation,* focusing on cutting back expenditure and stabilizing revenues, while redirecting revenue and expenditure policies to become more fully supportive of growth and employment objectives

(c) *Labor market reform,* directed at enhancing labor market flexibility by relaxing legal provisions on working arrangements (such as part-time work, self-employment, and fixed term contracts), by decentralizing collective bargaining, and discarding the minimum wage as an instrument of incomes policy, and by reforming the social assistance system.

The ultimate success of the policy reforms outlined in this report will depend to a great extent on *the government's capacity to strengthen the institutional framework in which those policies are conceived, decided upon, and executed.* Three priorities have been highlighted: (i) the reform of public expenditure management systems and practices needed to support a growth-oriented fiscal strategy; (ii) the consolidation of the recent decentralization moves as a prerequisite for further devolution, and (iii) a much overdue overhaul of the judiciary system.

CHAPTER I

STRATEGIC SETTING

The Slovak economy has this year experienced its best growth performance since it pulled out from the financial crisis of 1998. The economy is now on a recovery path, with output and private sector employment growth expected to reach 4 percent and 2 percent this year, respectively (see Table 1.1). However, no sooner had recovery gotten under way and begun to generate jobs, than macroeconomic imbalances resurfaced: the fiscal and external current account deficits hover around 8 percent of GDP, while more than 18 percent of the labor force remains unemployed.

The current situation *differs however from the pre-1999 situation in at least four important respects.*

(a) *First,* significant *structural reforms* implemented throughout the post-1998 period have managed to overhaul the supply side of the economy. The reforms have contributed to upgrading the business environment and stimulating investment, allowing the country to increase its penetration into international markets and to compete in the EU markets with more technologically sophisticated products. In parallel, the reforms have attracted strategic foreign investment that had previously eluded the country, allowing for a much-needed technological upgrade in production capacity.

(b) *Second,* while domestic demand drove growth in both periods, the *sources of domestic demand* are fundamentally different. In the pre-1999 period, domestic demand was mainly driven by state sponsored financial laxity in enterprises, whereas it is now led by greenfield foreign investment—which is good—and fiscal expansion, which is not.

(c) *Third,* while the economy is grounded in firmer fundamentals and able to compete more effectively in international markets, the ongoing expansion faces *a* less *supportive* international *environment.* Growth in the main market for Slovak products has decelerated, dragging down the demand for Slovak exports.

(d) *Fourth,* while the external environment for trade is less supportive now than in the past, the Slovak Republic has substantially greater access to *external* financing, especially to non-debt

TABLE 1.1: KEY ECONOMIC INDICATORS, 1995–2001

	1995	1996	1997	1998	1999	2000	2001
Real Economy							
Real GDP (growth rate)	5.8	5.6	4.0	1.3	2.2	3.3	4.0
Unemployment rate	13.1	11.3	11.8	12.5	16.2	18.9	19.4
Inflation (CPI, period average %)	9.8	5.8	6.1	6.7	10.6	12.0	7.3
Private Consumption/GDP	50.5	52.3	52.2	53.4	55.4	55.3	55.8
Gross National Savings/GDP	28.6	25.2	25.9	25.1	23.4	22.8	22.9
Gross Domestic Investment/GDP	26.5	35.6	35.2	34.7	28.2	26.4	31.9
Balance of Payments							
Trade Balance/GDP	−1.2	−11.2	−9.9	−10.7	−5.4	−4.5	−10.4
Exports of Goods and Services (growth rate in US$)	...	−0.5	8.3	10.2	−5.6	15.2	6.8
Imports of Goods and Services (growth rate in US$)	...	26.3	5.4	11.6	−13.4	13.2	15.3
Current Account Balance/GDP	2.0	−10.2	−9.3	−9.7	−4.9	−3.5	−8.6
Capital and Financial Account/GDP	7.2	12.0	8.6	8.3	7.6	7.5	9.1
Gross Official Reserves (billion US$, end-year)	3.4	3.4	3.3	2.9	3.4	4.1	4.2
Reserve Cover (months of imports of G&S)	...	3.2	2.9	2.3	3.1	3.4	3.0
Gross External Debt/GDP	...	...	47.4	55.2	53.0	55.7	56.3
External Debt Service (% of exports of G.S.I. & T.)	...	...	...	13.3	15.5	17.1	10.5
Public Finances							
General Government Balance/GDP	...	−3.2	−4.8	−5.1	−4.3	−9.1	−8.5
Idem, excluding extraordinary items	...	−1.4	−4.3	−4.7	−4.5	−6.0	−6.6
Public Debt/GDP (%)[1]	...	26.4	28.8	28.8	40.1	44.1	43.0
Interest Rates							
Average nominal lending rate (in percent)	16.9	13.9	18.7	21.2	21.1	14.9	11.2
Average real lending rate (deflated by CPI, in percent)	...	7.7	11.8	13.6	9.5	2.6	3.7
Average nominal deposit rate (in percent)	9.0	9.3	13.4	16.3	14.4	8.5	6.4
Average real deposit rate (deflated by CPI, in percent)	...	3.3	6.9	9.0	3.4	−3.2	−0.8
Money and Credit							
Money (annual growth)	...	15.8	−4.4	−11.4	4.2	21.5	21.3
Quasi-Money (annual growth)	...	16.4	18.3	14.6	15.0	12.5	7.7
Credit to Enterprises and Households (% growth)[2]	...	6.0	42.7	34.9	9.2	20.9	25.2
Labor and Wages							
Nominal gross wage growth (%, period average)	14.3	13.3	13.1	8.4	7.2	6.5	8.2
Real gross wage growth (%, period average)	4.1	7.1	6.6	1.6	−3.0	−4.9	0.8
Exchange Rates							
Nominal Exchange Rate (SKK per US$, average)	29.7	30.7	33.6	35.2	41.4	46.0	48.4
Nominal Exchange Rate (SKK per Euros, average)	40.6	39.9	38.0	39.2	44.1	42.6	43.3
Nominal Effective Exchange Rate (1995=100)[3]	100	100.7	105.8	103.6	93.4	94.5	93.2
Real Effective Exchange Rate (CPI, 1995=100)[3]	100	100.3	106.3	106.5	104.2	116.5	116.7
Real Effective Exchange Rate (ULC, 1995=100)[3]	100	108.6	120.0	115.6	110.6	111.0	109.8
Memo Items							
Gross Domestic Product (current SKK billion)	568.9	628.6	708.7	775.0	835.7	908.7	989.3
Gross Domestic Product (current US$ billion)	19.1	20.5	21.1	22.0	20.2	19.7	20.5
Per Capita Income (US$)	3,570	3,816	3,916	4,081	3,745	3,654	3,783

Notes: 1/ Includes debts assumed by the bank restructuring agencies in 1999–2000, and Sk 105 billion
(11 percent of GDP) in bank restructuring bonds issued in the first quarter of 2001.
2/ Adjusted by bank restructuring.
3/ Growth of the index indicates appreciation.

Sources: World Bank calculations based on Ministry of Finance, National Bank of Slovakia and Statistical Office of the Slovak Republic.

forms of financing such as FDI and privatization receipts. With ample privatization receipts, the country has found no major problems in financing the large current account deficits of the last two years. Indeed, the country has substantially increased its foreign reserves.

This chapter examines these four points in turn (the role of structural reforms, the sources of domestic demand, the external environment, and external financing). From this analysis of the current macroeconomic setting, the chapter identifies three key strategic objectives that the incoming government will want to pursue: (i) invigorating the economic recovery, and (ii) broadening the incipient employment growth, while (iii) securing external stability. Achieving all three objectives will require a combination of the following three instruments: continued trade and enterprise reform, fiscal consolidation, and labor market liberalization. The last three sections of this chapter discuss the specific policies involved, which are then examined in more detail in subsequent chapters of the report.

Role of Structural Reforms

A first important difference from the pre-1999 period is that growth is now underpinned by structural reforms rather than by over-investment. Structural changes imposed following the 1998 crisis managed to transform the supply side of the economy, setting new rules, altering the underlying system of incentives, reconfiguring ownership, and moving the public sector progressively away from the rampant interventionism and patronage of selected enterprises that characterized the previous period. Key among these changes were the revitalization of the privatization agenda and the dramatic transformation of the role of banks and credit allocation in the economic setting (see Chapter 2).

Before 1999, weak bankruptcy and foreclosure laws, incestuous relationships between enterprises and state banks, and political interference in the banks combined to loosen enterprise financial discipline. Not surprisingly, enterprises incurred large losses and accumulated substantial inter-enterprise and tax arrears. Two rounds of privatization, the second of which was tainted by corruption allegations, had succeeded in rapidly transferring ownership to the private sector, but did little to improve corporate governance and restore profitability. Quite the contrary, mass privatization and political interventions in the process benefited insiders, depriving enterprises of the type of capital and injections of know-how that were contributing to revamping the corporate sector elsewhere in the region. Considerable asset stripping and loose access to bank credit helped financed massive loses. Unsurprisingly, despite the good growth performance of the economy at that time (real GDP grew at an annual average 6 percent over the 1994–98 period), banks were building up record-high classified loans, surpassing those in other CEECs.[2] The public sector also played a role in allowing poorly managed enterprises to survive by providing subsidies, loan guarantees, and tax forgiveness. This contributed, in parallel, to rising fiscal deficits and building up contingent liabilities.

Aware of the country's reputation for cronyism during the previous administration, the government that took office in late 1998 took particular care to make its fresh round of privatization more transparent. This government moved to eliminate legal obstacles to the privatization of utilities and initiated their restructuring and sale as well as that of banks. By opening the process to foreign investors and improving transparency, the new government succeeded in attracting highly regarded strategic investors to key areas of the economy. These areas included: telecommunications (2000); the banking sector, with the three largest banks all privatized by 2001; and in 2002, the gas pipeline operator, and the three large power distribution companies. In all these cases, enterprise control was turned over to the strategic investor.

In addition to consolidating ownership and attracting foreign investment, structural reforms introduced since 1999 have helped to change the business environment. These reforms moved the underlying incentives away from the rent-seeking behavior based on inside positioning, preferred access to bank lending, and subsidization that characterized the pre-99 period. Legislative reforms in the commercial code, banking, and corporate governance underpinned this move. In the banking

---

2. See *Expenditure Policies towards EU Accession*, World Bank Technical Paper No. 533, 2002.

TABLE 1.2: DEMAND AND OUTPUT, 1995–2002
(percent)

	1995–98	1999–00	2001–02
Percent change			
Private consumption	6.9	0.6	4.5
Government consumption	6.9	−2.6	5.3
Gross capital formation	20.5	−10.5	10.4
Total domestic demand	9.7	−3.6	6.2
Exports	8.9	9.5	4.5
Imports	15.5	1.9	7.6
Gross domestic product	5.5	1.8	3.5
Contribution to GDP growth			
Gross capital formation	5.2	−3.6	4.4
Total domestic demand	9.8	−3.9	7.5
Net Exports	−4.3	5.2	−4.0
Gross domestic product	5.5	1.8	3.5

Note: The evolution in 2002 is estimated based on preliminary national accounts information as for 1st half 2002.
Source: World Bank calculations based on Statistical Office of the Slovak Republic

sector, in addition to the transfer of ownership of the largest banks to strategic investors, bank supervision has been strengthened.

Sources and Impact of Domestic Demand

Where domestic demand was formerly driven by (state sponsored) financial laxity among enterprises, it is now being fueled by greenfield investment, by changes in the pattern of consumption and credit, but unfortunately also by fiscal expansion (see Table 1.2). The distorted incentives of the pre-1999 period also generated distortions in domestic demand. Soft budget constraints generated by biased lending and indirect government subsidization fueled investment in the private sector while an ambitious highway program pushed public investment up. As a result, investment grew at unprecedented rates, averaging 20 percent in real terms over the 1995–98 period. Much of this investment however was not allocated efficiently.[3]

The depreciation of the exchange rate after the floating of the koruna in October 1998, and the strict austerity measures that ensued, caused domestic demand to contract, and led to a switch from the previously domestically driven growth to the significant increase in net exports that dominated the 1999–2000 period. Investment, which had played an expansionary role in the pre-1999 period, contracted particularly sharply. Households also contributed to the adjustment effort, as real wages fell in those two years for the first time since the end of the transition recession.

This contraction in domestic demand was, however, short lived. By 2001, domestic demand was expanding again briskly (at a pace of 6.2 percent annually over 2001–02) in response to a sharp deterioration of the fiscal position and a renewed momentum for investment. Minimum wage escalation added fuel to this expansion and acted in combination with growing labor market rigidities to stifle the supply response. As a result, after an initial depreciation in the wake of the floating of the currency in 1998, the real effective exchange promptly swung back, appreciating by 16 percent between January 1999 and April 2002 (see Figure 1.1).

---

3. The re-allocation of productive resources—essential to overhauling productivity in a transition economy—was further hindered at that time by requirements, attached to privatization deals, to maintain investment and employment levels in privatized enterprises.

FIGURE 1.1: REAL EFFECTIVE EXCHANGE RATE, 1995–2002

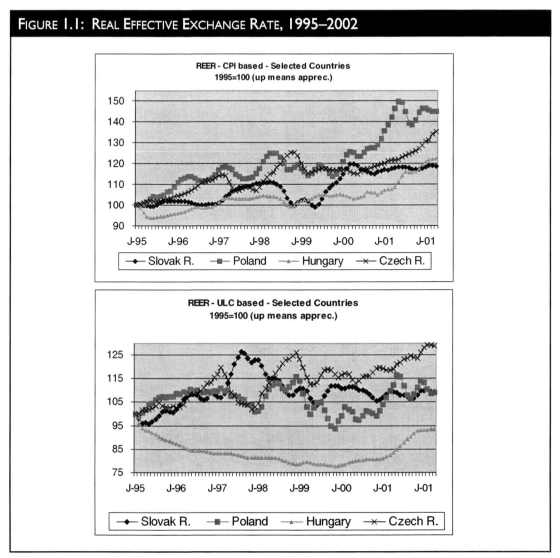

Source: World Bank calculations.

Private Demand

Following the 1998 crisis, a more welcoming approach to the outside world, together with structural reforms, began to attract FDI flows after 1999. The greenfield component of FDI and the investment brought by privatization deals (some of them specified in the privatization contracts), improved the quality of investment, though investment rates were more moderate than in the pre-1999 period. After contracting throughout the 1999–2000 period, investment surged after 2000, becoming once again the leading demand factor.

However, a sizable portion of the incoming privatization receipts was allowed to enter the domestic economy, and inflate domestic demand. Not only were privatization receipts used to finance the deficit, they were also allocated for different purposes, including repaying arrears, payments on called guarantees, and the financing of special development projects. Plans to use SPP receipts to retire domestic rather than foreign debt would add to this pattern. The redemption in cash of National Property Fund (NPF) bonds, amounting to 2 percent of GDP in 2001, also contributed to expand domestic demand. In this respect privatization receipts have contributed to financing a widening fiscal deficit without crowding out private demand. Indeed, domestic interest rates have fallen throughout the past four years (see Table 1.1).

Private consumption was further fueled by the enticement of new supermarkets and retail chains and easier access to credit for consumption (a new line of business for banks as will be seen in Chapter 2). Later on, increases in real wages also contributed to this increase.

Fiscal Expansion

Following a moderate tightening in 1999, the fiscal deficit has widened sharply thereafter. While fiscal deficits in the Slovak Republic were on the high side throughout the second half of the 1990s, they reached unparalleled levels in 2000–01, continuing to threaten stability in 2002 (see Table 1.1). The measures imposed in 1999 managed to cut spending and increase revenue collection temporarily, including through a temporary import surcharge. In this way, and despite a substantial expansion in net lending in that year, deficit levels were brought down to 4.3 percent of GDP. Since then, however, the overall deficit of the general government jumped to 9.1 percent of GDP in the year 2000 and to some 8.5 percent in 2001, when privatization receipts are excluded and the full cost of called guarantees and interest associated with the restructuring of banks is included. In turn, indications are that the deficit of the consolidated general government could reach some 7.5–8 percent of GDP this year.

This fiscal expansion comes at an inappropriate time. The fiscal expansion comes in the midst of economic recovery, with growth accelerating from 1.3 percent in 1999 to 3.3 percent in 2001. While some fiscal expansion may have contributed to sustaining demand at the time of the economic slowdown, as recovery consolidates, continuing the current policy stance may cause the economy to overheat.

The recent fiscal deterioration primarily reflects the impact of policy-driven revenue losses. To the general tariff reduction in the context of the Europe Agreement and the Uruguay Round, and the elimination of the import surcharges,[4] the government added a battery of fiscal measures that involved tax cuts in several areas with the aim of making the country more competitive and attractive to investors. As part of this strategy, the corporate income tax (CIT) rate was reduced while generous tax holiday schemes were implemented, benefiting some of the faster-growing components of the tax base (including VW and U.S. Steel, among others). Similar cuts were implemented in personal income tax (PIT). As a result, tax to GDP ratios fell by some 7.5 percentage points of GDP throughout the 1996–2001 period. The fall in tax to GDP ratios was spread over almost all taxes, but was concentrated in direct taxes and import duties. In addition, social insurance contributions fell in response to rising unemployment. Direct taxes decreased from 10.3 to 6.7 percent of GDP, while import duties and surcharges fell to one-quarter of their 1996 levels (in terms of GDP) and now stand at just 0.4 percent of GDP (2001). The drop in direct tax revenues is almost fully explained by the steep reduction in CIT, which brought CIT collection to 2.2 percent of GDP, from 5.5 percent in 1996.[5] Overall, the fiscal finance trend shows a pattern followed by many regional economies: a progressive reliance on indirect taxes and social security contributions, and a decreasing dependence on direct taxes.

The reduction of tax to GDP ratios in the Slovak Republic is part of a trend shared by all Visegrad countries, which reflects progress in transition, including further trade liberalization, changes in the tax bases due to the restructuring of the economy, and reductions in tax rates. However, in no other Visegrad country has the fall in tax to GDP ratios reached the levels in the

---

4. The government set a 7 percent import surcharge in mid-1999 to help contain the current account deficit and progressively reduced it during the following year and a half, before finally removing it in January 2001.

5. The CIT rate was cut from 40 percent to 29 percent in 2001 and to 25 percent this year.

Slovak Republic.[6] In fact, the reduction in taxes has pushed tax to GDP ratios in the Slovak Republic (at just 30 percent of GDP presently), to the bottom among Visegrad countries. Tax ratios in
the Slovak Republic are also at the very low end of those in EU countries.

   On the other hand, the promised expenditure retrenchment (as reflected in the PEP), that was
supposed to accompany the revenue decline, has never materialized. Consequently, while general
government revenues lost ground by as much as 8 percentage points of GDP between 1996 and
2001, total expenditure and net lending (excluding privatization receipts) shrank by only 2.5 percentage points of GDP over the same period. The uneven implementation of fiscal plans, with suc-
cesses in the reduction of taxes but failures in implementing expenditure reductions, reflects an
inability to break with the past and initiate structural reforms in key expenditure areas. On the contrary, some recent spending measures in the pre-electoral phase threaten to expand spending in
areas that are primary targets for reductions. These measures included a 17 percent increase in civil
service wages, a 5 percent hike in pensions, a ban on tuition for "external" university students, and
the universalization of previously income tested child allowances.

   The resulting *fiscal deficits are not sustainable* and need to be reduced promptly. Left to unattended, ongoing primary fiscal deficits would result in explosive public debt dynamics. According
to our simulations, ongoing fiscal deficit levels, if not corrected, will cause public debt indicators
to breach the Maastricht criteria as early as 2007.[7] Budget deficits are not the only risk involved.
Other risk arise also from (i) the significant amount of government guarantees that the Slovak
Republic has accumulated (equivalent to 18 percent of GDP as of end-2001), mainly to ensure the
continued financing of troubled state-owned enterprises, such as the railway and power companies;
(ii) the recurrent pressure to bailout critical sectors (e.g., health) after they have run up unbearably
high payment arrears; and (iii) unexpected banking troubles (until such time as the deposit insurance scheme is recapitalized). Moreover, even after the reforms of May 2002, the pension system's
deficits are projected to rise over the long run, further darkening the fiscal outlook.

   The result of our fiscal sustainability analysis shows that under reasonable interest rate and
growth assumptions, the sustainable level of *primary deficit* (the fiscal deficit less interest payments)
lies between *0.1 percent of GDP* (assuming 4 percent per annum GDP growth and real interest
rates at 5.5 percent) and *1 percent of GDP* (assuming GDP growth at 5 percent per annum and
interest rates at 4.25 percent). At the current primary deficit (at 4.5 percent of GDP in 2001), the
gap between the sustainable and ongoing primary deficits ranges from 3.5 to 4.4 percent of GDP.
This gives a first approximation of the long-term fiscal adjustment needed.[8]

Incomes and Labor Market Policies

*Rigidities in the labor market and an inconsistent combination of income and social assistance policies
have magnified the impact of domestic demand expansion.* The structural characteristics of the labor

---

   6. Based on the Pre-Accession economic programs (PEPs) for all ten candidate countries, the Slovak
Republic has the most radical plans to reduce both revenues and expenditures of the general government.
In fact, while on average, accession countries plan reductions in the order of 1.4 percentage points of GDP
in revenues between 2000 and 2004, the Slovak plan calls for a reduction of 6 percentage points during
that period (the 2001 Pre-Accession Economic Programs of candidate countries overview—Note by the
EU Commission).

   7. Simulations run on the basis of a continuation of General Government deficits at 2001 levels (4.5 percent of GDP) over the next years would result in a public debt to GDP ratio in the order of 63 percent of
GDP by 2007.

   8. The above approach to the analysis of fiscal sustainability is based on the government's present value
budget constraint, and the resulting sustainable balances represent the levels for which the present value
remains constant, that is, fiscal policy can be maintained over an infinite period. In doing so, privatization
receipts are excluded from the calculation of the sustainable deficit, as they do not impose any change in the
net worth of the government. In addition, the assumed real interest rates and GDP growth rates are entered
at their estimated sustainable values.

BOX 1.1: FISCAL SUSTAINABILITY

Fiscal sustainability entails more than the government's ability to finance itself; it requires a set of policies (fiscal, income and monetary) consistent with the expected growth, inflation, and interest rates. Fiscal sustainability does not require the cancellation of government's debt in the long run, but requires at the minimum that real debt rises more slowly than the real rate of interest paid on it. In other words, the government is accountable for the net real interest rate (real interest rate, r, minus the real growth rate, μ) paid on the debt to GDP ratio, b_0. This can be financed either with a primary surplus $g - \tau$, or with seignorage revenue, which is represented by the inflation tax paid on the money demand to GDP ratio, $L(r + \pi)$ (itself a decreasing function of the nominal interest rate, $(r + \pi)$). This sustainability condition is represented as:

$$\left(g - \tau\right) + \left(\pi + \mu\right) \cdot L\left(r + \pi\right) = \left(r - \mu\right) \cdot b_0$$

The resulting sustainable long-run deficit as presented in Table 1.3, is based on the following parameters and assumptions. Besides using the end-2002 estimated debt to GDP ratio of 43 percent, we estimated the sustainable primary debt for different growth and interest rates, with growth ranging form 4–5 percent while interest rates were set by using the 20-year average of the US Treasury Bond rate (5.4 percent) to approximate the long-run real interest rate, and setting an interval of 4–6 percent. While the net interest payments on debt account for most of the sustainability burden on the government budget, fairly modest seignorage revenues do not contribute greatly to reducing interest payments on debt. The inflation tax is calculated by the inflation rate (set at a long-run value of 4 percent) times the money demand to GDP ratio. Money demand is assumed to be a decreasing function of the nominal interest rate $L\,(\cdot)$ and is approximated accordingly. In this way, the impact of an increase in interest rates is twofold. It increases debt service payments while also decreasing seignorage revenue. The money demand function is estimated using the following form: $A \cdot e^{-\eta \cdot (r+\pi)}$ where $A = 0.109$ and $\eta = 1.99$ have been estimated using available quarterly data on money and interest rate.

TABLE 1.3: SUSTAINABLE PRIMARY BALANCES
(percent)

Real Interest rate	4.0	4.25	4.50	5.5	6.0
Real growth rate					
4.0	−0.6	−0.5	−0.4	0.1	0.3
4.5	−0.9	−0.8	−0.6	−0.2	0.0
5.0	−1.1	−1.0	−0.9	−0.5	−0.2

Note: For assumptions and methodology see Box 1.1.
Source: World Bank calculations

market and its institutional setting, including the wage setting mechanisms, have hindered the adaptation of the labor force to the new competitive environment favoring price rather than quantity responses. As a result, labor market rigidities have slowed employment growth, despite the latest acceleration in output, while contributing to continuing high unemployment. High welfare benefit levels relative to average wages contributed to reducing labor force participation. The legal framework regulating labor further hinders labor market flexibility.

To make matters worse, rapid minimum wage increases have outstripped average wage growth over the last four years, rising by as much as *86 percent* between 1998 and October 2002. This policy resulted in a sharp compression at the bottom of the wage distribution (see Table 1.4).[9] High

---

9. The increasing concentration at the lower end of the wage distribution is unusual for a transition economy, where wages tend to become less concentrated reflecting higher returns to education, among other factors.

TABLE 1.4: SELECTED LABOR MARKET INDICATORS, 1994–2002

	1994	1995	1996	1997	1998	1999	2000	2001
Minimum wage (Skk)	2,450	2,450	2,700	2,700	3,000	3,600	4,400	4,920
Average monthly wages (Skk)	6,294	7,195	8,154	9,226	10,003	10,728	11,430	12,365
o.w. in industry	6,464	7,477	8,508	9,527	10,371	11,349	12,718	14,013
Nominal growth of average wages (%)	17.0	14.3	13.3	13.1	8.4	7.2	6.5	8.2
o.w. in industry	17.6	15.7	13.8	12.0	8.9	9.4	2.1	10.2
Real growth of avg. wages (%)	3.1	4.1	7.1	6.6	1.6	−3.0	−4.9	0.8
o.w. in industry	3.6	5.3	7.6	5.5	2.0	−1.1	0.1	2.7
Minimum to avg. wage ratio (%, 1997=100)	133	116	113	100	102	115	132	136
Unemployment rate (%)	13.7	13.1	11.3	11.8	12.5	16.2	18.9	19.4
Unemployment rate for apprentices (%)	14.5	14.2	12.2	11.7	13.2	17.1	20.8	21.6

Source: Staff calculations based on Statistical Office of the Slovak Republic.

payroll tax rates, which, at 50.8 percent of gross wages, are currently at the very top among regional economies, raise labor costs and further contribute to pricing less qualified workers out of the market. Evidence of this is found in the particularly rapid growth in unemployment for the less qualified workers (see Table 1.4).[10] Differences in unemployment rates across education groups have widened over time. While in 1997 the unemployment rate[11] for a worker with an apprenticeship degree was three times higher than that for a worker with a college degree, by 2001 the unemployment risk for the apprentice was four times that for the college graduate, with the difference between the two groups' unemployment rates growing from 7.3 percentage points in 1997 to 14.7 in 2001.

A quick look at some comparative labor market indicators confirms these observations (see Table 1.5). In fact, not only has the Slovak Republic the highest unemployment rate of the Visegrad countries,[12] but it also has a relatively low employment to population ratio. Long-term unemployment and youth unemployment are on the high side, above average EU levels and close to the top among Visegrad countries. There is limited dynamism in those areas of employment that have contributed to generating more jobs in other countries. Self-employment, fixed-term contracts, and part-time employment are lower in the Slovak Republic than in any other Visegrad country. Less than 9 percent of those who have a job are self-employed or family workers, whereas these types of working arrangements reach almost 19 percent in the rest of the Visegrad countries and 16 percent in the EU. Part-time work represents a minuscule share of total employment in the Slovak Republic. At 2.4 percent of total employment, part-time work is at the very bottom among the Visegrad countries (averaging 6.4 percent) and is far below the average for the EU (18 percent). Given the high social assistance benefits relative to wages,[13] it comes as no surprise that the demand for these jobs is also low in the Slovak Republic. Only 2.4 percent of unemployed workers are looking for this type of arrangement, against 14 percent in the EU and 7 percent on average in the rest of the Visegrad countries.

---

10. Along these lines, evidence that wages are not set in line with productivity also comes from the high dispersion of wage to productivity ratios by region (see Chapter 3). Not surprisingly, the variation of unemployment by regions is also high, with higher unemployment in those regions with a comparatively high wage to productivity ratio.

11. Starting in 1997, minimum wages have grown faster than average wages.

12. Unemployment in the Slovak Republic remains at some 6.5 percentage points higher than the CC-11 and more than 12.0 percentage points above the EU.

13. Combined with a benefit structure that reduces welfare benefits by one koruna for every koruna earned.

TABLE 1.5: UNEMPLOYMENT RATES BY EDUCATION LEVELS
(percent)

	1994	1995	1996	1997	1998	1999	2000	2001
Primary	27.0	28.4	25.0	26.5	28.4	34.2	39.3	42.8
Apprenticeship	14.5	14.2	12.2	11.7	13.2	17.1	20.8	21.6
Secondary (without exam)	13.7	13.3	11.5	10.7	11.9	18.6	20.3	19.3
Apprenticeship (with exam)	16.9	11.6	9.6	9.6	10.6	13.9	18.9	18.5
Full secondary general	13.5	13.5	13.0	14.3	12.8	16.0	17.4	17.7
Full secondary vocational	9.3	8.2	7.4	8.5	8.4	12.7	14.0	14.8
Higher	.	.	3.7	5.5	6.1	5.1	7.5	9.5
Bachelor	.	.	.	.	.	.	11.2	11.8
University	4.1	3.0	2.7	3.4	3.6	4.7	5.4	4.6
Research qualification	.	.	5.1	–	5.6	4.3	3.0	14.4
Without school education	60.7	42.7	68.8	57.8	84.5	57.2	84.8	86.1
Total	13.7	13.1	11.3	11.8	12.5	16.2	18.9	19.4

Source: Slovak Labor Force Survey

The stability of the unit-labor cost-based real exchange rate throughout the period (see Figure 1.1) is therefore a misleading indication of the Slovak Republic's underlying wage competitiveness problems. To a large extent, this stability reflects the exit or downsizing of less productive firms under the pressure of competition. While some fast-restructuring enterprises were able to generate sufficient productivity gains to offset wage increases, other large segments of the economy struggled to compete, which led to heavy job losses and soaring unemployment, particularly among low-skilled workers. The consolidation of an export-oriented sector was paralleled by a move toward more skilled labor-intensive export products and, to a lesser extent, toward capital-intensive types of exports (see Chapter 2). While these (FDI-based and/or restructured) enterprises have been able to generate sufficient productivity gains to offset wage increases and to keep or expand employment, the move has left a second type of enterprise behind. The latter type remains unrestructured or has not been touched by FDI; these enterprises concentrate on non-tradable or import-competing activities, pay on average lower wages, and attract less-skilled types of workers. With little room for wage adjustments, owing in part to the growing compression in wages, less forthcoming access to credit, and increasing competition from imports, these enterprises failed in higher numbers, leading to mounting job losses among the low skilled.

External Environment

The return to rapid domestic demand expansion observed above has been taking place against a less supportive external environment than in the mid- to late 1990s. Growth in the main market for Slovak exports, the EU, is estimated to decelerate in 2001–02 to almost half that of the 1994–98 period. The growth rate of exports in 2001–02 is less than half that of the previous two years (see Table 1.2), while import growth quadrupled, due mainly to higher domestic demand. The current account widened in 2001, reaching deficit levels comparable to those experienced at the time of the 1998 devaluation. After reaching levels of more than 9 percent of GDP in 1998, current account deficits had initially fallen to 4.9 percent of GDP in 1999 and to 3.6 percent in the following year. By the year 2001, however, the current account balance fell back to deficits in the order of 8.6 percent of GDP, and it is estimated to remain at a similar level this year. As a result, after briefly driving growth in 1999–2000, net exports again dragged it down in 2001–02, reducing growth by 4 percent per year, as it had in 1995–98.

TABLE 1.6: LABOR FORCE INDICATORS IN SELECTED COUNTRIES, 2001 (percent)							
	SK	PLª	CZ	HU	SI	CC-11	EU-15
Employment							
Employment rate 15–24 years	27.7	21.4	34.4	31.4	30.3	27.0	40.4
25–54 years	74.6	69.5	82.0	73.1	83.8	73.8	77.0
55–64 years	22.5	30.5	36.9	23.7	23.4	34.6	38.2
15–64 years	56.7	53.8	65.0	56.3	63.6	57.8	63.9
Part-time employment	2.4	10.2	5.0	3.5	6.1	9.8	18.0
Employment in services/industry	153.0	163.2	134.8	172.0	133.0	152.7	233.8
Employment to population ratio							
−15–64 years	56.9	55.2	65.8	56.6	65.3	60.2	64.7
−15+ years	48.8	46.3	54.9	46.7	54.4	50.1	52.0
Self-employed & family workers-(% of tot. employm.)	8.6	28.0	15.3	14.6	17.1	27.1	15.7
Contract of limited duration	5.0	11.9	8.1	7.5	13.1	8.0	13.4
Unemployment							
Unemployment rate (% of labor force)							
−15–24 years	38.9	41.5	16.3	10.5	15.7	28.8	14.0
−25–64 years	15.9	15.6	6.9	5.0	4.6	11.3	6.5
−15 + years	19.4	18.4	8.0	5.7	5.7	13.0	7.3
Youth unemployment ratio 15–24 years (% of age pop.)ᵇ	17.6	15.2	6.7	3.7	5.7	10.9	6.6
Unemployment 12 months and more (% of tot. unempl.)	58.3	50.1	52.9	44.8	63.3	52.4	44.0
Unemployed seeking a part time job (% of tot. unempl.)	2.4	6.1	9.5	6.0	–	4.8	14.1

Notes: a/ Poland estimates cover only the population aged 15 and over.
   b/ 15 to 24 year old unemployed as percent of 15 to 24 year old total population.
SK-Slovak Republic, PL-Poland, CZ-Czech Republic, HU-Hungary, SI-Slovenia
Sources: EUROSTAT, Statistics in Focus, Population and Social Conditions, Theme 3—20/2002, staff calculations.

External Financing

Fortunately, the country has been able to finance the gap resulting from the discrepancy between absorption and output growth primarily through privatization receipts, instead of through international borrowing as was done in the mid-1990s. By opening the new round of privatizations to foreign investors and improving transparency, the new government succeeded in attracting highly regarded strategic investors to key areas of the economy. With renewed interest in greenfield investment also, net direct investment soared to about US$0.7 billion (or some 3.7 percent of GDP) in 1999 and to US$2.1 billion in the following year (or more than 10 percent of GDP). This late take-off of FDI started to compensate for the almost negligible levels of FDI inflows before 1999.[14]

The country's debt situation has strengthened as a result. The large FDI inflows contributed to stabilizing gross foreign debt to GDP ratios, which remain today at around the 1998 levels. Nevertheless, while the debt situation remains at a manageable level (of about 54 percent of GDP), there is a down side in its term structure, as short-term liabilities account for almost 40 percent of the total

---

14. FDI inflows in the Slovak Republic previous to 1999 were significantly lower than those received by the other CEECs. In particular, while Hungary averaged 5.1 percent of GDP in annual flows over the 1993–98 period and the Czech Republic and Poland averaged 3.2 and 2.8, respectively, the Slovak Republic only received an equivalent 1.3 percent of GDP over the same period.

debt. On the other hand, close to 70 percent of the foreign debt is owed by domestic corporations, part of which borrowed from parent companies (intra-enterprise lending), which is considered a less risky form of lending from a current account standpoint. With gross official foreign reserves on the order of US$ 4.2 billion net foreign debt stood at 35 percent of GDP by end-2001. However, helped by record high FDI inflows this year[15] (on the order of 15–16 percent of GDP), net foreign debt is estimated to drop to around 19 percent of GDP by the end of 2002, a decline of about 22 percentage points of GDP from the 1998 level. Helped by this evolution, and despite the large external imbalances, two of the major rating agencies have restored the Slovak Republic's debt to an investment grade rating, reversing the reduction in the rating in 1998. Sovereign bonds are now paying 70 percent lower spreads than at the time of the crises.

Strategic Challenges and Objectives

This situation of easy external financing will unfortunately not last. With the bulk of assets already privatized, privatization receipts are already shrinking. Unless the fiscal deficit is brought under control, the resulting interest rate hike will be sure to choke the recovery, bringing unemployment even higher. In fact, FDI inflows are expected to go back to more "normal" levels of 3–3.5 percent of GDP starting next year, making any further consolidation in the external position in the near future dependent on the narrowing of the current account balance.

In steering a policy course away from such troubled waters, one should remember that the Slovak Republic has been a latecomer to reform. The most successful transition countries in the region have managed to consolidate productivity gains while keeping exchange rate appreciation and rising labor costs at bay at the time of the initial accumulation of FDI. By doing this, they enable the export take-off to be sustained at the time of the FDI accumulation, allowing productivity gains to trickle down to salaries and government consumption only later on in the process. In this regard, a simple comparison of the Slovak Republic's real exchange rate trends now with those of other regional competitors (as in Figure 1.1) may not suggest an adequate policy stance. The Slovak Republic is at a relatively early stage of FDI accumulation and gains in productivity. Therefore, the Slovak Republic should now pursue income and fiscal policies that would allow the country to improve competitiveness and secure the export take-off, as countries such as Hungary did some years ago.

In this macroeconomic setting, the incoming government will want to pursue three objectives outlined above: invigorating the economic recovery, broadening the incipient growth in employment, and, at the same time, securing external stability. Achieving all three objectives will require a combination of the following three instruments:

(a) Continued trade and enterprise reform.
(b) *Fiscal* consolidation.
(c) *Labor* market *liberalization.*

Trade and Enterprise Reform

A dynamic, competitive enterprise sector will be the economy's prime engine to generate growth and productive jobs, as well as the exports to narrow the current account deficit. Thus, it will be a top priority for the new government to implement policies that will amplify the domestic supply response and to boost net exports. This is the focus of Chapter 2. Key items on this policy agenda include (i) speeding up farm restructuring before joining the EU's CAP, (ii) privatizing power generation and bringing forward the energy tariff adjustments required to set tariffs in line with EU directives; (iii) bringing down the internal border within the Czech-Slovak Customs Union (CSU) before EU accession; and

---

15. The sale of 49 percent of the gas company totaled some US$2.7 billion and the sale of the three power distribution companies for an additional US$ 0.6 billion, accounted for 95 percent of the total estimated privatization receipt for this year.

BOX 1.2: CURRENT ACCOUNT DEFICITS CONSISTENT WITH STABLE NET DEBT TO GDP RATIOS

Given the unusually high FDI inflows this year, net foreign debt (defined as gross debt net of gross official reserves) is estimated to fall from 35 percent of GDP (end of-2001) to around 19 percent by the end of this year. Under reasonable assumptions of real exchange rate appreciation, GDP growth, and foreign inflation over the next five years, we found that current account deficits at or below 5 percent of GDP will maintain net foreign debt to GDP at end-of-2002 levels.

Current account deficit that allows stable Net Debt to GDP ratio =

$$[1] \quad NFD * [g/(1 + g)] + net\ FDI = 4.8\ (percent\ of\ GDP)$$

where NFD represents the net foreign debt as a share of GDP, and g is the annual rate of nominal GDP growth in US$.

Assumptions regarding the evolution of the main variables over the 2003–08 period include: average external (EU) inflation at 2.2 percent per annum; the koruna's real annual exchange rate appreciation at 1.5 percent, which is lower than the average for the past six years; real GDP growth at 4.7 percent; and net foreign direct investment at 3.3 percent of GDP. End-of-2002 NFD is estimated at 19 percent of GDP, whereas the nominal rate of GDP growth in US$ (g) equals 8.5 percent; the result, in turn, of the combined effect of the assumptions regarding the REER, real GDP growth, and external inflation.

However, over the longer term the net FDI component should be reduced, as a growing part of earnings are expected to be transferred outside the country. Therefore, the longer-term current account deficit that assures stability to the net debt to GDP ratio falls to just the first component of equation [1] and a fraction of the second. If we assume that 50 percent of profits arising from FDI are not reinvested in the economy, then the longer-term sustainable current account deficit falls to just 3.4 percent of GDP.

(iv) strengthening the regulatory framework for bank operations while bottleneck debt resolution procedures. These measures would work in concert with the fiscal consolidation and labor market reform policies discussed below to create a sound environment for an efficient enterprise sector.

Fiscal Consolidation
Fiscal consolidation, the second fundamental leg of government's medium term strategy, is now required both in its own right (to arrest potentially explosive public debt dynamics) and to relieve current pressures on the balance of payments. The government needs to reverse past trends and rapidly reduce the fiscal deficit. This will compress public sector demand and thus make room for the ongoing investment expansion without unduly compromising external balances. However, while the need for fiscal consolidation is clear and relatively uncontroversial, the same cannot be said of the magnitude of the required consolidation nor of the means to achieve it. This chapter focuses on the size of the needed fiscal adjustment, while Chapters 3 and 4 discuss specific strategies to achieve it.

How much fiscal consolidation would be required? To answer this question we follow a two-step methodology proposed by the IMF staff in "The Road to EU Accession."[16] The first step involves the estimation of a current account deficit consistent with net debt to GDP ratios that remain stable over the next five years. The second step consists of estimating how much adjustment is needed in the public sector to allow the country to reach these current account deficits. In doing this, assumptions need to be made regarding the reaction of private sector saving-investment balances to changes in the fiscal stance (see Box 1.2).

---

16. Following the "Road to Accession," R. Feldman and C. Maxwell Watson, ed. IMF, mimeo, 2001, we assume that fiscal consolidation reduces private saving-investment balances irrespective of whether it is expenditure or revenue driven. The magnitude of the reduction depends on the importance of the *Ricardian* effects, which we assumed at 50 percent, following the above-mentioned report.

TABLE 1.7: PUBLIC SECTOR DEFICIT AND DEBT OUTCOMES—TWO SCENARIOS, 2001–09
(percentage of GDP)

	2001	2002	2003	2004	2005	2006	2007	2008	2009
Reform Scenario									
1. Gross debt level	43.0	42.0	43.1	44.3	44.1	43.3	43.0	42.8	42.8
2. Gross assets	30.2	34.7	33.4	31.3	27.4	27.4	27.4	27.4	27.4
3. Net debt	12.8	7.3	9.7	13.0	16.6	15.9	15.6	15.4	15.4
4. Primary deficit	4.5	3.6	2.6	1.5	0.5	−0.5	−0.5	−0.5	−0.5
5. Interest	3.9	3.9	3.2	3.2	3.1	3.0	3.0	3.1	3.1
6. Overall deficit	8.4	7.5	5.8	4.8	3.6	2.5	2.5	2.6	2.6
No Reform Scenario									
1. Gross debt level	43.0	42.9	45.9	50.0	53.8	58.2	63.3	68.7	74.3
2. Gross assets	30.2	34.7	33.4	31.3	27.4	27.4	27.4	27.4	27.4
3. Net debt	12.8	8.2	12.5	18.7	26.4	30.7	35.9	41.2	46.8
4. Primary deficit	4.5	4.5	4.5	4.5	4.5	4.5	4.5	4.5	4.5
5. Interest	3.9	3.9	3.3	3.5	3.5	3.9	4.4	5.0	5.6
6. Overall deficit	8.4	8.4	7.8	8.0	8.0	8.4	8.9	9.5	10.1
Common Assumptions									
7. Nominal GDP growth (PEP)	8.9	7.2	8.9	9.1	9.3	8.0	7.0	7.0	7.0
8. Privatization receipts for debt repayment	0.0	5.6	1.3	0.0	0.0	0.0	0.0	0.0	0.0

Source: World Bank estimates

The figures presented in Box 1.2 suggest that a medium-term target for the external current account deficit of about 4.8 percent of GDP might be appropriate to keep net foreign debt to GDP ratios at end-2002 levels throughout the next five years. Given the current account deficit is now at 8.6 percent of GDP, a reduction on the order of *3.8 percentage points of GDP* would be required. However, this adjustment will be facilitated by the expected expansion in EU transfers to the Slovak Republic. With *net* transfers from the EU estimated to increase by 2 percentage points of GDP, the required reduction in the goods, services, and income balance is then estimated to be close to 1.8 percent of GDP. To achieve this target would require bringing the overall fiscal deficit down to *about 2.5 percent of GDP* over the next four years (resulting in a primary fiscal surplus on the order of 0.5 percent of GDP by 2006).

To reduce the fiscal deficit (and the associated current account deficit) to the target levels would require a *fiscal consolidation on the order of 4.9 percent of GDP over the next four years.* Part of this contraction in the deficit, however, will result from the increase in transfers from the EU mentioned above.[17] Taking into account the potential contribution of EU transfers (see below), the size of the purely domestic fiscal effort would be around *3.5 percent of GDP* by 2006, a target that seems achievable.

The fiscal objective proposed for 2006 is within reasonable reach and could be met without resorting to unrealistically painful measures. However, it is important to stress that the calculations above assume a positive net impact of EU accession in the range of 2 percent of GDP over the medium term. This is composed of agriculture and structural funds transfers from the EU to the Slovak Republic, net of tax transfers from the Slovak Republic to the EU. The net fiscal gains will be realized *only if* structural funds are applied to "existing" expenditure programs (as recommended in Chapters 3 and 4) and *not* used to finance new spending over and above these pro-

---

17. Assuming that CAP-related transfers and structural funds do not add to the existing spending levels.

grams. If these assumptions fail to materialize, then the fiscal adjustment needed will be correspondingly larger.

What is more important is that this interim fiscal objective be seen as setting the country on a path to reduce its macroeconomic deficits further, enabling it to meet the demands of the Growth and Stability Pact once it is in the EU (and therefore in the EMU), as well as later to meet the Maastricht criteria on debts and deficits for joining the euro zone at an appropriate time. To reconcile growth, fiscal, and external balance objectives, the primary deficit of the general government would need to be reduced over the next four years and turned into a primary surplus of about 0.5 percent of GDP by 2006. This fiscal outcome should also allow stabilizing the ratio of total government debt (domestic and foreign) to GDP at around 43 percent of GDP and should restore external sustainability, stabilizing net foreign debt to GDP ratios at end-2002 levels.

The adjustment through domestic fiscal efforts of about 3.5 percent of GDP over four years, while challenging, seems feasible. Consistent with the experience of successful fiscal adjustment in other OECD countries, the government should pursue the following three-prong trategy:

(a) The bulk of adjustment should be achieved through expenditure cuts, primarily in enterprise subsidies and transfers and in the government's wage bill.
(b) The revenue reduction proposed under the country's pre-accession economic program[18] should be postponed until the expected cutbacks in expenditure actually materialize.
(c) Revenue and expenditure should be redirected and restructured to reinforce growth and employment objectives.

As discussed in Chapter 4, key expenditure retrenchment measures would involve cutting back enterprise subsidies (currently the highest in the CEECs), and raising the retirement age, thereby lowering projected pension deficits and providing scope for more adequate and secure pensions for future generations. In addition, expenditure reforms proposed for education and health, and consolidation of the decentralization program, should, over time, reduce the government's wage bill (the highest in the CEECs), in part through a reduction in the currently bloated numbers of employees in education and health, and in part through avoiding fragmentation and duplication in the decentralization process. In the longer run, reforms in benefit levels and structures should slow the growth in spending on other social benefits, especially by encouraging a more rapid transition from welfare to work.

On the revenue side, given the steep tax reduction implemented in the last four years, the time has come to postpone any further overall tax reductions until fiscal consolidation objectives are accomplished. While keeping overall revenue ratios close to the current levels, there is substantial scope for important changes in the structure of revenues in the Slovak Republic and to broaden the base of general revenues, thus allowing a reduction in payroll taxes. This rebalancing of revenues should include an expansion of non-tax revenues, particularly those linked to revenues from participation in gas and electricity enterprises, as well as an expansion of the tax base in both the CIT and PIT. For example, there is room to expand the CIT base by limiting tax incentives for investment to EU-compatible levels. In addition, significant revenues are possible from the special levy proposed in Chapter 2 to tax windfall profits expected in the gas company from the planned increase in regulated prices.[19] A similar effort should be made for the PIT. In addition to efforts to formalize areas of the economy, those categories of income currently exempted from PIT should be brought into the tax base. This concerns, in particular, pensions (which would need to be appropriately rebased) and child allowances, if they continue to be available to all parents.[20] There is also room for expanding

---

18. From 38 percent of GDP in 2000, to a projected 35 percent of GDP, to a 33 percent of GDP target in 2004.
19. While this may require some compensatory social policies for the most needy, the net outcome is expected to improve the fiscal balance.
20. This would leave the redistribution role to the progressive rates embedded in the tax system.

some other taxes, particularly the VAT and excises. Increasing excises for beer and tobacco and unifying VAT tax rates at the current top level would be the most relevant measures in this area.

These measures to broaden the revenue base would allow reductions in payroll taxes in the areas discussed in Chapter 4 (notably health, sickness insurance, and possibly pensions). The Slovak Republic's payroll taxes are currently the highest of all Visegrad countries. A reduction in payroll taxes would in turn reduce country's unemployment, which is also the highest in the region, while reducing incentives to remain in the informal sector.

Finally, *current and future inflows of privatization receipts* from abroad should be used to retire *foreign rather than domestic debt*. Not only is this needed to keep such inflows from spilling over into excessive domestic demand, such approach would also be consistent with a strategy to optimize the currency structure of public debt and to deepen the domestic debt market. At present 52 percent of public debt is in foreign currency, which is relatively high, and about a third of that foreign debt is currencies other than the euro, which may be unduly risky given the country's prospect of joining ERM-2 in the not too distant future. On the other hand, the domestic debt market is under-developed, lacks predictability and transparency: there is, for instance, no firm issuance program, making it difficult for market participants in turn to plan and manage their own cash flows. To overcome this deficiency, the government would therefore be well advised to

(a) Integrate cash and debt management within the Ministry of Finance (international experience would seem to advise against delegating that task to a separate debt management agency in circumstances where oversight capacities are weak).

(b) Rely primarily on regular, non-discretionary debt issuances designed to create liquid benchmarks spread along the yield curve.

(c) Develop an asset/liability management strategy in line with best practices among EU members and develop attendant risk management systems.

Labor Market Reform

Reducing unemployment is perhaps the clearest mandate emanating from the recent elections and is consequently a priority for the forthcoming government. It will be a challenging mandate to fulfill, as unemployment in the Slovak Republic has proved to be resilient, rising in spite of increased economic activity over most of the past four years. Given the structural changes in the input composition of export and import products, an export-oriented strategy alone may not suffice to reduce current unemployment to levels similar to those in countries such as Hungary. In particular, with unemployment concentrated at the very bottom of the education-wage distribution, and with wage mechanisms that favor wage concentration by artificially forcing wage increases at the bottom of the distribution, growth alone will probably not suffice. In addition, high social assistance benefits relative to wages obstruct increases in labor force participation. A recent OECD report[21] lays out in comprehensive detail the policy agenda involved, and many of these themes are also discussed in Chapter 4 of this report in the context of restructuring expenditure for education and social protection.

On the labor demand side, it is necessary to reduce labor costs by reducing payroll taxes. This in turn will require, on one hand, the transfer of the costs of the social welfare components from the social insurance system to general taxation. It will also require further restructuring in the financing of the social insurance system (especially in health) to enhance efficiency and reduce costs. Chapter 4 also discussed these possibilities in more detail. To improve labor demand further it is necessary to reduce tax pressure on the SMEs, a dynamic segment of the enterprise sector that has been proven to generate the greatest number of jobs in other economies. In this regard, reducing the tax exemptions on foreign investment (as recommended in Chapter 2) will reduce the current bias against domestic enterprises, particularly against SMEs, and allow them to compete on a level playing field.

---

21.   *The Slovak Republic, 2002 Annual Review*, OECD, Paris, 2002.

Increased flexibility in labor relations and wage setting mechanisms should also boost labor demand. In this regard, it is highly recommended to put an end to the deliberate policy of increasing minimum wages more rapidly than other wages, and, more broadly, to stop attempting to use the minimum wage as an instrument of incomes policy.[22] As presented in the PEP, the current approach intends to "gradually increase the proportion of the minimum to the average wage level." While this policy may encourage some extra workers to participate, it is also sure to reduce labor demand, particularly at the low end of the wage scale. It would also be desirable to limit the extension of regional or sectoral collective agreements only to those firms that participated in the negotiations. The extension to firms not involved may result in wage awards that are not justified by improvements in productivity. Along these lines, the decentralization of wage bargaining will enable wage agreements to reflect productivity conditions at the firm level more accurately.

Furthermore, the easing of many of the restrictive regulations currently embedded in the new labor code could facilitate job creation and the reallocation of the labor force following the structural changes in the enterprise sector. Regulations should be modified to improve flexibility in the areas of part time employment and limits on working hours, to reduce the labor union's role in management of personnel issues, to reduce red tape for the creation of SMEs, and to soften some of the most protective employment provisions of the labor code for SMEs.

On the supply side of the labor market, it will also be necessary to encourage labor force participation by reforming the benefit levels and structure of social assistance (following a new household survey) to reduce the work disincentives in the current system, while containing expenditure growth (see Chapter 4). The gap between benefit levels and wages should be wide enough to maintain a strong work incentive. Labor force participation would also benefit from changes in the structure of social assistance, making its activity tests more effective, and possibly tapering the withdrawal of benefits as recipients earn income from gainful employment.[23] In the longer term, efforts should be aimed at adapting the supply of human capital to the new market requirements. Promoting general as opposed to vocational secondary education and gradually expanding enrollment at the tertiary level would contribute to this end (see Chapter 4). Further liberalization of the housing market would also improve labor mobility.

Conclusions

The external current account and fiscal deficits (net of privatization receipts) remain unsustainably high (at about 8 percent of GDP in 2002). With a capital account surplus in the range of 20–22 percent of GDP this year, the country may not find it particularly difficult to finance those deficits in the short run. However, this favorable situation will not last. Furthermore, this policy mix, through its impact on the real exchange rate, undermines the employability of large segments of the population (particularly those with low skill levels) and will ultimately choke growth (projected at 4 percent for 2002). While much policy attention has gone into stimulating investment, future growth will also depend on raising the employment rate, currently one of the lowest among the CEECs at 50 percent of the working age population.

This chapter has laid out the broad thrust of a policy strategy to invigorate the economic recovery and bring the economy toward EU convergence. Such a strategy consists of three key elements:

(a) *Continued trade and* enterprise *reform*. This is the main topic of Chapter 2.
(b) *Fiscal consolidation*, focusing on cutting back expenditure and stabilizing revenues while redirecting revenue and expenditure and expenditure policies to become more fully supportive of growth and employment objectives. The discussion above provided the

---

22. An appropriately low minimum wage could still play a useful role in protecting workers against abuses by unscrupulous employers.
23. At present social assistance benefits are reduced by the full amount of any earned income, resulting in a marginal tax rate of 100% up to the social assistance benefit level.

macroeconomic context and estimated the size of fiscal adjustment needed, while Chapters 3 and 4 discuss specific strategies for reduce and redirect expenditures.

(c) *Labor market and social protection reform* to enhance labor market flexibility, including more flexible working arrangements (such as part-time work, self-employment and fixed-term contracts), as well as decentralized wage setting mechanisms, better matching between labor market demands and education system outputs, and measures to reduce both work disincentives in social assistance programs, and job creation disincentives from high payroll taxes. The discussion above provided an overview of the policy agenda of labor market reform, while the review of expenditure programs in Chapter 4 presents some specific policy options in the areas of social protection.

The substance of this strategic approach is the focus of the rest of this report. The success of this strategy, however, is predicated on enhancing the country's governance framework, including the capacities to design and implement reforms and manages public expenditures. Chapter 5 focuses on the policy options involved in realizing this objective.

CHAPTER 2

STRUCTURAL
TRANSFORMATION

The previous chapter drew attention to the macroeconomic factors behind the current recovery, as well as behind the imbalances that have reemerged during the process. Underpinning these macroeconomic developments are more profound structural developments in the performance of the enterprise sector. The 1998 crisis constituted in many respects a traditional crisis of crony capitalism. State assets had been seized upon by friends of the regime and their operation had been shielded from market tests and bankrolled by state-owned banks. A fixed exchange rate regime was integral to that scenario, but proved increasingly hard to sustain in the face of rampant laxity (and corruption) in the conduct of financial affairs. The currency crisis of (October 1998) brought that episode to an end and forced a reconsideration of the entire policy scenario.

After four years of reform, one can judge the magnitude of the change. As loss-making firms were weeded out under tighter financial conditions, overall profitability surged, and firms—articularly foreign-owned firms—are again creating jobs. The same firms are also driving the country's integration into the production networks of EU-based multinational corporations (MNCs), while on the domestic side network industries are being unbundled and privatized (also to strategic foreign investors).

Certain key issues remain, however which the new government will now need to tackle, including the following: (i) performance has been lagging behind in the agriculture sector, owing in part to a government policy to pursue food self-sufficiency and to support inefficient large corporate farming with large subsidies; (ii) anti-small business biases in the business framework have arisen from the preferential tax treatment provided to large (and largely foreign) investors and from the absence of actionable debt resolution procedures; (iii) bank lending is thus guided more by the degree of enforceability of creditors' rights than by underlying economic rationales, and is in practice available only to top-echelon firms; (iv) conversely, there is a risk that banks, now highly liquid, will seek to branch out rashly into new lines of business, such as real estate and commercial properties, in a bid to boost their currently low profits; (v) the country's trade specialization may be veering too rapidly away from labor-intensive products; (vi) the maintenance of an internal border within the Czech-Slovak Customs Union (CSU) is hindering trade expansion and has allowed the country to fall behind in aligning its trade regime with EU requirements; and (vii) energy tariffs, particularly for gas, remain heavily distorted in favor of residential users.

This chapter takes stock of the reform progress and identifies the outstanding policy agenda. In the discussion below, the first section provides an overview of firm performances since 1998. Banking sector restructuring has played a key role in the turnaround, and the second section outlines this role and discusses the next steps. The third section deals with issues of trade integration and specialization and highlights the role of EU accession on the one hand, and of the CSU on the other, in the process. The next two sections turn to sectoral issues in agriculture and energy, respectively. The final section concludes by summing up the chapter's policy recommendations for bringing forward enterprise reform.

Enterprise Restructuring

The last few years have seen a sharp turnaround in enterprise performance. Interestingly enough, most of the improvement observed at the aggregate level is due not so much to the performance of profitable firms as to the weeding out of loss-making firms under the tighter financial discipline faced by the latter. This section looks at the nature and sources of this turnaround, and sets the stage for the discussion in the following sections of the remaining policy agenda in the areas of financial sector development, trade integration, agriculture (a sector in which restructuring has been lagging behind), and energy.

The most striking manifestation of the turnaround in enterprise performance has been the sharp upswing in profitability recorded between 1998 and 2002. Depending on which series one looks at (see Table 2.1), this upswing would have ranged anywhere between 9 and 11 percent of

TABLE 2.1: EVOLUTION OF ENTERPRISE PROFITABILITY, 1998–2002
(percent of GDP)

	1998	1999	2000	2001	1Q2002	Change 2002 (Q1)/1998	Percent Contribution
By firm size							
0–9 employees	1.9	2.5	2.2	2.6	2.5	0.7	6.1
10–19	0.2	0.3	0.9	1.4	0.6	0.3	3.2
20–49	0.5	0.3	1.0	1.1	1.2	0.8	7.1
50–249	0.5	0.8	0.9	1.6	3.4	3.0	27.7
250–499	−0.1	0.1	1.0	0.5	1.1	1.2	11.4
500–999	−0.5	−0.1	0.7	1.4	1.6	2.1	19.5
1,000–	0.4	5.0	3.0	5.0	3.1	2.7	25.0
Total	2.8	8.8	9.7	13.6	13.5	10.7	100.0
By form of ownership[a]							
Public sector	0.0	0.8	1.2	2.2	3.4	3.5	38.4
Private sector	0.7	1.7	4.2	6.5	6.3	5.5	61.6
o.w.							
Domest. owned	−0.2	−0.1	2.0	2.1	3.1	3.4	37.3
Cooperative	−0.1	−0.1	−0.1	0.1	−0.1	0.0	0.3
Other[b]	1.1	2.0	2.2	4.3	3.2	2.2	24.1
Total	0.7	2.6	5.4	8.7	9.7	9.0	100.0

[a]Non-financial enterprises employing more than 19 employees only.
[b]Including foreign-owned enterprises.
Source: Statistical Office of the Slovak Republic and staff calculations

GDP. The turnaround was particularly impressive among state-owned and domestically owned private firms (Table 2.1, first panel). Taken together, these two types of enterprises were forced to turn their books from red to black: the level of profit of each of these two categories of firms improved by about 3.5 percent of GDP. Foreign-owned enterprises also continued to improve their profitability, albeit from already positive positions at the start of the reforms.

Most of the improvement in performance has been concentrated among medium and large-scale enterprises (Table 2.1, first panel), perhaps because it was these enterprises that benefited most from the previous climate of financial laxity. In 1998, the worst losses were reported among firms ranging from 250 to 1,000 employees. Small-scale firms, in contrast, had probably operated under hard budget constraints all along and continued to post steady profits.

A few factors may help explain this phenomenon. First, the government managed to privatize or close down about 40 percent of those enterprises that remained in state hands as of 1998. As Table 2.2 shows, this affected mainly medium and large-scale enterprises, smaller ones having all been privatized earlier on in the transition.

Better still, the quality of privatization improved considerably. Until 1998, privatization had officially focused on the building of a "domestic capitalist class" and had resulted in little foreign direct investment and enterprise restructuring. In practice, asset sales had been non-transparent and mired in cronyism and political abuse. The new government abolished the previous Act on Strategic Enterprises, which was an obstacle to the privatization of utilities, published a list of auctioned enterprises, reconsidered disadvantageous privatization agreements, and initiated the restructuring and sale of large banks and utilities. The process gained credibility with markets, thanks to unusually transparent behavior and procedures and to well selected advisers, and resulted in attracting reputable strategic investors.

TABLE 2.2: ENTERPRISE OWNERSHIP STRUCTURE
(percent)

	0–9[a]	Oct-49	50–249	250–499	500–999	1,000 +	Total	Change 2002/1998
1998								
Public	0.7	4.9	15.2	20.3	15.9	42.6	2.3	
Private	99.3	95.1	84.8	79.7	84.1	57.4	97.7	
Foreign[b]	20.4	13.2	9.6	10.9	13.9	7.8	18.8	
Private domestic	77.0	74.7	52.3	50.7	58.9	47.5	75.0	
Cooperative	1.5	6.0	21.0	16.5	8.6			
Associations[c]	0.2	0.2	0.4		1.3			
Other[d]	0.3	0.9	1.5	1.6	1.3	2.1	0.4	
Total	100.0	100.0	100.0	100.0	100.0	100.0	100.0	
2002 (June)								
Public	0.6	2.8	6.0	11.5	10.1	30.2	1.3	−40.9
Private	99.4	97.2	94.0	88.5	89.9	69.8	98.7	3.4
Foreign[b]	19.4	14.3	17.0	21.4	29.2	23.6	18.6	1.5
Private domestic	80.0	82.9	77.0	67.1	60.7	46.2	80.1	9.4
Total	100.0	100.0	100.0	100.0	100.0	100.0	100.0	2.4

a/ Including enterprises with an uncertain number of employees.
b/ Foreign and international enterprises.
c/ Also political parties and churches.
d/ Other calculated as a residual.
Source: Statistical Yearbook of the Slovak Republic, 1997–2001

TABLE 2.3: AVERAGE PROFIT MARGINS BY OWNERSHIP TYPE, 1996–2001
(percent)

	1998	1999	2000	2001
Public	−0.1	1.8	3.3	5.9
Private	−0.3	0.1	2.1	3.0
Foreign	3.2	4.4	3.2	5.5
Total	0.4	1.4	2.7	4.4

Note: Non-financial enterprises with more than 24 employees, 1997 and later with more than 19 employees.
Sources: Statistical Office of the Slovak Republic and staff calculations

Second, public tariffs were raised, sometimes drastically (see below on energy prices), allowing public utilities to restore their profit and self-financing margins (see Table 2.3). Tariff increases in the energy sector alone ranged from 200 to 300 percent between 1998 and 2001.

Third and perhaps most important, enterprises began to face tighter financial conditions. Banking sector reforms broke up the old-boys' club mentality that used to tie together banks and their corporate borrowers. On its part, the government became less willing to underwrite corporate borrowing through a disorderly use of government guarantees (although the latter remained a key features of the financial operations of utilities and railways). Enterprises in turn proved more reluctant to extend credit to their clients. As a result, inter-enterprise overdue receivables, contracted through the 1998–2002 period (see Figure 2.1).

The result was to force enterprises to restructure or to go out of business. The number of loss-making firms dropped abruptly across the economy (see Figure 2.2). Even those that stayed in business were forced cut back their losses substantially (see Table 2.4). Indeed, most of the improvement in aggregate profits observed above (Table 2.1) can be attributed to what happened to loss-making firms. In contrast, if the number of profitable firms increased somewhat between

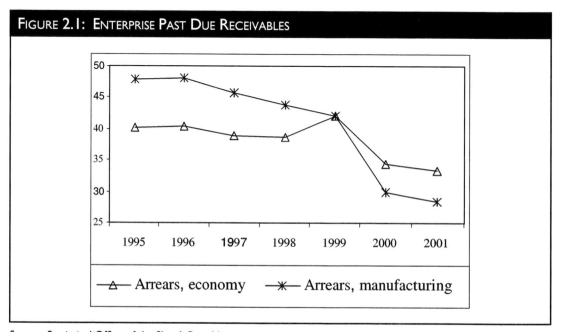

FIGURE 2.1: ENTERPRISE PAST DUE RECEIVABLES

—△— Arrears, economy   —✳— Arrears, manufacturing

Source: Statistical Office of the Slovak Republic.

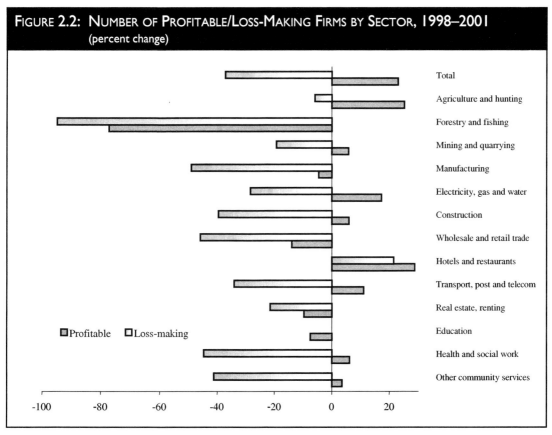

FIGURE 2.2: NUMBER OF PROFITABLE/LOSS-MAKING FIRMS BY SECTOR, 1998–2001
(percent change)

Source: Statistical Office of the Slovak Republic and staff calculations.

TABLE 2.4: EVOLUTION OF PROFIT MARGINS BY SECTOR, 1998–2001
(percent)

	All Enterprises[a]				Profit-Making Only[a]				Loss-Making Only[a]			
	1998	1999	2000	2001	1998	1999	2000	2001	1998	1999	2000	2001
A. Agriculture, Hunting	−2.7	−3.7	−1.1	0.9	15.2	5.6	5.0	5.5	−23.5	−14.6	−10.2	−10.4
B. Forestry & Fishing	1.8	−0.1	1.0	0.8	15.7	4.8	1.2	1.0	−11.0	−4.6	−4.0	−5.8
C. Mining & Quarrying	3.9	2.9	7.9	9.7	9.6	8.3	15.1	18.9	−10.9	−6.3	−3.8	−3.1
D. Manufacturing	−1.4	0.8	2.9	4.8	7.4	5.7	5.8	6.9	−18.6	−11.7	−9.4	−9.4
E. Electricity, Gas & Water	7.4	11.8	6.1	6.6	14.2	12.3	6.5	11.1	−9.7	−5.3	−3.8	−8.2
F. Construction	1.4	1.0	1.5	3.2	9.2	6.6	4.6	6.1	−16.1	−10.6	−9.4	−9.6
G. Wholesale & Retail Trade	1.3	0.3	2.4	2.1	5.9	4.8	4.0	3.7	−9.7	−6.4	−3.0	−4.0
H. Hotels & Restaurants	−0.6	2.3	3.4	5.1	14.2	10.8	7.8	9.6	−26.7	−20.2	−10.2	−6.4
I. Transp., Post & Telecom.	−3.9	−4.2	−1.3	7.9	18.1	11.6	6.7	13.4	−20.4	−19.2	−13.7	−3.3
J. Real estate and Housing	2.0	3.6	4.2	6.1	16.0	11.2	10.6	10.3	−24.8	−14.0	−14.2	−13.7
K. Education	−4.4	−4.2	−3.2	4.1	9.6	4.3	3.7	7.4	−14.4	−8.0	−6.5	−5.6
L. Health & Social Welfare	6.8	7.3	5.9	4.5	17.7	11.2	7.9	6.3	−15.4	−8.3	−4.7	−6.8
M. Other Community Serv.	4.5	2.0	2.6	2.1	12.2	10.1	8.1	9.7	−17.4	−11.2	−7.2	−13.7
Total	0.4	1.4	2.7	4.4	9.1	7.0	5.6	7.1	−16.4	−10.8	−8.1	−7.2

a/ Non-financial enterprises employing more than 19 people only.
Source: Statistical Office of the Slovak Republic and staff calculations.

1998 and 2002 (with particularly strong performances in such sectors as transport equipment, chemicals, textiles, leather, pulp and paper, and utilities), their profit margins remained essentially unchanged. This may be associated with the growing degree of competition brought about by trade liberalization and EU integration (see below).

One main way in which enterprises adjusted was by shedding labor. By 2001, those firms that survived employed on average 25 percent fewer people than in 1998. The worst hit were the traditionally labor-intensive construction firms (which further suffered from a contraction in the volume of public works contracts), but all sectors were affected to varying degrees (see Table 2.5, first panel). Only foreign-owned firms appear to have been able to buck this trend and expand their respective payrolls (Table 2.5).

Financial Sector Reform

As already noted, the above developments in the enterprise sector owe much to the major restructuring of the banking sector that the government undertook in 1999–2001. A series of bank failures in 1999–2001, and the resulting banking resolution, eliminated the sick banks in the system and hardened the firms' budget constraints. Building on these stronger premises, banking sector growth is likely to be fueled in the future by expansion into consumer finance, leasing, housing finance, and small business sector lending. Indeed, as we have observed, corporate sector ownership is rapidly changing in the Slovak Republic and larger entities are being privatized and are increasingly foreign owned. Although there will be regular growth in credit facilities to these larger private corporations, a significant part of such funding will be provided through cross-border credit

TABLE 2.5: AVERAGE FIRM SIZE BY SECTOR AND BY FORM OF OWNERSHIP, 1996–2001 (1998=100)

	1995	1996	1997	1998	1999	2000	2001
				By Sector			
A. Agriculture, hunting	n.s.	n.s	n.s	n.s	n.s	n.s	n.s.
B. Forestry and fishing	n.s.	n.s	n.s	n.s	n.s	n.s	n.s.
C. Mining and quarrying	31.2	122.2	103.2	100.0	92.0	75.8	61.2
D. Manufacturing	103.9	114.1	110.1	100.0	85.9	76.6	67.0
E. Electricity, gas and water	99.5	105.1	113.3	100.0	93.8	91.7	68.3
F. Construction	132.5	106.7	107.8	100.0	79.7	67.0	35.3
G. Wholesale and retail trade	117.4	159.9	130.3	100.0	116.9	99.8	75.6
H. Hotels and restaurants	278.0	n.a.	50.7	100.0	124.8	83.2	n.a.
I. Transport, post and telecom	167.0	140.2	113.0	100.0	102.6	76.9	76.3
J. Financial intermediation	n.a.	n.a.	n.a.	n.a.	n.a.	n.a.	n.a.
K. Real estate, renting	129.0	85.1	94.1	100.0	100.2	81.6	66.7
O. Other community services	n.s.	n.s.	n.s.	n.s.	n.s.	n.s.	n.s.
Unidentified	83.2	52.4	65.6	100.0	98.6	17.8	146.0
				By Form of Ownership			
State	95.8	105.0	110.9	100.0	111.6	99.8	86.9
Private–domestic	99.1	111.3	104.4	100.0	93.8	82.0	57.8
Private–foreign	106.0	86.8	100.4	100.0	115.5	128.9	150.7
Unidentified	80.2	56.0	70.3	100.0	85.8	15.9	130.7
Total	96.3	97.8	102.7	100.0	97.3	87.5	76.5

Note: n.s. = not statistically significant.
Source: Statistical Office of the Slovak Republic and staff calculations.

facilities and FDI. With the forthcoming EU integration and euro-zone participation, there is also less incentive for the growth of Slovak equity and fixed income markets. Several factors encourage many larger companies to raise capital abroad—foreign ownership, EU integration, and deeper, more liquid, more reliable and cheaper markets. This would leave banks to focus on household and small business needs.

Two risks are involved in this scenario, however. One is that banks, now highly liquid, will seek to branch out too rashly into new, high-risk business activities in a bid to boost their currently low profits. Hence, there is a need to step up supervision. The second risk is that bank lending will be guided more by the degree of enforceability of creditors' rights in different business segments and will remain atrophied in the small business segment in the absence of an effective bankruptcy framework. Hence, the need to remove the latter bottleneck (including through judiciary measures) is a matter of the utmost priority.

Impact of Bank Restructuring

The banking sector has gone through a major overhaul. In 2000–2001, the three large state-owned banks (Slovenska Sporitelna (SSP), VUB, and IRB) were restructured through recapitalization and the transfer of non-performing loans to two state-owned asset management companies—SKA and Konsolidacna Banka (KBB), later merged into SKA—and subsequently privatized. In the process of selling the state-owned banks to private foreign strategic investors, the government replaced SKK 113 billion (13 percent of GDP) in non-performing loans (NPLs) with government bonds.

As a result, the system's soundness has increased substantially (Table 2.6). The sector is now more than 90 percent foreign owned (with all of the major banks controlled by *much larger* foreign banks) and is at much greater arm's length from its borrowers. NPLs not covered by provisions (net NPLs) in the system fell from 25 percent of total loans in 1998 to 7–8 percent in 2001. Furthermore, banks are generally very well capitalized now and the entry of foreign owners is expected to strengthen credit culture and governance, as well as to bring in new, modern risk management systems.

Bank liquidity is also at an all-time high. This high liquidity reflects the impact of the debt carve-outs (as banks acquired large amounts of government securities) and of the result of the central bank's sterilized purchases of capital inflows. Excess liquidity has cut into banks' operating profitability in the post-restructuring environment, as their loan books have shrunk and low-yielding assets now dominate their balance sheets. The rate of return on assets shows the system at near-zero profitability for the past three years.[24] Total loans between 1997 and 2001 went down from nearly SKK 355 billion to SKK 293 billion, and the loan-to-total assets ratio fell from 47 percent to 31 percent during the same period.

This situation may put banks under pressure to reach for higher yield by taking on new kinds of risks, especially market risks. In order to increase profitability, the larger banks are likely to introduce new services and step up competition for existing financial services in the sector. This will change the risk environment of banking operations and will create pressures for relatively weaker or unsuccessful banks to further consolidate, or to exit the system.

Regulation and Supervision

Hence, there is a need to step up regulation and supervision. Bank regulation, on the one hand, has been significantly strengthened through the recent adoption of a new banking law. The new law (effective January 2002) provides a stronger framework for corporate governance, risk management, enforcement, and consolidated supervision. The procedures for dealing with problem banks

---

24. While net income has improved significantly in recent years, this gain is based in large part on non-recurring items, such as a reversal of funds previously committed to specific provisions or to the general risk reserve.

TABLE 2.6: FINANCIAL SOUNDNESS INDICATORS FOR THE BANKING SECTOR, 1997–2001
(percent)

	Dec-97	Dec-98	Dec-99	Dec-00	Dec-01
Capital Adequacy					
Regulatory capital to risk-weighted assets*	8.0	6.6	12.71	13.08	19.72
Asset Quality					
Sectoral distribution of loans to total loans					
Individuals	5.2	6.5	8.7	10.7	15.3
Government	2.0	2.1	2.0	1.7	3.7
Agriculture	4.5	3.8	4.6	3.6	4.2
Mining	0.7	0.9	0.7	0.6	0.7
Manufacturing	29.5	28.7	20.7	18.6	19.7
Transportation	1.8	2.1	1.3	1.2	3.9
Financial services	5.0	2.3	2.7	2.5	3.8
Other services	51.2	53.6	59.3	61.2	48.6
FX loans to total loans	7.4	8.2	9.1	8.3	7.8
NPLs to gross loans*	27.2	31.6	23.7	15.3	14.01
NPLs net of provisions to capital	22.5	25.2	15.7	6.9	7.9
Liquidity					
Liquid assets to total assets[a]	13.5	9.7	12.1	18.1	27.5
Liquid assets to short term liabilities[b]	47.8	38.6	59.7	90.7	61.4
Customer deposits to loans (ratio)	1.22	1.20	1.34	1.59	2.13
Customer FX deposits to total deposits	11.6	16.2	16.2	17.4	18.3
Earnings and Profitability					
Net income (ROA)	0.09	−0.48	−2.27	1.41	1.07
Operating profit (ROA)	1.40	1.37	−0.10	0.07	−0.09
ROE	2.81	−13.39	−36.53	25.16	25.26

*Excluding KOBL
a/ Liquid assets include government securities of all types and maturities, cash and reserve balances at NBS
b/ Defined as liquid assets to highly volatile liabilities in the NBS Supervisory Information System.
Source: National Bank of Slovakia (NBS).

have also been substantially strengthened. The supervisor now possesses the explicit authority to require corrective action plans from banks, including requirements for a capital plan, plans for strengthening a bank's financial position, and other action that the National Bank of Slovakia (NBS) deems necessary. Subsequent enforcement actions may be taken if NBS requirements are not met. Supporting regulations to further define selected aspects of the new law and to implement various provisions (for example, regulations addressing classification of assets, market risk and risk management, capital adequacy, and large exposures) are currently being drafted and are expected to be in place by late 2002. Against this backdrop, the government has opted to integrate regulation and supervision for all banking and non-banking markets under the jurisdiction of the NBS by 2005.

While the decision may be a pragmatic one, it will be important not to lose the focus on building the supervisory capacity of the NBS (and the FMA) in the interim period. Indeed, although meaningful steps have been taken to strengthen bank supervision, the Slovak Republic is still well short of meeting many of the Basle Core Principles for Effective Supervision. Fundamental changes in the way supervision is implemented must still take place if supervisory capacity is to be effective and consistent with international best practices. The supervisory process remains heavily compliance-based, with a

BOX 2.1: OVERVIEW OF THE FINANCIAL SYSTEM

The Slovak financial sector is dominated by banks that constitute nearly 88 percent of the sector's assets (see table below), followed by insurance companies at 6.3 percent and leasing companies at 4.7 percent. Overall, the financial sector at 110 percent of GDP as of end 2001 is of a reasonable size compared with other European Union (EU) accession countries. Total assets in the financial sector have grown in absolute terms from Sk 841.0 billion in 1997 to nearly Sk 1061.0 billion in 2001. Monetization of the economy as measured by the ratio of broad money to GDP remained steady during 1998–2001 at 60 percent, reflecting a fairly high degree of confidence in the Slovak koruna and the banking system.

The non-banking sector is growing rapidly, but from such a low base that to date it has not had much impact on the size of the overall financial sector. Total non-bank assets were 10 percent of total financial sector assets in 1997 and had grown to around 12 percent in 2001. As a percentage of GDP they have grew from 11.3 percent to 13.5 percent. Pension funds are the most rapidly growing segment but remain the smallest, while the more slowly growing insurance sector is the largest non-bank sector.

The private insurance sector in Slovakia is one of the smaller but faster developing insurance markets in the region. As of end 2001 there were 28 companies operating in the market, and total insurance premiums written increased from Sk 14.0 billion in 1996 to Sk 32.0 billion in 2001. Insurance density, expressed as total premiums in US$ per capita, was US$45.50 for life insurance and US$64.00 for non-life insurance. These figures rank Slovakia ahead of Turkey but lower than the Czech Republic, Hungary, and Poland.

STRUCTURE OF THE FINANCIAL SYSTEM, 1997–2001

	1997	1998	1999	2000	2001
Percentage of GDP					
Deposit money banks	110.4	103.5	90.6	94.0	97.0
Insurance companies	6.0	6.3	6.0	6.0	7.0
Investment funds	0.3	0.3	0.4	0.7	0.9
Pension funds	0.0	0.1	0.2	0.4	0.6
Leasing companies	5.0	4.3	3.4	4.3	5.2
Total	**121.8**	**114.5**	**100.6**	**105.4**	**110.6**
Number of financial institutions					
Dealer/brokers	132	148	154	141	130
Deposit money banks	29	27	26	23	21
Insurance companies	23	26	28	29	28
Investment management companies	12	18	19	6	9
Leasing companies	41	44	44	42	35
Pension funds	2	3	4	4	4

Sources: National Bank of Slovakia (NBS), Financial Markets Authority (FMA), industry associations, and staff estimates.

continued need to conduct more qualitative assessments on bank safety and soundness, management practice, systems, and risk management. Enhanced and reoriented supervision capabilities will need to include at least the following actions: (i) interpreting and applying banking legislation more flexibly, especially as concerns the authority of the NBS to set regulatory reporting standards for banks and to issue regulations/guidance in areas not specifically referenced in the banking law; (ii) enhancing market risk supervisory capabilities and improving the reporting of exposure to market risk; (iii) intensifying information sharing with other banking supervisors, especially those in the countries of origin of the strategic foreign owners of the banks; and (iv) enhancing the accuracy of regulatory and accounting information.

Accounting and Auditing

As of this date, financial statements are still prepared in accordance with inadequate Slovak accounting standards and do not present an accurate picture of the financial condition of firms. Among the CEECs, the Slovak Republic stands alone with Romania in not (yet) mandating the use of international accounting standards (IAS)—not even by financial institutions, despite the clear public interest nature of their activity. There is, unfortunately, a large gap between Slovak accounting requirements and IAS.[25] Although listed companies are required to prepare financial statements in accordance with IAS, in addition to statutory annual financial statements, there is no mechanism to monitor and enforce this requirement. As a result, many of the statements presented as IAS financial statements do not fully comply with IAS. Furthermore, Slovak disclosure requirements fall short of IAS disclosure standards.

In the auditing area, too, a number of problems indicate the need for a well-organized reform program. Among these problems are: the failure of auditors to comply with internationally comparable independence and ethical requirements; the inadequate capacity of the Slovak Chamber of Auditors to properly regulate the profession; shortcomings in educational and training arrangements with regard to the practical application of high-quality accounting and auditing standards and requirements; and the absence of effective mechanisms for enforcing established rules and regulations.

The authorities have agreed to design and implement a Country Action Plan (CAP) to bring Slovak accounting and auditing standards and practices in line with IAS/ISA and international best practices standards. Proactive implementation of the Plan will be key to the future growth of all segments of the financial system and, hence, financial intermediation in support of economic growth.

Deposit Insurance

An urgent effort is also required to strengthen the finances of the Deposit Protection Fund (DPF). The recent bank failures have depleted DPF's resources. Without a capital injection, a minimum prudent insured deposit coverage ratio of 1.5 percent will not be reached before end-2010. At the same time, deposit insurance coverage levels are rising rapidly. The government and/or the NBS should therefore urgently inject funds into the DPF and put in place emergency funding arrangements to allow it to manage any unforeseen future bank failures. Furthermore, inappropriate allowances for the DPF and the new Investor Guarantee Fund (IGF) to provide emergency liquidity support to banks and securities firms under temporary administration, and for insurance companies to sell deposit insurance and investor protection coverage over and above the insurance/coverage provided by the DPF and the IGF should be abolished.

Debt Resolution Framework

Significant remaining weaknesses in creditor rights will need to be addressed if the banking sector is to expand into such potential growth areas as small business sector lending. As a general rule, creditor rights remain weak, collateral systems (other than for the traditional mortgage) are poorly developed, and enforcement procedures are slow and unreliable through the courts. As a result, credit is largely inaccessible to all but the upper echelon of corporate borrowers and, more recently, mortgage borrowers (see growth in lending to individuals, Table 2.6). To offset the high regulatory risk this situation creates, lenders have adopted a policy of requiring fully secured loans in nearly all corporate transactions. Similarly, the process of insolvency remains slow, inefficient, and poorly regulated, although recent changes in the law have led to improvements. Legal and regulatory weaknesses have fueled a growing business in lease finance, where ownership resides in the lender or creditor, making asset recovery more efficient and predictable.

Court system weaknesses and inefficiencies are the most significant impediment to debt enforcement. While the Foreclosure (Execution) Law has greatly enhanced the ability of creditors to foreclose

---

25. For example, Slovak standards do not require banks to use fair valuation of collateral assets or non-accrual of interest on distressed assets, and this results in misrepresentation of bank income and capital.

TABLE 2.7: BANKRUPTCY AND SETTLEMENTS
(number of firms)

	1993	1994	1995	1996	1997	1998	1999	2000
Bankruptcy proceedings initiated	538	1,115	1,530	1,321	1,755	1,831	2,161	2,008
Processed:	169	466	591	672	488	702	1289	1547
Petition withdrawal	20	104	113	—	—	—	—	—
Cessation of proceedings	85	267	388	272	275	279	451	514
Cases handed over to locally authorized bodies	57	69	64	—	—	—	—	—
Rejection due to lack of assets	7	26	26	66	100	219	425	574
Other	—	—	—	334	113	204	413	415
Declaration of bankruptcy	11	32	74	198	427	654	665	638
Non-processed	369	649	939	2,663	3,896	5,025	5,897	6,358

Source: Ministry of Justice, as cited in OECD 2002 Annual Review—The Slovak Republic

on assets, mostly real estate, the creditor is unable to avoid court proceedings and continue enforcement without the cooperation of the debtor, which rarely occurs. Another notable deficiency in creditors' ability to secure their debts is the lack of a registry for pledges on movable property. Currently, possession is required to effect a pledge on movables. A new law and pledge registry for pledge of movables is being developed; its adoption should significantly enhance asset-based lending.

At present, bankruptcy presents the worst option for a creditor to choose in recovering debt. Though amending of the Bankruptcy Law as of August 1, 2000, has strengthened creditors rights in bankruptcy proceeding creditors continue to find that participation in bankruptcy proceedings is not fruitful (see Table 2.7). Courts are weak as an institution in the Slovak Republic, and bankruptcy courts are no exception. The lack of professional development and regulation of trustees, important players in the bankruptcy process, represents another significant institutional weakness in the bankruptcy system.

This situation has hindered the resolution of the SKK 100 billion or so in bad loans that the government carved out from the banking sector and has reduced the recoveries.[26] Unfortunately, this also increases the moral hazard involved in the bailout operation, and, perhaps worse, delays the release of assets from failed owners (many of whom acquired them in questionable transactions during the Meciar years) and their return to more productive use.

An Interagency Commission established in February concluded that the defects in the current bankruptcy framework were so profound as to require comprehensive reform. Key elements of such reforms include:[27] (i) a modernized legislation, providing among other features an effective

---

26. This is currently the responsibility of SKA, a joint stock company owned by the state, whose investment board (staffed with independent domestic and foreign experts) must endorse all NPL resolution actions proposed by management. SKA has adopted a three-pronged strategy for NPL recovery, comprising sales of claims to third parties, recovery using third party solicitors, and in-house action. A package of Sk 13 billion (US$280 million equivalent) of claims was sold through tender in June 2001 to a consortium of a foreign investment bank and a local industrial holding company, for 4.7 percent of its nominal value. Through parallel legal collection actions SKA has additionally resolved approximately Sk 4 billion as of end February 2002 with an average recovery rate of 10 percent. Further, SKA plans include: (i) preparation of packages of claims on individuals up to Sk 10 million by region, for sale to third parties (the total of such small claims on individuals being held by SKA was Sk 5 billion as of February 2002); and (ii) sale of individual large claims of over Sk 100 million each (the total of such claims was Sk 8 billion as of the same date). SKA may also transfer selected large claims to a turnaround fund to be created with EBRD participation. Based on the above strategy, SKA is planning to complete its NPL resolution efforts and cease to exist by end 2004, as originally envisaged.

27. See the recently completed "Report on Observance of Standards and Codes for Insolvency and Creditor Rights," IMF-World Bank.

reorganization mechanism (rather than only liquidation) when the enterprise is potentially viable and greater creditor initiative and participation; (ii) a more limited scope for debtors, land registry offices, and other parties involved in bankruptcy cases to delay proceedings; and (iii) more resources to bankruptcy courts, better training of judges, and stronger regulation of trustees with a view to reducing the current backlog and making proceedings more foolproof. Implementing the recently adopted amendment to the tax laws allowing corporations to deduct overdue claims as business expenses would lift a serious impediment to the informal workout procedures.[28] This would represent major progress, as formal procedures may not become truly dependable until the structural bottlenecks in the judiciary system have been eliminated (see Chapter 5).

Trade Integration

Alongside of the hardening of budget constraints, trade integration has been the second most powerful driver of enterprise restructuring, particularly in the manufacturing sector. Made possible by trade liberalization and driven by foreign investors, the process permitted the insertion of Slovak manufacturing into global manufacturing networks, and facilitated a redirection of production following the breakup of Czechoslovakia. Two patterns of trade have emerged: (i) trade with the EU has expanded briskly through the 1990s and the export specialization has shifted toward more skilled labor-intensive products; while (ii) trade with the Czech Republic has contracted and the export content reverted to less processed goods.

Recent export developments raise three concerns: (i) export growth seems to have lost its earlier momentum, and this has been associated with a perhaps excessively rapid emergence from unskilled labor-intensive industries; (ii) while the country' external tariff is already one of the most liberal in the CEECs, the country still has a long way to go to meet EU requirements in terms of standards, intellectual rights, etc.; and (iii) a destructive tax competition for foreign investors has set in among Visegrad countries.

Under the circumstances, the government would be well advised to take the following steps. First, it should seek to eliminate the internal border within the Czech-Slovak Customs Union (CSU) ahead of EU accession—not only to reinvigorate trade with a country that remains the Slovak Republic's second largest trading partner, but also to catch up with EU requirements, if only "by osmosis." Second, it should support any initiative taken in the context of the competition chapter of the EU accession negotiations to harmonize the tax incentives offered by Visegrad countries at the lowest possible level.

Recent Trade Development

In contrast to the experience of other Central European economies, not just one but two shocks (i.e., the dissolution of the CMEA and that of Czechoslovakia) have shaped Slovak trade performance. Following the collapse of intra-CMEA exchanges, trade with the Czech Republic also contracted dramatically after the breakup of former Czechoslovakia (minus 20 percent in nominal terms between 1994 and 2000) (see Table 2.9).

Aggressive trade liberalization has helped redirect Slovak trade to third country partners, particularly the EU (see Table 2.9). The CSU has pursued that policy at both the regional and the multilateral level. At the regional level, it is part of a single European trading bloc organized within the Pan-European Cumulation Agreement encompassing 28 European countries. As of January 1, 2002, trade in industrial products among these countries is duty-free and subject to diagonal cumulation of rules of origin. The latter implies that imports originating in any of 28 signatories of the Agreement are treated as local inputs. In parallel, the MFN Common External Tariff CET of the CSU has been cut back following the implementation of the Uruguay Round Agreements. As a

---

28. The law now recognizes as legitimate business expenses the write-off of claims overdue since January, 1.2002 (25 percent of provision if claim is due for more than 18 months, 50 percent, 24 months, 75 percent, 36 months, 100 percent, 48 months).

TABLE 2.8: EVOLUTION OF EXPORTS AND IMPORTS VOLUMES, 1993–2000
(percent change)

	1993	1994	1995	1996	1997	1998	1999	2000
Total exports	56	23	28	3	9	11	−6	18
Total imports	63	4	33	25	7	11	−15	15
Exports to the EU	n.a.	42	37	14	25	32	0	18
Imports from the EU	n.a.	19	38	32	27	28	−12	9

Source: Based on Slovakia data as reported to the UN COMTRADE database and ECE 2002 for the estimates of values of total exports and imports in 1992.

result, the CSU's MFN bound tariff rates second lowest (after Estonia with a free trade regime), among CEECs and its bound tariff rates are the lowest. The bulk of Slovak trade, however, is with preferential partners (at lower than MFN rates). In 2002, preferential partners accounted for three-fourths of Slovak imports and for more than 90 percent of Slovak exports (Table 2.10).

Trade with the EU

Overall Development. Following the opening up of EU markets under the country's 1993 Europe Agreement, exports to those markets surged. Except for 1999, the rates of growth were in a double-digit range. As for other CEECs, the share of the EU in total exports thus increased from 35 percent to 59 percent between 1994 and 2000 (Table 2.9). The increase on the import side was

TABLE 2.9: GEOGRAPHIC DISTRIBUTION OF SLOVAK FOREIGN TRADE, 1994–2000

Country	1994	1995	1996	1997	1998	1999	2000
			Export Value (US$ million)				
European Union	2,343	3,208	3,645	4,539	5,970	5,977	7,024
CEEC-10 (excl. Czech R.)	662	956	1,033	1,174	1,349	1,205	1,566
Czech Rep.	2,502	3,024	2,738	2,455	2,179	1,820	2,068
TOTAL	6,690	8,577	8,824	9,634	10,718	10,057	11,885
			Export Share (in percent)				
European Union	35	37	41	47	56	59	59
CEEC-10 (excl. Czech R.)	10	11	12	12	13	12	13
Czech Rep.	37	35	31	25	20	18	17
Other	18	16	16	15	11	10	10
			Import Value (U$ million)				
European Union	2,213	3,049	4,030	5,136	6,553	5,753	6,245
CEEC-10 (excl. Czech R.)	321	511	573	629	757	677	784
Czech Rep.	1,958	2,434	2,682	2,503	2,402	1,857	1,880
TOTAL	6,611	8,770	10,936	11,727	13,071	11,131	12,774
			Import Share (in percent)				
European Union	33	35	37	44	50	52	49
CEEC-10 (excl. Czech R.)	5	6	5	5	6	6	6
Czech Rep.	30	28	25	21	18	17	15
Other	32	32	33	29	26	26	30

Source: Based on Slovakia as reporter from UN COMTRADE Statistics.

TABLE 2.10: SHARE OF "FREE TRADE" PARTNERS IN FOREIGN TRADE

Trading partner	Share of total imports in 2002 (Jan.–June)	Share of total exports in 2002 (Jan.–June)	Simple average tariff rate in 2001
EU	49.8	59.9	2.3
EFTA	1.5	1.8	2.4
CEFTA	22.5	30.0	
o.w. Bulgaria	0.1	0.3	2.1
Czech Republic	15.1	16.6	0.0
Hungary	2.6	5.4	2.0
Poland	3.2	5.8	1.9
Romania	0.2	1.0	2.1
Slovenia	0.7	1.0	2.0
Estonia	0.0	0.0	2.4
Israel	0.1	0.1	2.5
Latvia	0.1	0.2	2.2
Lithuania	0.1	0.2	2.2
Turkey	0.3	0.3	2.5
TOTAL	74.3	92.5	

Source: Derived from Slovak official foreign trade data and tariff data from WTO 2001.

smaller but significant also (from 33 to 49 percent over the same period of time).[29] The expansion of exports to the EU (from US$1.6 billion in 1993 to US$6.5 billion in 2000) occurred in two huge leaps: one over 1994–95, when the value of exports more than doubled, and the second in 1998, when it increased 36 percent.

As in other CEECs, this export expansion was driven by foreign investment. After lagging behind the other CEECs for most of the 1990s, foreign investment began to pour in as reforms got under way in earnest after 1998 (Table 2.11). Companies with foreign capital exceeding 10 percent of their total equity (referred to hereafter as foreign investment enterprises or FIEs) now account for the majority of the country's exports and imports (Table 2.12). The fact that the overall contribution of FIEs to the trade balance is slightly negative should not come as a surprise. Its small size is encouraging for the future, as it should turn strongly positive once the impact of initial, one-time imports of capital goods subsides.

After loosing momentum in 1999–2000, the Slovak penetration of EU markets would seem to be gathering steam again. Until the late 1990s, the Slovak performance in exporting to the EU compared favorably with that of other EU applicants. Over the 1993–2000 period, it ranked second only to that of Estonia (see Table 2.13). Slovak growth rates fell behind the total for other CEECs in 1999 (3 percent as compared with 5 percent) and again in 2000 (2 percent as compared with 10 percent). The Slovak share in total CEEC-10 exports to the EU declined as a result from 7.9 percent in 1998 to 7.2 percent in 2000.[30] Preliminary data for 2001 suggest that Slovak

29. Where the Slovak Republic differs from other CEECs, however, is that its exports to CEFTA members (other than the Czech Republic) also expanded with the share growing from 10 percent in 1994 to 13 percent in 2000.

30. A significant discrepancy should be noted between the Slovak data on exports to the EU and those reported in EU statistics on imports from Slovakia. The Slovak data show a growth of 0.1 percent (as compared with 3.4 percent recorded in EU data) in 1999, and of 17.5 percent (as compared with 2.1 percent). While the value of exports was 3 and 4 percent below the EU import data in 1998 and 1999, respectively, it was 8 percent higher in 2000.

TABLE 2.11: FOREIGN DIRECT INVESTMENT, 1998–2002

USD	1995	1996	1997	1998	1999	2000	2001	1Q02
Official data[a]								
Equity capital and reinvested earnings								
net annual change		370	215	527	403	2,155	1,198	84
valuation changes		–85	–148	–69	–259	–705	–233	36
cumulative	1,162	1,447	1,671	2,128	2,272	3,722	4,687	4,808
Balance of payments[b]								
Direct investment in SR	300	301	220	684	390	1,925	1,475	70
Equity capital and reinvested earnings			204	505	365	2,155	1,179	84
Other capital			16	179	25	–230	296	–14
SKK	**1995**	**1996**	**1997**	**1998**	**1999**	**2000**	**2001**	**1Q02**
Official data[a]								
Equity capital and re invested earnings								
net annual change		11,334	7,220	18,582	16,689	99,561	57,921	4,051
valuation changes		467	–272	1,879	781	–19,199	–7,139	–2,001
cumulative	34,345	46,146	58,107	78,568	96,038	176,400	227,182	229,232
Balance of payments[b]								
Direct investment in SR	8,913	9,223	7,399	24,105	16,165	88,953	71,324	3,376
Equity capital and reinvested earnings			6,867	17,783	15,128	99,561	57,007	4,061
Other capital			532	6,322	1,037	–10,608	14,317	–685
Discrepancy, %[c]			5	4	10	0	2	0

a/ Monetary Survey, NBS, July 2002. Methodological changes: In 1996, CZK was included to convertible currencies. In 1997, capital in SKK was included (in 1996 only capital in foreign currency).
b/ Reporting format in 1995–1996 does not permit distinguishing between FDI and other capital.
c/ A difference between equity capital and reinvested earnings in official data and balance of payments.
Source: National Bank of Slovakia.

TABLE 2.12: SHARE OF FOREIGN INVESTMENT ENTERPRISES IN FOREIGN TRADE, 2000–01

	Exports of FIEs		Imports of FIEs	
	(SKK million)	**% of total exports**	**(SKK million)**	**% of total imports**
2000	335,194	61.1	352,756	59.7
2001	316,148	51.8	378,343	53.0

Sources: Hoskova, Adela, 2001, "Impact of Foreign Direct Investment on the Economy of Slovakia," National Bank of Slovakia, Institute of Monetary and Financial Studies, Bratislava, and Hoskova, Adela, 2002, "Priame Zahranicne Investicie," mimeo, National Bank of Slovakia, Institute of Monetary and Financial Studies, Bratislava.

exporters have started again to gain market shares in EU external imports.[31] Quarterly data indicate a continuation of this trend up to the second quarter of 2002 (when an uptick was registered following the coming on stream of a new car production line).

Export Specialization. A number of factors indicate that the country's export position in EU markets is strong. First, despite the slump in export performance, Slovak exporters did not lose

---

31. The share of Slovakia in EU external imports (i.e., excluding 'internal' trade among EU members) was 0.76 percent in 1999, 0.67 percent in 2000, and 0.80 percent in 2001 (derived from data in Comext).

TABLE 2.13: EU IMPORTS FROM CEEC-10, 1993–2000
(millions of US dollars)

	1993	1994	1995	1996	1997	1998	1999	2000
Bulgaria	1,201	1,719	2,435	2,202	2,413	2,547	2,355	2,442
Czech Republic	6,496	8,224	11,844	12,370	13,385	16,530	17,922	19,581
Estonia	356	738	1,307	1,568	1,883	2,133	2,137	3,094
Hungary	5,747	7,274	10,047	11,325	13,378	17,026	18,962	19,779
Latvia	878	1,274	1,653	1,859	1,945	1,859	1,517	1,915
Lithuania	854	1,051	1,382	1,529	1,565	1,671	1,757	2,117
Poland	10,019	12,211	16,145	15,769	16,635	18,631	18,916	21,624
Romania	2,106	3,364	4,508	4,616	5,167	5,624	6,103	6,852
Slovak Republic	*1,649*	*2,659*	*4,045*	*4,292*	*4,532*	*6,148*	*6,359*	*6,493*
Slovenia	3,732	4,512	5,628	5,513	5,346	5,868	5,707	5,557
TOTAL	33,039	43,026	58,996	61,042	66,249	78,037	81,734	89,442

Source: Derived from trade data as reported by the EU to UN COMTRADE database.

TABLE 2.14: SHARE OF SLOVAK EXPORTS IN TOTAL EU IMPORTS, 1993–2000
(percent)

	1993	1994	1995	1996	1997	1998	1999	2000	2001	Index, 2001 1993=100
Share in EU imports	0.12	0.17	0.21	0.22	0.23	0.30	0.30	0.30	0.32	375

Source: Derived from trade data as reported by the EU to UN COMTRADE database.

ground to competitors from the rest of the world. In both 1999 and 2000, Slovak exporters retained their share in EU imports (Table 2.14).

Second, the Slovak initial position of an exporter specializing in manufactured products has been sustained (see Table 2.15). Within broad categories of manufactures, however, there was a significant change in terms of new specialization patterns. The case of transport equipment, whose share in EU-oriented exports more than tripled between 1994 and 2000 (from 9 percent to 31 percent) is the most spectacular example. Together with electric and non-electric machinery, exports of transport equipment shaped the dynamic of Slovak export to EU markets in the second half of the 1990s. These three product categories accounted for 57 percent of Slovak exports of manufactures to the EU in 2000—up from 23 percent in 1994.

Encouragingly, "sunrise" sectors account for 21 percent of total Slovak exports to the EU (see Table 2.16). These are products that exhibit both outstandingly good export performance and exceptionally strong demand on EU markets.[32] Such positioning augurs well for sustaining future export growth in EU markets. Moreover, expanding markets offer better prospects for firms simply because the "area" of competition expands which does not compel them to sell at discounted prices.

---

32. Defined as 4-digit SITC product categories whose value of EU-oriented exports from Slovakia exceeds US$5 million, whose average annual growth rate was at least 10 percent over 1998–2000, and for which EU-external imports experienced an annual average growth rate of at least 5 percent during 1998–2000.

TABLE 2.15: EXPORT SPECIALIZATION INDICES OF SELECTED PRODUCT CATEGORIES, 1994–2000

Product (SITC Rev. 1)	1994	1995	1996	1997	1998	1999	2000
				Export Specialization Index			
All Manufactures (5+6+7+8–68)	1.3	1.3	1.1	1.3	1.2	1.2	1.3
Chemical Elements (51)	1.1	0.7	0.7	0.9	0.7	0.6	0.7
Leather Goods (61)	1.4	1.2	1.2	2.4	1.8	2.8	2.5
Wood Manufactures (63)	3.1	2.9	2.5	1.9	1.7	1.8	1.8
Textiles, Yarn and Fabric (65)	2.5	2.1	1.2	1.6	1.3	1.4	1.4
Iron and Steel (67)	10.4	8.0	2.9	6.1	3.8	3.7	3.5
Metal Manufactures (69)	2.7	2.7	2.4	2.1	1.7	1.9	1.9
Non-Electric Machinery (71)	0.4	0.4	0.4	0.5	0.4	0.6	0.6
Electrical Machinery (72)	0.5	0.6	0.7	0.9	0.9	0.9	0.8
Transport Equipment (73)	1.3	1.2	2.3	2.6	3.7	3.2	3.9
Furniture (81)	4.0	4.0	3.7	3.1	2.4	2.1	3.1
Clothing (84)	1.1	1.0	0.9	1.6	1.3	1.3	1.2
Footwear (85)	1.5	1.7	1.6	2.3	2.1	2.2	2.4
Scientific Instruments (86)	0.1	0.1	0.1	0.2	0.2	0.1	0.2

Note: The Export Specialization Index is calculated as a ratio of shares of Slovak exports to the EU to the shares of the EU external imports.
Source: UN COMTRADE Statistics.

Role of Global Production Networks. This reflects the country's growing, albeit still uneven, integration in global production networks. Overall, about US$2 billion worth of Slovak exports was associated with such networks in 2000 as compared with less than US$130 million in 1993. Exports associated with the network accounted for about one-third of the Slovak Republic's manufacturing exports to the EU, and the overall trade balance in this network was positive and equal to US$0.57 billion in 1998 and US$0.37 billion in 2000. While in absolute values the Slovak Republic's involvement in EU-based networks is less pronounced than that of Hungary, it is comparable, in terms of its share in EU-destined manufacturing exports, to the performance of the Czech Republic and Poland.

As Table 2.17 confirms, the country's most salient success has been the spectacular increase in its participation in the EU-based automotive production network. While in 1993 Slovakia exported only US$43 million of automobiles, this figure was 31 times higher in 2000, amounting to US$1.37 billion. While this increase in automobile production has been accompanied by a large increase in imports of parts and components, the statistics also indicate growing exports of domestically produced parts and components.

TABLE 2.16: "SUNRISE" SECTORS IN EU-DESTINED SLOVAK EXPORTS, 2000

	No. of "sunrise" sectors	Share in "sunrise" exports (%)	Share in total Exports
Capital Intensive	14	48.3	25.0
Natural Resources	8	19.0	10.8
Unskilled Labor	5	18.0	17.9
Skilled Labor	7	14.7	46.3

Source: Computations based on UN COMTRADE Statistics.

TABLE 2.17: PARTICIPATION IN EU-BASED NETWORK TRADE
(millions of US Dollars)

	Czech Republic			Estonia			Hungary		
Automotive Network	**1993**	**1998**	**2000**	**1993**	**1998**	**2000**	**1993**	**1998**	**2000**
Final product exports	382	1856	2415	1	3	14	20	525	1283
Final product imports	487	916	1009	46	202	179	638	1037	1171
Exports of p&c	94	975	1539	1	7	11	168	3011	3097
Imports of p&c	176	1162	1588	5	46	40	206	1311	1465
Final exports minus p&c imports	206	694	827	−4	−43	−25	−186	−786	−181
Shares in manufactures exports to EU (%)	9	19	22	1	1	1	5	24	25
Overall Balance	−187	753	1358	−50	−238	−194	−656	1189	1745
Information revolution network									
Final product exports	23	69	278	0	160	541	32	1192	1635
Final product imports	93	273	708	2	81	64	86	284	395
Exports of p&c	53	280	460	2	118	258	202	859	1199
Imports of p&c	286	599	1143	4	298	449	396	1645	2465
Final exports minus p&c imports	−263	−530	−864	−4	−138	92	−364	−452	−831
Shares in manufactures exports to EU (%)	1	2	4	2	23	41	6	14	16
Overall Balance	−302	−523	−1112	−4	−100	286	−248	123	−27
Furniture network									
Final product exports	147	219	240	9	84	93	90	120	134
Final product imports	94	123	107	3	34	27	93	114	105
Exports of p&c	60	412	459	3	31	50	38	152	180
Imports of p&c	34	150	137	1	10	9	24	75	96
Final exports minus p&c imports	113	69	103	8	74	84	66	45	38
Shares in manufactures exports to EU (%)	4	4	4	8	9	7	3	2	2
Overall Balance	79	358	455	8	71	107	11	83	113
All Networks									
Final product exports	552	2144	2934	9	247	648	142	1837	3052
Final product imports	674	1312	1823	52	317	270	817	1434	1671
Exports of p&c	207	1667	2458	6	157	319	408	4022	4476
Imports of p&c	495	1912	2868	10	354	498	625	3030	4026
Final exports minus p&c imports	56	233	66	0	−106	150	−483	−1193	−974
Shares in manufactures exports to EU (%)	14	26	31	10	33	50	13	40	43
Overall Balance	−411	588	701	−46	−267	199	−893	1395	1831

TABLE 2.17: PARTICIPATION IN EU-BASED NETWORK TRADE (millions of US Dollars) (CONTINUED)								
	Poland			**Slovakia**			**CEEC-10**		
Automotive Network	1993	1998	2000	1993	1998	2000	1993	1998	2000
Final product exports	536	1220	1552	43	1653	1369	1307	6184	7,365
Final product imports	950	1622	1992	73	294	178	3058	5675	5,991
Exports of p&c	75	489	1879	9	266	301	482	5068	7,181
Imports of p&c	418	1720	1836	36	1054	1120	1248	6091	6,801
Final exports minus p&c imports	118	−501	−284	7	599	250	59	94	564
Shares in manufactures exports to EU (%)	9	12	20	4	34	29	7	17	19
Overall Balance	−758	−1633	−396	−57	571	374	−2517	−513	1,754
Information revolution network									
Final product exports	4	528	571	2	4	27	83	2000	3,192
Final product imports	113	750	891	19	133	85	385	1894	2,552
Exports of p&c	85	328	295	5	140	173	372	1819	2,758
Imports of p&c	403	989	1256	74	254	239	1350	4365	6,428
Final exports minus p&c imports	−399	−461	−685	−72	−250	−213	−1267	−2366	−3,236
Shares in manufactures exports to EU (%)	1	6	5	1	3	4	2	6	8
Overall Balance	−428	−883	−1282	−85	−244	−125	−1280	−2441	−3,029
Furniture network									
Final product exports	519	1223	1398	52	94	91	1242	2300	2,570
Final product imports	85	187	178	17	36	28	365	709	597
Exports of p&c	77	287	405	13	43	73	298	1342	1,663
Imports of p&c	35	126	154	5	50	24	125	495	504
Final exports minus p&c imports	484	1097	1244	46	44	67	1117	1805	2,066
Shares in manufactures exports to EU (%)	9	10	10	5	3	3	6	6	6
Overall Balance	476	1197	1471	42	51	112	1050	2438	3,132
All Networks									
Final product exports	1058	2971	3521	97	1751	1487	2632	10484	13,127
Final product imports	1148	2559	3061	109	463	290	3808	8278	9,140
Exports of p&c	236	1104	2579	27	448	547	1152	8229	11,602
Imports of p&c	855	2835	3245	115	1358	1383	2722	10951	13,733
Final exports minus p&c imports	203	136	276	−18	393	104	−90	−467	−606
Shares in manufactures exports to EU (%)	20	28	35	9	39	36	16	29	33
Overall Balance	−709	−1319	−207	−100	378	361	−2746	−516	1,857

Source: Computations based on EU data in UN COMTRADE Statistics.

The country's participation in the "information revolution" network, encompassing office machinery and telecommunications equipment, has been less impressive, however, and the overall trade balance within the networks remains negative. Similarly, while some progress has been made in the furniture network, the Slovak performance in this area is less impressive than that of a number of other CEECs. Still, furniture is one of the most dynamic exports to the EU, and the furniture networks as a whole generate a positive trade balance.

Vertical Linkages. Also on a positive note, there are indications that, while difficult to quantify, foreign investment enterprises are developing backward linkages with domestic firms. Casual observation and anecdotal evidence suggest that (i) foreign investors who entered the Slovak Republic are putting down roots in the country and are being followed by key foreign suppliers; and (ii) local sourcing by foreign investment enterprises is slowly but steadily on the rise. For example, Volkswagen Slovakia has been followed by more than 10 foreign investors (involved in the production of electrical equipment, machinery, metallurgical products, and industrial chemicals) and, partly as a result, has been successful in increasing its sourcing from firms operating in the country (albeit not all of them domestically owned). While in 1997 VW had only 4 direct suppliers and 9 indirect ones, this number increased to 30 and 35, respectively, in 2000 (see the experience of Siemens, Box 2.2).

Factor Intensity. The country's pattern of trade specialization may be changing more rapidly than the underlying factor endowment would warrant(quasi-full employment of skilled labor but high unemployment of unskilled labor; one of the lowest levels of enrollment in tertiary education in the region). As the country's revealed comparative advantage in unskilled labor-intensive products (as measured by the Export Specialization Index) (see Table 2.18) eroded, the export of products requiring a highly skilled labor force experienced the most rapid growth in recent years (at an average annual rate of 28 percent), followed by capital-intensive products. Capital-intensive goods are even more disproportionately represented among "sunrise" sectors (see Table 2.16). As a result, the combined share of skilled labor-intensive and capital-intensive products in the Slovak Republic's total EU-oriented exports was 71 percent in 2000, up from 58 percent in 1995. Conversely, unskilled labor-intensive products doubled their shares of imports.

BOX 2.2: INTEGRATION INTO INTERNATIONAL PRODUCTION NETWORKS

The Slovak Republic's impressive performance in the automotive network has been driven by multinational corporations, such as Volkswagen, Siemens (cable harnesses, lights), INA Werke Schaffeler (ball bearings), Sachs Trnava (coupling assemblies for passenger cars), to name a few. Siemens has stakes in 14 Slovak companies, which employ more than 8,900 people. Siemens subsidiaries in turn make a growing contribution to the Slovak Republic's exports in the automotive network. For example, Osram Slovakia (part of the Siemens group) contributed to the growth of exports of electrical lighting and signaling equipment being sold to the EU and the Czech Republic. Siemens is also the driving force behind exports of pumps, which is one of the fastest growing product categories exported to the EU.

Siemens subsidiaries are very closely integrated with their customers as well as their suppliers abroad. SAS Automotive is one example. Formed in Bratislava in 2000, it supplies Volkswagen with complete assembled cockpits. Modules consist of dashboards, electronic components, air-conditioning, airbags, steering rods, and pedals. The module must be assembled error-free and delivered directly to the production line of the specific car within two hours from receiving the order. Supplies of the just-in-time mode require very precise coordination, logistics, and production. Logistics ensure the supply of more than 100 parts from various European countries and their effective storage and removal from the warehouse. Both the production staff and workers carry out continual high quality assembly to ensure the timely supply of cockpits in order to comply with the high standards set by Volkswagen.

TABLE 2.18: SPECIALIZATION AND FACTOR INTENSITY OF SLOVAK TRADE WITH THE EU, 1995–2000

Factor Intensity	1995	1996	1997	1998	1999	2000	Average annual growth 1996–2000
			Exports to the EU (US$ million)				
Natural Resources	587	627	814	753	822	731	5
Unskilled Labor	668	651	1,020	1,149	1,096	1,216	15
Capital Intensive	730	800	1,131	1,377	1,462	1,701	19
Skilled Labor	1,079	1,018	1,571	2,688	2,593	3,146	28
							Index in 2000
			Composition of Exports to the EU (%)				(1998=100)
Natural Resources	19.2	20.3	17.9	12.6	13.8	10.8	85.3
Unskilled Labor	21.8	21.0	22.5	19.3	18.3	17.9	92.9
Capital Intensive	23.8	25.8	24.9	23.1	24.5	25.0	108.5
Skilled Labor	35.2	32.9	34.6	45.0	43.4	46.3	102.8
							Index in 2000
			Export Specialization Index				(1998=100)
Natural Resources	0.6	0.5	0.6	0.5	0.5	0.4	82.5
Unskilled Labor	1.6	1.3	1.6	1.3	1.3	1.4	107.8
Capital Intensive	0.6	0.6	0.7	0.6	0.6	0.7	113.7
Skilled Labor	2.4	2.1	2.5	2.8	2.7	3.4	120.1
							Average annual growth
			Composition of Imports from the EU (%)				1996–2000
Natural Resources	15.5	17.2	17.9	15.0	10.5	11.0	12
Unskilled Labor	7.4	9.4	14.5	16.2	11.3	14.3	41
Capital Intensive	53.5	60.9	58.1	54.4	38.9	47.0	17
Skilled Labor	24.4	36.5	38.4	42.0	27.1	35.1	34

Note: The Export Specialization Index is calculated as a ratio of the shares of Slovak exports to the EU to the shares of the EU external imports.
Source: Computations based on Slovakia as reporter from UN COMTRADE Statistics.

This observation (of a shift out of unskilled labor-intensive activities) corroborates the findings of an earlier study of outward processing trade (OPT) transactions[33] between the EU and the Slovak Republic. The later study found traditional unskilled labor-intensive OPT activities (such as the production of textiles, clothing, footwear, and furniture) making way for more skilled labor activities linked to FDI (such as the production of power generating machinery, specialized machinery, telecommunications and sound recording equipment, and electrical machinery).[34] While it might be desirable for the Slovak Republic to move up in the value chain over time, one

---

33. Eltero, Andrea, 1998, "The Impact of FDI on the Foreign Trade of Four Smaller CEE Countries," Institute for World Economics, Hungarian Academy of Sciences Working Paper No. 96, Budapest, Hungary. OPT takes place when a manufacturer shifts some or all of its production process (often labor-intensive parts, easily separable from other stages of the manufacturing process) to a foreign country to take advantage of difference in factor prices (e.g., lower labor costs). The manufacturer often supplies its subcontractors in the foreign country with all inputs as well as product designs. After being processed in the foreign country, products are exported back to the home country of the manufacturer with the duty assessed based only on the foreign value added.

34. The share of the latter group in total OPT transactions increased from 13.7 percent in 1993 to 21.4 percent in 1997, while the share of traditional OPT products declined from 82 to 73 percent. Shifts in the same direction have also been observed in the Czech Republic and Hungary.

could wonder whether the overall policy framework (including the real exchange rate and wage setting arrangements) is not inducing a faster "graduation" than would be desirable, and threatening to leave large segments of the population.

Trade within the Czech-Slovak Customs Union

Overall Developments. Trade developments with the Czech Republic have taken almost the exact opposite direction from those with the EU (Table 2.19). First, as noted above, the contraction in mutual trade was dramatic in both relative and absolute terms. Following the "velvet divorce" of the Czechoslovak federation on 1 January 1993, trade between the two new sovereign states immediately fell compared with their respective "domestic" sales in 1992. The quick disappearance of a monetary union, followed by the devaluation of the Slovak koruna against the Czech koruna, the establishment of an internal border and of complicated payment systems, as well as "creeping" differences in technical standards, exacerbated the decline, which the creation of a Czech-Slovak Customs Union failed to stop. Unsurprisingly, the share of mutual trade in their respective totals kept falling through the first quarter of 2002.

This is not to say that a close coordination of foreign and customs policies has not been maintained within the CSU. Yet, the CSU has failed to deliver one of the two major potential advantages of a customs union over a free trade area. The arrangement has allowed the two countries to eschew very costly rules of origin among members, as all products entering the customs union are subject to CET and other taxes and charges collected by customs. However, trade between the two countries has remained subject to customs controls. International experience suggests that the transaction costs created by inefficient customs clearance procedures often exceed tariffs. Furthermore, the internal border has allowed for a considerable discretion in decisions affecting imports, such as the temporary imposition of import surcharges (on the Slovak side) or import deposits (on the Czech side), and the introduction of other technical barriers to trade.

Trade Patterns. Patterns, as well as the volume, of trade have been drastically affected. The Slovak export basket to the Czech Republic has shifted toward (i) agricultural products and raw materials—the share of manufactures fell from 79 percent in 1994 to 70 percent in 2000; and (ii) less processed goods—the combined share of foods, feeds and beverages, and industrial supplies and materials (a good proxy for low processed goods) rose from 19 percent to 30 percent over the period.

The previous division of labor within the industrial sectors also began to disappear. Trade within the automotive network provides a good illustration of that phenomenon: the share of parts and components originating in the EU in Slovak total imports of automotive parts and compo-

TABLE 2.19: SHARE OF THE SLOVAK AND CZECH REPUBLICS IN THEIR RESPECTIVE TRADE, 1993–2000
(percent)

	1994	1995	1996	1997	1998	1999	2000	2001	Memo: Index 2000, 1994=100
Czech Republic									
Share in exports	16	14	14	13	11	8	7	7	44
Share in imports	14	12	10	8	7	6	5	5	36
Slovak Republic									
Share in exports	37	35	31	31	21	18	17	17	47
Share in imports	30	27	25	22	19	17	15	15	49

Source: Direction of Trade Statistics Yearbook, IMF, Washington D.C., various issues, and official government website: http://www.statistics.sk/webdata/english/tab/fot/iae01.htm

TABLE 2.20: FACTOR INTENSITY OF SLOVAK TRADE WITH THE CZECH REPUBLIC, 1995–200

Factor Intensity	1995	1996	1997	1998	1999	2000	
	Exports to Czech Rep. (US$ million)						Annual Growth in 2000 (%)
Natural Resources	580	480	628	594	604	394	−34.8
Unskilled Labor	367	326	268	224	180	200	10.9
Capital Intensive	759	662	636	543	435	452	4.0
Skilled Labor	1,076	695	921	817	599	682	13.9
	Composition of Exports to Czech Rep.						
	(percent)						Index in 2000 (1995=100)
Natural Resources	20.3	18.7	25.6	27.3	33.2	22.8	112.5
Unskilled Labor	12.8	12.7	10.9	10.3	9.9	11.6	90.3
Capital Intensive	26.5	25.9	25.9	24.9	23.9	26.2	98.6
Skilled Labor	37.6	27.1	37.5	37.5	32.9	39.5	105.0
	Export Specialization Index						Index in 2000 (1998=100)
Natural Resources	0.8	0.8	1.1	1.3	1.7	1.0	76.3
Unskilled Labor	1.1	1.1	0.9	0.9	0.8	1.0	117.2
Capital Intensive	0.7	0.6	0.7	0.6	0.6	0.6	106.0
Skilled Labor	1.6	1.1	1.5	1.4	1.3	1.6	109.7
	Composition of Imports from Czech Rep.						
	(percent)						Annual Growth in 2000 (%)
Natural Resources	25.3	22.9	24.3	25.1	27.5	26.7	−2.6
Unskilled Labor	11.9	11.3	11.7	12.5	11.6	12.1	4.5
Capital Intensive	27.5	26.0	25.5	22.9	23.7	24.6	4.2
Skilled Labor	34.6	32.2	38.5	39.5	37.1	36.6	−0.9

Note: The Export Specialization Index is calculated as a ratio of shares of Slovak exports to the EU to the shares of the EU external imports.
Source: Computations based on Slovak data as reported to UN COMTRADE database.

nents increased from 36 percent in 1995 to 92 percent in 2000, while the share of Czech suppliers fell from 51 percent to 4 percent over the same period.[35] More generally, the Czech-Slovak trade shows little specialization in terms of factor intensity (see Table 2.20). Skilled labor-intensive products account for a dominant share of their mutual trade. It should be noted, however, that the combined share of unskilled labor-intensive and natural-intensive products in Slovak Czech-destined exports has not declined as it did in the EU trade: it expanded rapidly between 1996 and 1999, before falling back in 2000.

Stimulating Trade

Chapter 1 underlined that the Slovak Republic needed to boost it net exports. Where could such fresh impetus come from? First and foremost, of course, it could come from policies that promote wage competitiveness and prevent real exchange rate appreciation (see Chapter 1). Formal accession to the EU will give trade another boost, particularly as Slovak farmers secure access to European markets (the calculations presented below suggest that they could be quite competi-

---

35. In contrast to parts, trade in final product (i.e., cars and trucks) does not seem to follow the same pattern, with Czech producers of passenger cars recording a significant increase in their share of cars imported into the Slovak Republic.

tive in a CAP framework). A pre-condition for membership, however, is that the Slovak Republic fully align its trade regime with the *acquis communautaire*. This will still require considerable progress and efforts.

What this report suggests is that removing the internal economic borders within the CSU could not only help regain lost trade opportunities but could also serve as a crucial stepping-stone to integration into the EU. The proposed enhanced regulatory cooperation within the CSU and the elimination of internal economic borders could yield rapid and substantial improvement in the overall business environment and would obviate the need to attract FDI through costly tax incentives (see below).

Removing the Internal Border within the CSU

Consistent application of the mutual recognition approach (that is, products meeting Slovak or Czech regulations offer equivalent levels of protection as those provided by domestic regulations) standards would provide an extra boost to the integration of domestic firms into international supply chains spread out over several countries, as common standards reinforce linkages between component manufacturers, assembly operations, and distributors in the final product markets. This should not be problematic, as both countries have special arrangements for mutual recognition of certificates and test results. Both countries will have to implement the EU requirements on standardization. Both have been moving in that direction, but at a different pace.[36]

Strengthening the regime of intellectual property rights is also crucial for investment in creative industries and industries intensive in research and development. Here again, closer CSU coordination would help. The current Slovak system has a long way to go to fall in line with the *acquis communautaire*.[37] In contrast, all areas pertinent to intellectual property rights protection in the Czech Republic have been reformed and the Czech regime is highly compatible with that of the EU. Merging the two regimes would be an expedient way for the Slovak Republic to catch up.

Those benefits (plus a reduction in transaction costs at the border) could be obtained with little administrative difficulty. Both countries have a modern and well-run customs administration, which augurs well for the proper distribution of customs revenue between two countries. Both countries observe the rules of the WTO Customs Valuation Agreement requiring that members levy customs duties on an imported good's transaction value rather than on notional reference prices constructed by government. Both countries maintain accurate and up-to-date computer databases of prices that they use to detect fraudulent invoicing. The remaining difference in tax rates could easily be addressed, it would seem, in negotiations between the two governments.

Scaling Back Tax Incentives to Investment

Such improvements in the business climate could pave the way for scaling back the currently excessive tax incentives provided to investors. After expressing skepticism, if not outright opposition to them, Visegrad countries have gradually slipped to all-out tax competition in this field. In the Slovak case, the pendulum has swung all the way from discriminating in favor of domestic

---

36. The transposition level in the Czech Republic–as of November 2000—amounted to about 90 percent of the total European standards while the corresponding level of transposition in the Slovak Republic in 2001 was about 60 percent. The EU's CE mark and CE conformity are not yet accepted for most products, whereas they are accepted in the Czech Republic. While the number of purely national standards has been on the decline in the Czech Republic, this has not been the case in the Slovak Republic.

37. With the split of the former Czech and Slovak Federal Republic, most of the staff, equipment, and know-how stayed in the Czech Republic. The Slovak intellectual property rights protection was established from scratch.

BOX 2.3: TAX INCENTIVES FOR INVESTMENT

The current incentive package has the following features.

First, the Income Tax Act offers a 100 percent five-year tax credit and an extra 50 percent tax credit for another five years if the investment continues. In other words, for up to ten years, the investor's profits will not be taxed at the current rate of 25 percent. In order to qualify for the 100 percent tax credit, the following conditions must be met:

- A minimum of 60 percent of the investment must be in the form of registered capital *coming from abroad*.
- The minimum qualifying investment, varying depending on sector and location, is
    - ⇒ 4.5 million for investment in the production of goods
    - ⇒ 3.0 million for investment in the production of goods in an area with the unemployment rate exceeding 10 percent
    - ⇒ 2.0 million for investment in the provision of selected services
    - ⇒ At least 60 percent of the revenue must come from the production of goods or selected services.
- An additional 50 percent tax credit over the next five years is available for companies investing and extra † 4.5 million (for the production of goods) or † 3 million for selected services, provided the investment is in an area with an unemployment rate exceeding 10 percent.
- Companies already established in the Slovak Republic qualify for tax exemptions if they have yet to realize a profit.

For companies registered after January 1, 2002, the tax credit cannot exceed 50 percent of the cumulative value of investment in tangible fixed assets or 25 percent in intangible fixed assets. But this may not be effective in capping tax credits, as the absence of tax profits in one year can be rolled forward until the end of a five-year period and the wording of the law appears ". . . to allow tax credits to be gained several times on the same capital expenditure."

Second, the law allows for tax credits for newly created jobs and offers compensation for the retraining of newly hired employees. A subsidy equivalent to the average annual wage (SKK 140,000–150,000) is granted for each job created by a greenfield investment in high unemployment areas.

Third, foreign firms are exempted from paying duties on imports of capital equipment.

---

investors to offering ever-growing preferences to foreign investors. The process started in 1998 when the government offered a tax credit allowing exemptions from corporate income tax for particular activities. Subsequently, the incentive package was amended several times, with the last changes being introduced in December 2001 (see Box 2.3).[38] The most recent innovation has been the almost indiscriminate promotion of industrial parks (the state covers 70 percent of the development of industrial parks by the municipalities). In the Czech Republic,[39] Poland, and Hungary, the view that incentives are crucial to attracting investment flows has similarly prevailed.

---

38. See "Act of December 4, 2001 on Investment Incentives and on Changes and Amendments to Certain Laws," *Collection of Laws No. 565/2001*, Bratislava.

39. A recent convert, the Czech Republic introduced an aggressive investment incentive package in 1999, subsequently amended in 2000. The package offers a waiver on corporate income tax during the first five years and a tax bonus equal to the amount waived to be offset against taxation in subsequent years, a zero customs duty on imported machinery, deferral of VAT payments for 90 days, and low cost land. This package is available only to investors willing to commit at least US$10 million or US$5 million in high unemployment areas. Two new programs recently introduced (June 2002) extended the existing framework of investment incentives for the manufacturing industry to strategic services and technology centers. Last but not least, grants and loans at interest rates below market rates are available to foreign and domestic investors.

The resulting tax competition is destructive. Most research indicates that the impact of tax incentives on investment decisions is marginal relative to other host-country determinants, and is negative for the rest of the economy. As the tax base is narrow, tax rates tend to be higher than they would otherwise need to be. In this sense, the package discriminates against small firms—they cannot qualify for tax exemptions and their profits are taxed at 25 percent rather than the zero rate that recipients of tax incentives enjoy. Moreover, the provision in the Slovak law compelling the state budget to cover 70 percent of the development cost of the creation of an industrial park incurred by the municipalities, even without the prior commitment of an investor to locate there, is an invitation to waste.

The prospect of EU accession offers a golden opportunity to break the vicious circle and initiate a climbdown. The harmonization of tax incentives has emerged as a major item in the negotiations of the accession treaties. The Slovak authorities would be well inspired to *support any initiative to harmonize tax incentives at the lowest possible level.* Furthermore, without denying the advantages that industrial zones can provide, it would be in the country's own interest to condition any incentive for their creation upon the fulfillment of *two market tests:* (i) the demonstrated commitment of an interested investor; and (ii) the presence of a majority private sector stake in the industrial zone itself.

To sum up, the discussion above lends support to three policy recommendations:

(i) To enhance the competitiveness of low-skill labor through the macroeconomic and labor market measures discussed in Chapter 1
(ii) To remove internal economic borders in the Czech and Slovak Customs Union even prior to accession to the EU
(iii) To scale back the existing regime of tax incentives to foreign investors and to overhaul it.

Agriculture

The restructuring of the agriculture sector has lagged behind that of the rest of the economy. However, the country would stand to benefit most from the adoption of the EU Common Agricultural Policy (CAP) if it enters it with a restructured farming sector. Otherwise, there is a danger that the large subsidies associated with EU agricultural policies will serve to mask enduring inefficiencies in the sector rather than to modernize it, leaving it as a constant drag on overall economic performance. The government would thus be well advised to focus its immediate attention on speeding up farm restructuring ahead of the adoption of EU agricultural policies upon accession. As discussed below, this would involve:

(a) Completing the post-socialist land reform by expeditiously privatizing the remaining 25 percent of "unclaimed" land still under government control
(b) Tightening the budget constraint for farms among other ways by employing a more effective collection of tax and utility arrears, and by speeding up bankruptcy proceedings against delinquent debtors
(c) Removing the current policy emphasis on self-sufficiency and the policy bias in favor of large-scale farms (expressed in a range of price support measures and direct production incentives)
(d) Scaling back sectoral support to CAP-compatible instruments only, without, however, applying them at EU-levels before membership
(e) Expediting the adoption of EU compliance in food safety standards by the Slovak Republic's food processing industry, which is currently lagging dangerously behind.

Agriculture over the Transition

Overall, agriculture's performance has been much worse than that of the rest of the economy over the transition. While GDP rebounded after the initial downturn to reach 110 percent of the 1990

FIGURE 2.3: GDP AND AGRICULTURAL VALUE ADDED

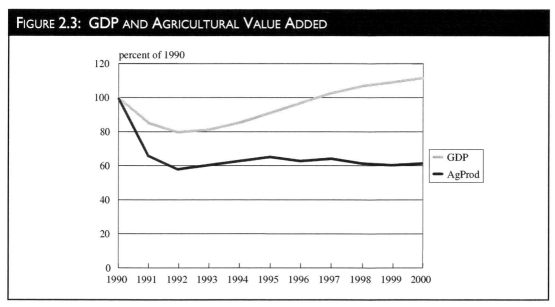

Source: Statistical Office of the Slovak Republic.

level by 2001, agricultural value added did not: it hovered at about 60 percent of the 1990 level for the past decade (Figure 2.3).

This counter-performance reflects to some extent the impact of adverse terms of trade developments, common to most transition economies (Figure 2.4). After a sharp swing at the beginning of the decade, however, agricultural terms of trade, rather than steadying, continued to erode through 2001. One of the beneficiaries was the food industry: its own terms of trade improved markedly (see Figure 2.4). The sources of this phenomenon are not fully understood, but they might be related to the different levels of trade protection that the agricultural and

FIGURE 2.4: TERMS OF TRADE OF THE AGRICULTURE AND FOOD SECTORS

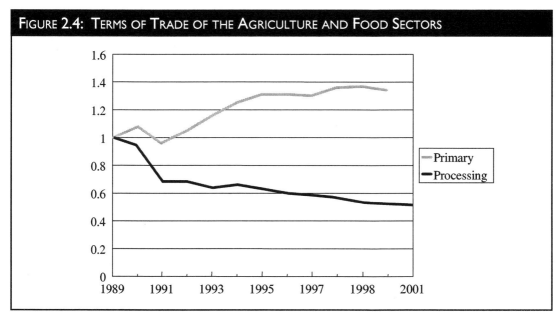

Source: World Bank calculations.

food sectors have obtained. MFN tariffs for agricultural products average around 13 percent (compared to about 4 percent for non-agricultural products), but range beyond 100 percent for foodstuffs.[40]

In response to the resulting profit squeeze, farms resorted to cutting back on labor and input usage, and to run down their equipment and livestock. As a consequence, recorded agricultural employment contracted sharply. With labor productivity at an annual rate of 4.7 percent between 1993 and 2000, the sector began to purge some of its traditionally under-employed labor force.[41] Similarly sharp declines in the livestock herd (from 2 million standard head in 1990 to 1 million in 1999) led to a significant recovery in livestock productivity: livestock output per standard animal increased in 1999–2000 to roughly 120 percent of the 1990 level. But as fertilizer use dropped by 75 percent and the availability of tractors by one-third, the productivity of land (as measured by the value of crop output per hectare of arable land) declined sharply. It stabilized at only two-thirds of the 1990 level, with crop yields and livestock production parameters at between 40–70 percent of EU levels.

Impact of Agricultural Policies

Misguided sectoral policies have made things worse. As output collapsed in the early 1990s, the emphasis of agricultural policies gradually shifted from privatization and market reforms to food self-sufficiency. This objective was to be championed by the large corporate farms that emerged from the former collective farms,[42] and to be backed by a complete battery of policy interventions targeted to them.[43]

The level of support provided to corporate farms may have declined over the years (see Figure 2.5), but the underlying policy direction has largely remained unchanged to this day. Witness the recent "Concept of Agricultural and Food Policy of the Slovak Republic Until 2005," which continues to interpret food security primarily as self-sufficiency in food production. Even at the current reduced level, the Slovak Republic spends twice as much (as a percentage of GDP) on agricultural support as the average CEEC (2.4 percent of GDP compared to 1.2 percent in 2000, respectively).

The hopes that largely unrestructured corporate farms would lead agricultural modernization have been frustrated. Indeed, individual farms—commercial and subsistence operations combined—currently achieve a level of productivity four times higher than corporate farms do, producing 30 percent of the agricultural output on 7 percent of the agricultural land, thus (Figure 2.6 illustrates this productivity gap between individual and corporate farms).

The lower productivity of corporate farms in turn translates into poor profitability. While the commercial individual farms show a small aggregate profit as a subsector, corporate farms reported aggregate losses until 2000. This is because nearly half of the corporate farms reported losses, com-

---

40. It should be noted that, high as they are, most Slovak tariffs on agricultural products are considerably lower than the EU ad valorem equivalents. Indeed, the Slovak Republic and the Czech Republic rank among the only OECD countries with ad valorem tariffs not exceeding 150 percent.

41. Nevertheless, increases in agricultural labor productivity lag behind the increases in the overall productivity of labor in the economy, where GDP growth combined with decreasing labor produces fairly high rates of change in labor productivity (6.4 percent per year for 1993–2000).

42. The corporate farms are substantially smaller than in the socialist era–averaging about 1,500 hectares per farm compared to over 2,500 hectares before 1990. Yet they are much larger than the average commercial farm in market economies (100–200 hectares).

43. Including price support measures with "guaranteed" prices and export subsidies for the main commodities; financial support for investments in the agro-food sector, in the form of direct subsidies, subsidized credits, and credit guarantees; direct payments or compensation to farmers; environmental measures; support for more general agricultural services such as research, animal and crop breeding, information dissemination, training, and extension services. A key feature of this system is a bias against small farmers, since most of the farmer-related payments have conditions regarding the minimum size of operations (e.g., output values corresponding to five cows or five hectares of land).

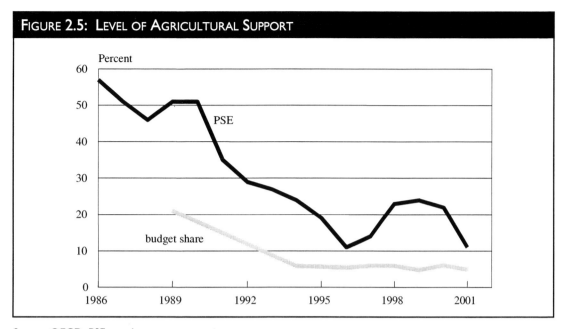

FIGURE 2.5: LEVEL OF AGRICULTURAL SUPPORT

Source: OECD; PSE: producer support estimate.

pared with only about 30 percent among the commercial individual farms. In the aggregate, corporate farms barely break even after all of the production and operating costs, and are thus unable to cover their interest charges. They have traditionally stayed afloat by running up arrears to banks, state-owned utilities (for their energy inputs), the Tax and Social Security Administrations, and state-owned input suppliers.

Another lifeline has been the availability of state land on attractive terms under leasing arrangements with the State Land Fund. The Fund retains huge landholdings pending the completion of

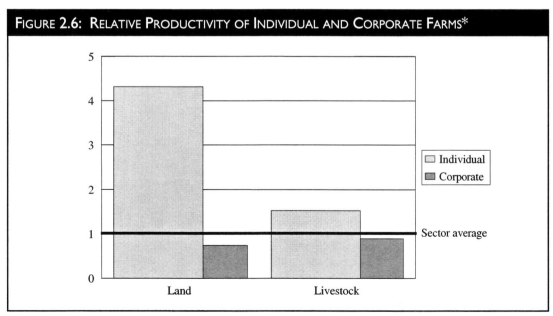

FIGURE 2.6: RELATIVE PRODUCTIVITY OF INDIVIDUAL AND CORPORATE FARMS*

Source: World Bank calculations.

the ongoing restitution process. That process has been slow. If about 8 percent of agricultural land has been restituted to previous owners, three times as much—600,000 hectares—remains in the State Land Fund. The deadline for obtaining restitution, after being postponed several times, has now been set for 2005. In the meantime, a quarter of the land used by corporate farms is leased from that source.

Nevertheless, there are indications that corporate farms are beginning to face harder budget constraints. First, banks are increasingly reluctant to lend. As a result, the share of bank (and government) loans in the debt of corporate farms dropped from 27 percent to 17 percent between 1995 and 2000. Unless profitability improves, this trend is likely to accelerate now that the main agricultural bank (the former Polnobank) has been privatized (to the UniCredito Italiano Group). Furthermore, and for the first time in recent history, the agricultural sector enterprises, taken a as whole, reported a small aggregate profit in 2001, reflecting a sharp drop in the number of loss-making agricultural enterprises. Their numbers dropped from about 725 in 1999 to about 400, leading to an overall consolidation in the sector (the total number of agricultural enterprises fell from 1,215 to 940 over the same period).

The adoption of the CAP upon EU accession is expected to give sectoral profitability a further boost. The exact increase would depend on the amount of direct payments granted to Slovak farmers. Even without direct payments, however, farmers' income would rise by an estimated 18 percent as prices adjust to EU levels. The flip side of these price increases would be to depress average household income (by an estimated 1.3 percent in real terms), the impact being worse at the lower income levels (an estimated minus 1.9 percent).

Although there are pressures for immediate increases in support and protection to EU levels before accession, such moves should be resisted in order to maintain the current pressure on farms to restructure complete reforms and to remain within budgetary constraints and WTO commitments. While policy instruments should be aligned with CAP requirements, the levels of support offered should be adjusted to EU levels only after the accession and with EU funding. In the meantime, policies should focus on the following:

(i) *Scaling Back and Redirecting Support Policies towards the CAP.* First, government support program needs to be pruned of all non-CAP compliant programs (including most credit subsidies, supports for modernization and restructuring to agro-processors, and tax refunds on diesel fuel used for farming purposes). Second, other support programs need to be refitted to CAP requirements, including by adjusting *market support system*s to incorporate the potential use of quotas and to reform the current intervention scheme from an ex ante system (based on short-term forecasts on production and consumption) to an ex post system (based on the observed evolution of EU market prices); and by shifting the intervention point from the farmgate to the wholesale level for most products. *Direct payments and other current structural support measures* should also be adapted to the EU format. Third, much remains to be done to prepare farms and food industries to compete in EU-wide markets. For this purpose, it is indispensable that food legislation and the ability of enforcement agencies be made fully compatible with the EU directives on food hygiene, inspection and certification, and the legal responsibilities of producers. Not only is this crucial for entering the single market (to avoid non-tariff barriers within the single market), these measures are also needed to control the products imported into the EU from third countries through Slovak borders. Substantial work and educational efforts are still required to implement the relevant *acquis* (including, as concerns animal registers, meat testing and inspection, and the certification of food processing industries).

(ii) *Completing Land Privatization.* A strict deadline should be set for the identification and resolution of "unclaimed" land ownership. Beyond that deadline, much of the State Land Fund should be expeditiously privatized through auctions. If at all possible, the 2005 deadline for filing restitution claims should be brought forward (and late claimants given financial compensation instead).[44]

(iii) *Further Tightening of Budget Constraints.* Following the privatization of banks and major energy utilities, and with reduced subsidies, arrears on tax and social security contributions remain the main loophole to close.

Energy

Public utilities reform, particularly in the energy sector, is a powerful contributor to overall recovery, not only in terms of improved sectoral performance but also in its offer of more competitive services to the rest of the economy. In many respects, the Slovak Republic has been catching up with the leaders in the field among EU candidate countries as it unbundled and privatized key assets to strategic investors, began to adjust tariffs toward cost-recovery levels (although that process came to a halt since January 2001), and established independent regulation. Completing this process will result in increased efficiency, improved financial viability, and better service to all energy consumers. The key next steps will involve the privatization of power generators, the opening of electricity and gas markets to competition, and the elimination of administrative pricing and the corresponding final elimination of cross-subsidies ahead of EU accession. Because of the delays that have recently occurred in the process of price adjustment, the resulting price adjustments will be more abruptly painful for households, particularly at the lower end of the income scale, than they might have been. This might call for specific mitigation measures, as suggested below.

Restructuring and Privatization

The restructuring of the energy sector is well advanced. The gas sector utility—Slovensky Plynarensky (SPP)—has been sold together with its pipeline business (at a price equivalent to 13 percent of GDP) to a consortium comprising Gasprom, RuhrGas, and Gaz de France. Although the company was sold as a going concern, it remains desirable for it to spin off its distribution assets. The unbundling of the power sector was completed in 2001 with the split of Slovenske Elektrarne (SE, the former integrated power utility) into a transmission and a generation company (distribution had already been separated in 1993). The three regional electricity distribution companies are being privatized to strategic investors in 2002, and the government has announced that it plans to privatize generation next. Only transmission would remain fully state-owned.

In privatizing SE, the best option from the point of view of speed, flexibility, and privatization revenue is to sell nuclear and non-nuclear generation facilities separately, rather than as a single corporate entity. One reason for this is that there is no precedent for the sale of nuclear plants in this region (or indeed outside of the United Kingdom and the United States), and therefore it is difficult to predict how long selling the Slovak facilities as part of a combined package might take, or whether it is even feasible.[45] It would be better not to let that question delay the whole privatization process.

---

44. Most countries in the world maintain a certain proportion of agricultural land in state ownership, but the administrative and bureaucratic traditions surrounding state property in market economies are entirely different from those in former socialist countries. Given the former socialist tradition, with its abusive bureaucratic tendencies and the goals of reducing government intervention, it is recommended that the Slovak Republic privatize as much of the State Land Fund as possible in the near future.

45. One question concerns the due diligence process of prospective investors related to the nuclear plants—financial, looking especially at the debt situation for Mochovce, and environmental, looking at both operational safety considerations and the extremely important decommissioning issues. Bohunice 1 and 2 may in fact not attract investors, since decommissioning will take place in 2006–2008. Bohunice 3 and 4 and Mochovce 1 and 2 are less problematic in this regard, but would still represent a significant challenge.

Competition and Regulation

There is a more fundamental reason to prefer a sale of SE on a plant-by-plant basis: namely, to enhance competition at the generation level, thereby providing incentives to reduce generation costs. This would be in line with developments on the demand side. Under the current schedule, electricity markets should gradually be opened to eligible consumers. This will be done by reducing the eligibility threshold from an annual consumption of 100 GWh in 2002 to 9 GWh in 2005, and by opening up the Slovak market to foreign suppliers in 2003. Foreign access will initially be subject to a cap of 5 percent of domestic consumption. As the Slovak Republic reaches agreements on a reciprocal basis, as it should seek to do, the number of actors on the electricity market will gradually expand.

The gas market has similarly begun to open up (up to 20 percent of the market, as of January 1, 2002). Access should gradually expand, first to all power and heat plants and for consumers of more than 20 million m3/year, and later to all non-household consumers. Until 2008 (i.e., when the import contract with Gazprom expires), the government should impose an obligation on SPP to offer gas to eligible customers at the import points under prices and conditions equivalent to the import contracts.

A side benefit of competition in energy markets is to alleviate the task of the newly created Regulatory Office for Networks Industries (RONI). Experience has pointed to the inherent difficulty for regulators to establish their independence and authority. Thus, it would be better to pursue a limited agenda than to spread ambitions too widely. For example, the existence of competition in the wholesale level of markets should limit the need for RONI to regulate prices, essentially to the operation of natural monopoly networks serving residential and small commercial consumers. The separation of generation, transmission, and distribution similarly reduces the danger that network operators would use their monopoly powers in one sector to bolster their competitive position in another.

For such a market model to work, there needs to be third-party access to the networks. The principle of such access was introduced in a decree of the Ministry of Economy of December 2001. This decree is now being amended to fall in line with the EU directives on the gradual opening of gas and electricity markets. RONI is also responsible for setting charges for third party access. The price regulation regime has already been defined in electricity distribution and gas transportation. The next step will involve electricity transmission charges, which will need to be set later in 2002 based on regulated companies' filings.

Pricing

It will also be the role of RONI to oversee the adjustments of residential tariffs to EU-compliant, full cost-recovery levels. Despite an initial round of tariff adjustments (electricity prices tripled and gas prices doubled between 1998 and 2000), power and especially gas tariffs are still far from complying with EU directives. Prices for households, in particular, are considerably below those observed in the rest of OECD Europe. Among accession countries in Central Europe, the Slovak Republic has one of the lowest tariffs for both electricity and gas. Although cross-subsidization has been reduced, the ratio of residential to industrial electricity tariffs remains at about two third of the OECD Europe level and as low as one-quarter of the levels observed in OECD Europe for gas. Following the 2002 adjustment of industrial gas tariffs, the ratio of residential to industrial tariffs slipped back below one (compared to 2.7 in the OECD) (see Tables 2.21 and 2.22). A side effect of such low prices has been the overstimulation of energy consumption, putting undue pressure on the balance of payments.[46]

In the case of gas, low prices are linked to the non-transparent way in which SPP has been able to manage its lucrative transit business (SPP operates a key gas pipeline between Russia and

---

46. In the face of falling real prices for electricity, residential power consumption increased by 53 percent between 1993 and 1999.

TABLE 2.21: END-USER PRICES FOR ELECTRICITY AND NATURAL GAS

Electricity (US cent/kWh)	1993	2000	2001
Industry			
Slovak Republic	5.00	4.2	4.4
Czech Republic	5.25	4.3	4.6
Hungary	5.29	4.9	4.8
Poland	3.30	3.7	4.4
OECD Europe	7.21	6.5	n.a
Households			
Slovak Republic	3.00	5.0	6.3
Czech Republic	2.92	5.4	6.1
Hungary	4.28	6.5	6.4
Poland	4.63	6.5	7.4
OECD Europe	11.13	13.0	n.a
Natural Gas (US$/10^{7}Kcal)	**1993**	**2000**	**2001**
Industry			
Slovak Republic	120.9	101.8	102.5
Czech Republic	131.4	147.6	154.4
Hungary	127.9	1524.9	148.4
Poland	115.9	133.0	n.a
OECD Europe	149.5	151.3	n.a
Households			
Slovak Republic	75.5	108.6	112.6
Czech Republic	95.4	214.1	222.6
Hungary	117.0	166.3	172.2
Poland	153.9	247.5	254.7
OECD Europe	398.6	404.7	n.a

Sources: IEA and MoE.

TABLE 2.22: RATIO OF HOUSEHOLD PRICES TO INDUSTRIAL PRICES FOR ENERGY

	1993	2000	2001
Electricity			
Slovak Republic	0.60	1.19	1.43
Czech Republic	0.56	1.26	1.33
Hungary	0.81	1.33	1.33
Poland	1.40	1.76	1.68
OECD Europe	1.80	2.00	n.a
Natural Gas			
Slovak Republic	0.62	1.07	1.10
Czech Republic	0.73	1.45	1.44
Hungary	0.91	1.33	1.16
Poland	1.33	1.86	n.a
OECD Europe	2.67	3.98	n.a

Source: Staff calculations based on IEA and MoE figures.

Western Europe). Parts of the related location rents go to subsidize industrial users, parts go to subsidize residential users, and much of the rest finances the company's own internal inefficiency. SE, on the other hand, does not have that luxury. As the scope for cross-subsidization has diminished, SE's financial and commercial viability has deteriorated to the point at which it is unable to refinance its debt without state guarantees.

Bringing tariffs in line with EU directives may now require residential tariff increases in the range of 40 percent in the case of electricity and more than 100 percent in the case of gas. The pattern adopted for electricity is to raise residential tariffs at four times the rate of inflation until the target rate is reached. No such schedule exists as yet for gas (in part because RONI will only assume responsibility in this field from the Ministry of Finance as of January 1, 2003). With the expected date of EU accession fast approaching, and with the urgent need for fiscal adjustment, there is now little scope for gradualism in phasing in the new gas tariffs. Under the circumstances, the government would be well advised to advance the process as much as possible, even into 2002. It should also consider introducing in parallel a special royalty to tax away the windfall rent that would otherwise accrue to the privatized SPP.

Mitigation Measures
The social impact of such abrupt energy tariffs may be high. Slovak households currently devote 11 percent of their net incomes to energy; that percentage could rise to 18 percent after the tariff adjustments. Much of the gas tariff increase would be felt indirectly though its impact on heating costs. The situation would be worse for low-income users who could see their energy bill rise from 18 percent to 32 percent of their net income; this percentage could potentially go all the way up to 50–60 percent for pensioners, or for single parents.

As explained in Chapter 3, the existing housing allowance is ill-designed to help low-income family cope with such a burden. A better way to proceed might be to rely on the following instruments:[47]

(i) A targeted lifeline tariff for the first block of basic electricity consumption (estimated at 100 kWh for cooking, lighting, and refrigeration) at half the standard rate. The cost of this program (estimated at 0.1 percent of GDP, with an eligibility threshold at 1.5 times the minimum subsistence level) could be covered by a special fee on all residential users.

(ii) A targeted subsidy for basic heat (and hot water) consumption. Assuming income eligibility at the same level as for the above lifeline electricity tariff and a subsidized block equivalent to half the average consumption level (of 116 GJ per year per household), this program would impose a cost of about 0.15 percent of GDP on the budget (other funding options being impractical). This compares to the almost 1 percentage point of GDP that the tariff increase would raise from the consumer (two-thirds of which the government should recapture in the form of profit tax, royalties, and dividends from SPP).

These temporary subsidies could be phased out over time, as the increased cost of energy is incorporated in a revised MLS, based on fresh household survey data (see Chapter 3).

Conclusions
The turnaround that the enterprise sector has undergone in recent years has been, in many respects, remarkable. As a result, those firms that survived the adjustment process are now on a sounder financial footing, and are more likely to be integrated into and to compete in the EU-wide market. Formal accession to the EU is likely to give this process a further boost. To prepare for

---

47. See Vol, Sarah, and Andrej Juris, *"Alleviation of Social Impacts of Energy Tariff Rationalization in Slovakia,"* National Economic Research Associates, Washington, June 2002.

that moment of reckoning, the discussion above has pointed out the need to keep up reform efforts along a broad front, highlighting the following priorities:

(i) Removing bottlenecks to debt resolution procedures—including launching a long over-due reform of the judiciary (see Chapter 5), with a view toward facilitating a second round transfer of asset ownership away from those who acquired assets during the Meciar years (including through a resolution of the SKA portfolio) and removing a critical obsta-cle to bank lending to SMEs.

(ii) Strengthening the regulatory framework for bank operations, among other ways by man-dating the use of IAS first by banks, and then by other corporations, and by not allowing the creation of an integrated financial sector regulator to distract from the efforts to enhance the supervisory capacity of the exiting regulatory bodies (NBS and FMA).

(iii) Stoking up farm restructuring ahead of joining the EU's CAP, among other ways by expediting the privatization of "unclaimed land" and scaling back and redirecting support policies toward the CAP format.

(iv) Bringing down the internal border within the Czech-Slovak Customs Union (CSU) ahead of EU accession with a view towards removing barriers to mutual trade with a country, but also as a means of expediting the alignment of the trade regime with EU requirements.

(v) Encouraging any initiative taken in the context of the competition chapter of the EU accession negotiations to harmonize the tax incentives offered by Visegrad countries at the lowest possible level.

(vi) Bringing forward the energy tariff adjustments required to set tariffs in line with EU directives (i.e., in the range of 40 percent for electricity and more than 100 percent in the case of gas), with targeted lifeline blocks for low-income consumers.

(vii) Privatizing power generation (with nuclear and non-nuclear generation facilities being sold separately).

CHAPTER 3

REGIONAL DIMENSIONS

With the approach of EU accession, the issue of regional development—a major EU policy concern—is fast becoming a top policy issue in the Slovak Republic. The magnitude of the funding potentially involved is considerable (up to 4 percent of GDP in EU transfers plus counterpart funds) and could conceivably help fuel the country's convergence toward EU standards. In the absence of a carefully thought out strategy, however, this potential could easily be squandered.

This chapter suggests that while substantial regional disparities exist in terms of output per capita, their significance for policy and planning purposes should not be misjudged. First, there is little indication that these disparities are particularly large by European standards. Second, these disparities are not widening. Third, they are hardly reflected in disparities in household income. This is due in part to the way labor market structures operate (centralized collective bargaining and single wage tariff at the national level) and also to the impact of uniform social transfers. The combination of those two factors unfortunately contributes to the persistence of wide regional disparities in terms of unemployment. The first section below takes stock of these various dimensions of regional disparities and the related policy implications.

The experience of other low-income countries in joining the EU seems to indicate that rapid income convergence may be associated with an initial widening of regional differences in GDP per capita, as growth first takes hold within localized "growth poles." The second section discusses how that experience applies to the Slovak Republic.

Based on this, the final section draws the contours of what a regional convergence strategy might involve for the Slovak Republic. One aspect might be to focus investments on a limited number of growth poles—starting with Bratislava—where external effects on productivity are likely to be highest, and then gradually spreading externalities toward the East. In view of fiscal consolidation objectives, such public intervention policies would need to be pursued by redirecting, rather than expanding, government programs toward those key strategic objectives (regions, sectors). To be successful, such a strategy would require both labor and social welfare reform in order to give people a greater incentive to move to where the jobs are being created and to induce firms to establish themselves outside of the Bratislava growth pole.

Level and Sources of Regional Disparities

As most observers of the Slovak economy have stressed, a significant cleavage exists between the modern and well-performing Bratislava region and the much less prosperous rest of the country. With about 11 percent of the Slovak population, Bratislava produces more than 22 percent of the Slovak GDP. If we use a regional decomposition into eight NUTS 3 regions (following the nomenclature used by the Eurostat), we find that the GDP per capita in the Bratislava region reaches twice the level of the national average and more than three times that of the poorest Slovak region, Prešov (see Table 3.1).

These disparities arise from differences in both productivity levels and employment rates (see Table 3.2). Bratislava comes out ahead of the rest of the country on both counts.

TABLE 3.1: REGIONAL GDP PER CAPITA AT PPS, 1996–99
(percent)

	% of EU average				% of Slovak average			
	1996	1997	1998	1999	1996	1997	1998	1999
Bratislava	92	100	99	100	203	203	202	197
Trnava	51	51	50	55	106	106	103	109
Trenčín	44	44	44	46	92	93	91	92
Nitra	37	39	40	42	82	82	83	83
Žilina	38	40	41	42	84	84	84	83
Banská Bystrica	42	43	44	45	91	91	90	90
Prešov	30	31	32	32	66	66	66	65
Košice	44	44	47	50	93	93	97	99
Slovak Republic	46	48	49	50	100	100	100	100

Sources: Statistical Office of the Slovak Republic, Eurostat, and staff calculations

TABLE 3.2: REGIONAL DIFFERENCES IN PRODUCTIVITY AND EMPLOYMENT

	Productivity[a] (% of average)	Employment Rate[b]
Bratislava	158.7	60.2
Trnava	105.5	50.1
Trenčín	88.9	50.2
Nitra	89.7	44.9
Žilina	82.3	48.9
Banská Bystrica	95.3	45.8
Prešov	67.8	46.5
Košice	109.6	43.8
Total	100.0	48.5

[a]Regional value added per person employed, 1999.
[b]As of 2001.
Source: World Bank calculations based on Statistical Office of the Slovak Republic.

Sources of Regional Differences in Productivity

Many factors combine to make Bratislava more productive than the rest of the country: the nature of its productive structure, the density of its small and medium-scale enterprises (SMEs), higher investment rates, a greater attractiveness for foreign direct investment, linked in part to the region's proximity to EU markets and accessibility to them, and its comparative concentration of university graduates.

Productive Structure.   The structural change from an industrial economy focused around large state-owned enterprises, many of them in heavy industry, to an economy predominantly based on services and with a predominance of small and medium enterprises, has not been equally rapid and successful in all of the regions. The two richest regions, Bratislava and Košice, are also those that have made the greatest progress toward a service-based economy and that currently have the highest share of services in output among all Slovak regions (see Figure 3.1). Services account for almost three-quarters of value added and employment in Bratislava. At the other extreme are large parts of southern and eastern Slovakia that have suffered from substantial declines in agricultural production (see Chapter 2) as well as those industrial towns that were hit by the collapse of military production.

Role of SMEs.   Small and medium-size enterprises (SMEs) have typically driven the transformation process. On this count, again, Bratislava's performance is much better than that of all other regions. Although the Bratislava region accounts for 11 percent of the Slovak population, more than 32 percent of all Slovak small enterprises with less then 50 employees are based there (see Table 3.3).

Investment Rates.   The larger part of the country's capital stock is concentrated in the Bratislava region. Its investment to GDP ratio has consistently reached almost twice the national average (see Table 3.4). In per capita terms, investment in Bratislava has been 6.4 times higher than the average for all other regions and 14 times higher than for the region of Prešov.

Foreign Direct Investment.   One factor behind such high investment rates is that Bratislava has attracted the bulk of the incoming FDI (see Table 3.5). By the end of 2001, 51.4 percent of

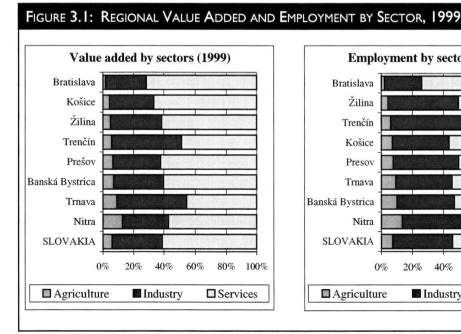
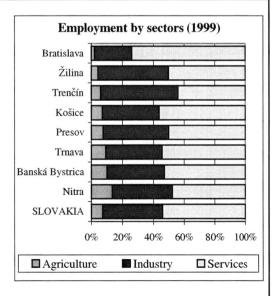

FIGURE 3.1: REGIONAL VALUE ADDED AND EMPLOYMENT BY SECTOR, 1999

Source: Statistical Office of the Slovak Republic.

TABLE 3.3: REGIONAL DISTRIBUTION OF SMALL AND MEDIUM ENTERPRISES, 2001
(percent)

	Less than 50 employees	50–250 employees	Population (%)
Bratislava	32	20	11
Trnava	8	11	10
Trenčín	10	12	11
Nitra	8	13	13
Žilina	10	12	13
Banská Bystrica	11	11	12
Prešov	10	12	15
Košice	13	10	14
SLOVAKIA	100	100	100

Source: Statistical Office of the Slovak Republic.

TABLE 3.4: GROSS FIXED CAPITAL FORMATION BY REGION, 1996–99
(percent of GDP)

	1996	1997	1998	1999	Average
Bratislava	68.7	67.4	68.2	61.3	66.4
Trnava	18.3	19.8	21.7	15.2	18.7
Trenčín	20.8	31.7	31.4	21.5	26.4
Nitra	28.5	31.4	42.8	31.0	33.4
Žilina	24.6	24.3	26.9	20.5	24.1
Banská Bystrica	24.9	26.6	27.3	19.3	24.5
Prešov	17.1	17.9	17.8	13.1	16.5
Košice	29.8	30.9	31.7	26.6	29.7
Total	34.2	35.9	38.0	30.4	34.6

Source: Statistical Office of the Slovak Republic.

TABLE 3.5: FOREIGN DIRECT INVESTMENT BY REGION, 1999–2001

	Corporate						Total (Including Banking Sector)					
	million USD			%			million USD			%		
FDI Stock	1999	2000	2001	1999	2000	2001	1999	2000	2001	1999	2000	2001
Bratislava	1,035	1,749	1,856	53.1	51.9	51.4	1,342	2,069	2,550	59.5	56.0	59.3
Trnava	201	200	197	10.3	5.9	5.5	201	200	197	8.9	5.4	4.6
Trenčín	153	143	144	7.9	4.2	4.0	153	143	144	6.8	3.9	3.3
Nitra	86	94	145	4.4	2.8	4.0	86	94	145	3.8	2.6	3.4
Žilina	78	175	194	4.0	5.2	5.4	78	175	194	3.4	4.7	4.5
Banská Bystrica	111	112	188	5.7	3.3	5.2	111	112	188	4.9	3.0	4.4
Prešov	99	98	110	5.1	2.9	3.1	99	98	110	4.4	2.6	2.6
Košice	187	802	773	9.6	23.8	21.4	187	802	773	8.3	21.7	18.0
SLOVAKIA	1,949	3,373	3,608	100	100	100	2,256	3,692	4,302	100	100	100

Source: National Bank of Slovakia.

TABLE 3.6: SHARE OF UNIVERSITY GRADUATES AMONG THE UNEMPLOYED AND IN THE ECONOMICALLY ACTIVE POPULATION, 2001
(percent)

	Unemployed (%)	Economically Active Population* (%)
Bratislava	5.3	24.1
Trnava	2.1	9.4
Trenčín	2.5	9.6
Nitra	2.9	9.4
Žilina	2.8	9.1
Banská Bystrica	2.9	9.2
Prešov	3.6	10.0
Košice	2.7	8.6
Total	3.0	11.2

*Population 15 years and over.
Source: Statistical Office of the Slovak Republic.

FDI stock in the corporate sector was concentrated in Bratislava. The only region that has come close has been Kosice, following the purchase of VSZ by U.S. Steel Corp.

Geographic Location and Distance from Markets.   As in other economies in Central and Eastern Europe, geography has played an important role in shaping FDI decisions. Empirical studies of investment patterns confirm that foreign investments are motivated by market proximity.[48] Regions situated in the west and along major transportation corridors perform much better than those situated along the eastern borders with Hungary, Poland, and Ukraine. Western European centers situated close to borders with the accession countries exercise a particular influence on the neighboring border regions.[49] Bratislava has a particular advantage in its proximity to Western markets, access to decision-makers, good infrastructure, and existence of network economies. Proximity to Bratislava and Austria may explain to a large extent the high FDI inflow into the Trnava region.

The eastern regions face an opposite situation. They border similarly poor and economically problematic regions in the neighboring countries and are quite remote from their main future markets in the EU and from deep-water ports such as Rotterdam and Hamburg. Potential investors in the region, in agricultural processing and light industry as well as in tourism, are deterred by poor road accessibility.

Concentration of University Graduates.   Another reason why investors choose Bratislava over other locations is its high concentration of university graduates (see Table 3.6). Bratislava has an almost 2.5 times higher share of university graduates in the labor force than the national average. This helps to account for the high productivity and low unemployment rates in Bratislava. Even in regions with very high unemployment, someone with a university degree is approximately three times less likely to be unemployed.

48. Boeri, T., et al. (2000), *The Impact of Eastern Enlargement on Employment and Labour Markets in the EU Member States,* Report for European Commission's Employment and Social Affairs Directorate, European Integration Consortium (DIW, CEPR, FIEF, IAS, IGIER), Berlin/Milan, Germany/Italy; Döhrn, R. (1996), *EU Enlargement and Transformation in Eastern Europe: Consequences for Foreign Investment in Eastern Europe,* Konjunkturpolitik, Vol. 42, No. 2–3, pp. 113–132.
49. Gorzelak, G., and Zarycki, G. (1995), *Regional Development and Policy in Poland after 1990,* EUROREG, University of Warsaw.

Mitigating Factors

Nevertheless, the significance of these regional differences should be not blown out of proportion. There are good reasons to believe that the existing statistics (although fully consistent with the Eurostat methodology) overstate the underlying reality. First, regional GDP per capita statistics record, in Bratislava, the value added generated by the large workforce that commutes from outside the region. Dividing the regional output by the number of residents (irrespective of the number of people employed) inflates the output per capita figures in the region of Bratislava accordingly. Furthermore, statistics on regional GDP per capita at PPS are calculated on the basis of a single set of prices for the whole country. The prices are taken from a survey in Bratislava only, where prices are higher than in the rest of the country, thereby leading to the underestimating of comparative GDP levels in outlying areas.

Second, leaving aside the outliers of Bratislava and Presov, the regional variation in GDP per capita is actually fairly small. All other regions range between 42 and 55 percent of the EU average (see Table 3.1). Third, it is worth noting that regional differences in GDP per capita have been narrowing, not widening in recent years (see Table 3.1).

Fourth, the gap observed between the capital city and the rest of the country is not exceptional at a European level. The gap between the GDP per capita in the region of Prague or inner London and their respective national averages is even greater than that in the Slovak Republic (see Table 3.7). Actually, the magnitude of the gap between the capital city region and the rest of the country depends crucially on the geographical size of the statistical region that includes the capital city. The smaller the size of the capital region, the higher its GDP per capita gap is likely to be, reflecting a growing density of economic activities as one moves toward city centers. In Poland and Hungary, the gap in GDP per capita between the capital region and the rest of the country may look narrower, but this in part because the NUTS-3 regions of Bratislava, Prague, and inner London are very small, while the NUTS-3 regions of Warsaw and Budapest also include a wide circle of surrounding areas.

Impact on Living Standards

Furthermore, reflecting the impact of social safety nets as well as labor market outcomes, there is much less disparity in household income across regions than there is in output per capita (see Table 3.8). Barely 34 percent separates the average disposable incomes of the top and bottom of the range. It would be surprising if regional differences in cost of living were much smaller.

However, the mechanisms at play exacerbate the one truly worrisome form of regional disparity: that in (un)employment rates. Reflecting, on the one hand, the impact of centralized collective bargaining (and of the nation-wide wage tariffs collective bargaining arrangement set) and of a uniform minimum wage, there is far less wage variation across regions than the underlying dif-

TABLE 3.7: RELATIVE LEVEL OF GDP PER CAPITA IN SELECTED CAPITAL REGIONS, 1999
(percent of national average)

Inner London*	238
Prague	212
Bratislava	**198**
Brussels*	152
Mazowieckie (Warsaw)	151
Kozep-Magyarorszag (Budapest)	149
Vienna*	146

*Data for 1998.
Sources: Statistical Office of the Slovak Republic, Eurostat, and staff calculations.

TABLE 3.8: GROSS AND NET MONEY INCOME PER PERSON PER MONTH, 2000
(percent of national average)

	Gross Money Income	Net Money Income
Bratislava	125	122
Trnava	96	96
Trenčín	97	97
Nitra	98	100
Žilina	93	93
Banská Bystrica	99	99
Prešov	90	91
Košice	102	101
Total	100	100

Source: Statistical Office of the Slovak Republic.

ferences in productivity would warrant (see Table 3.9). The case is particularly stark in the industrial sector: while industrial productivity varies by a factor of 3.5 between the most and the least productive regions, the difference in industrial wages between these the two regions is less than 50 percent.

The net result is that higher unit labor costs price out the most depressed regions, irrespective of what transport costs and other aggravating factors (see above) might be. Conversely, it comes as little surprise that the employment rates that we observed at the outset of this discussion (see Table 3.2) are highest in those regions where the wage/productivity ratio is most favorable, or that those same regions also attract most foreign direct investment.

The presence of large social transfers to the unemployed makes the situation tolerable and limits its impact on household disposable income (as seen in Table 3.8). The impact of social transfers goes beyond that, however. As benefits are uniform, they provide a higher purchasing power in depressed regions than in more affluent ones. Thus, it is not surprising that, in spite of large differences in employment rates between Bratislava and the rest of the country, the Slovak Republic

TABLE 3.9: REGIONAL DIFFERENCES IN PRODUCTIVITY AND WAGES
(percent of national average)

	Economy		Industry[c]	
	Productivity[a]	Average Wage[b]	Productivity	Average Wage
Bratislava	159	138	205	132
Trnava	106	98	124	93
Trenčín	89	96	93	94
Nitra	90	89	80	93
Žilina	82	94	71	90
Banská Bystrica	95	91	100	90
Prešov	68	84	61	84
Košice	110	103	104	103
Total	100	100	100	100

[a]Regional value added per person employed, 1999.
[b]As of 2001.
Source: World Bank calculations based on the Statistical Office of the Slovak Republic.

TABLE 3.10: REGIONAL UNEMPLOYMENT RATE, 1997–2001					
	1997	1998	1999	2000	2001
Bratislava	4.1	5.1	7.2	6.4	5.8
Trnava	10.6	12.5	16.3	14.9	15.5
Trenčín	8.3	10.8	13.5	12.7	12.7
Nitra	14.3	17.6	21.5	21.7	23.1
Žilina	10.8	14.1	17.7	16.8	16.4
Banská Bystrica	14.9	19.7	23.1	21.8	23.6
Prešov	17.8	22.1	26.0	22.1	24.0
Košice	17.1	20.8	25.1	24.4	25.6
Total	12.5	15.6	19.1	17.9	18.6

Source: Statistical Office of the Slovak Republic

would have the lowest inter-regional labor mobility in the OECD area.[50] Only 3 persons per 1,000 population moved between regions in the Slovak Republic in 2000, compared to regional mobility rates of 10 to 25 migrants per 1,000 population in most OECD countries.

Nevertheless, this uniform approach to labor relations and social welfare contributes to entrenching regional unemployment and therefore to exacerbating, rather than lessening, regional disparities. While the unemployment rate has consistently remained at a relatively low level in Bratislava and significantly below the national average (see Table 3.10), it increased dramatically in all other regions between 1997 and 1999. The unemployment rate in the region with the worst performing labor market was 4.4 times higher than in Bratislava.

Impact of EU Accession

The experience of existing EU members suggests that the Slovak government may face some stark choices in fueling convergence toward EU levels while dealing with inter-regional equality. Indeed, while all Cohesion countries (that is Greece, Ireland, Portugal, and Spain) have experienced at least some degree of income convergence at the national level, convergence at the subnational level has been meager. In countries that have converged at very rapid rates, national growth has tended to be driven by growth poles (usually around capital cities and major agglomerations), with the relatively lower growth in other parts of the country resulting in widening regional disparities.

This trade-off between economic efficiency (in this case, rapid convergence at the national level driven by a small number of growth poles) and inter-regional equality has been confirmed and quantified in several studies.[51] While all regions in Ireland, for example, converged rapidly toward average EU incomes between 1991 and 1997, the performance of the southern and eastern regions was comparatively stronger; disparities thus widened. Similarly, between 1980 and 1996, Spain's convergence was driven by rapid growth in regions such as Madrid and Catalonia. Almost all regions also converged toward EU levels but at a slower pace; regional differences thus increased.

This observation is in line with the findings of the "New Economic Geography" types of models that analyze the ways in which spatial patterns of agglomeration of economic activities may lead to differences in income levels. These models predict that more advanced economies (including

---

50. This statistics is based on administrative data on people's residence that may underestimate the magnitude of migratory flows.

51. See, for example, De la Fuente, A. (1996), *Inversión pública y redistribución regional: el caso de España en la década de los ochenta*, Papers de Treball, No 50.96, Barcelona.

regional economies) will benefit more from a partial integration, as firms will exploit economies of scale by concentrating there. However, as integration advances beyond a certain threshold, industries will move to regions where they can benefit from labor cost advantages, enabling poorer economies that have retained such advantage to catch up.

The Slovak Republic appears to be at the stage at which relatively low trade costs induce firms to exploit economies of scale by concentrating their production in or close to the Bratislava region, where there are more customers and suppliers, knowledge spillovers, and other location-specific benefits. This results in a process of endogenous concentration in which more and more firms and works are attracted to the region. The benefits that these firms derive from their location in this agglomeration boost productivity and outweigh higher (absolute) wage levels, giving rise to a growth pole syndrome in the region of Bratislava. The models suggest that as the economic integration deepens, trade costs become lower and tend to disappear, higher wage costs in Bratislava should lead industries to move to other regions that have preserved their lower labor cost advantages.

In the initial stage after Slovakia joins the EU, however, the economic importance and concentration of economic activities in the Bratislava region may increase rather than decrease. Situated only 65 km from Vienna and with a new highway connecting the two cities scheduled to be completed by 2005, Bratislava will probably experience rapid economic integration with Vienna. Firms situated in Vienna are likely to take advantage of the demand in a rapidly growing Bratislava by paying increased attention to this market. Moreover, servicing each other's markets from the other city will become significantly easier once Slovakia joins the EU and the Schengen Area as the border controls are removed and laws and regulations become highly harmonized. Thanks to Bratislava's high productivity—which is already comparable to that in the neighboring Niederoesterreich region[52] and its relatively low labor costs, many Austrian firms may also relocate their production there. Domestic Slovak firms located in Bratislava will also be able to benefit from the opportunities provided by the Vienna market. Moreover, after the transition period of labor migrations, labor markets between the two cities are likely to become much more integrated, with a significant number of employees initially commuting from Bratislava to Vienna.

Conversely, as most of the neighboring eastern regions in Poland and Hungary are as depressed as the Slovak areas, EU accession is not likely initially to boost the local demand for Slovak firms situated in the east. Although economic integration with the EU should provide major economic benefits and should stimulate the convergence of the Slovak Republic as a whole, it may also, if not properly addressed, exacerbate economic disparities between the capital and the rest of the country.

Outline of a Regional Development Strategy

The appropriate response is not to suppress the growth potential of the capital region (for example, by diverting resources away from it) but to maximize it while facilitating the diffusion of the convergence process to other regions, first of all through labor markets (to improve the wage competitiveness in poorer regions) and social welfare reforms (also to help poorer regions and to stimulate labor mobility). Improving transport access between Bratislava and the east would help make Bratislava a springboard toward those regions that establish or maintain wage competitiveness.

Investment Priorities

The EU structural funds have the potential to help the country make the transition. As a candidate for EU membership, the country has already benefited from EU grant funding through its access to the pre-accession funds. Upon entering the EU, the amount of available EU funding from the Cohesion Fund and the Structural Funds (the so-called "structural funds") could increase substan-

---

52. Weise, C., et al. (2001), *The Impact of EU Enlargement on Cohesion*, Preparatory study for European Commission's "Second Report on Economic and Social Cohesion," Brussels.

tially. While the current inflows of EU grant assistance amount to less than 1 percent of the Slovak GDP, they could eventually reach up to 4.0 percent of the Slovak GDP.

In planning for the use of the structural funds, two important considerations should be kept in mind. First, *the country should seek to maximize the related supply (as different from demand) effects.* The inflow of structural funds may lift demand and disposable income in the short term, but without supply side effects (arising from the improved stock of human and physical capital, physical infrastructure, and broader market environment), the impact of Structural Funds will be ephemeral. In the short term, the magnitude of demand effects may be higher (close to the amount of actual spending), but it is their impact on lifting the recipient country's potential growth rates that will make a lasting difference in the longer run. Various studies suggest that the direct supply side effects added approximately one half of one percentage point to the real GDP growth rate in Ireland and Portugal over the course of the 1990s.[53]

How large these effects will turn out to be will depend crucially on the strength of the economic rates of return that the related investments are going to generate. The higher the economic return is, the higher the supply effect will be. In practice and in the light of the discussion above, *it may well be that many of those high return investment opportunities lay in the richer Bratislava region.* This should not be a reason to ignore them.

On the contrary, the government would be well advised to reconsider the recent decision to exclude the region of Bratislava from the benefit of EU funding under Objective 1 (which benefits from the largest allocation of Structural Funds). Even though a support of the Bratislava growth pole might initially lead to some exacerbation of regional disparities in output per capita, the increased regional variation should be socially sustainable in the short term.[54] Perhaps the simplest way to achieve this would be to revise the NUTS-3 structure of the country to subsume Bratislava within its surrounding region.

In addition to Bratislava, the government may wish to explicitly foster the later development of other growth poles. There are some signs that such a pole may be emerging around Košice. In addition to a relatively fast shift to a service-based economy, the regional economy has been growing more rapidly since 1997 than any other region in the Slovak Republic. Košice has a relatively good endowment of human capital, thanks to several major universities and a relatively high stock of foreign direct investment.

An important aspect of stimulating the regional economies and the outflow of economic activities from Bratislava to other regions will be to reduce trade costs through *significant improvements in transportation infrastructure* (including a high speed road link connecting the eastern part of the country and Bratislava). Building on the experience that the Slovak authorities have already acquired in the pre-accession period with the ISPA Fund, this could be the main focus of Cohesion Fund resources.

The second priority area of public investment should be *human capital*. The importance of investment in human capital has been confirmed by several recent empirical studies and experiences of the current EU members.[55] A major focus on education policy is particularly important in order to create the appropriate conditions for generating endogenous growth processes and attracting

---

53. These estimates are based on conservative assumptions, and the true magnitude of the supply-effects of the structural funds may actually be larger see, for example, Pereira, A., and Gaspar, V. (1999), "An Intertemporal Analysis of Development Policies in the EU," *Journal of Policy Modeling,* Vol. 21, No. 7, pp. 799–822, and Barry, F., et. al. (2001), "The Single Market, the Structural Funds and Ireland's Recent Economic Growth," *Journal of Common Market Studies,* Vol. 39, No. 3, pp. 537–52.

54. In the post-2006 programming period, which should also coincide with a full integration of the Slovak Republic into the Schengen area, Bratislava may increasingly benefit from an economic integration with Vienna. At this point, focused public development initiative may no longer be justified in Bratislava.

55. Alesina, A. et al. "Redistribution through public employment: the case of Italy," IMF Working Paper, No 177, 1999 and European Commission, "The economic and financial situation in Italy" Office for Official Publications of the European Communities, Luxembourg, 1993.

industries with leading technologies. While medium tech and high-tech industries are expanding toward the periphery in the EU, studies find that their location remains sensitive to countries' endowments in terms of researchers. Although the Slovak Republic has a fairly good endowment of researchers in technical disciplines, government support of R&D is currently very low compared to other European technological leaders. With a full accession into the EU, researchers will face further strong incentives to relocate to other EU member countries. This could lead to an accelerated "brain drain" process, with a strong negative impact on long-term growth prospects in the Slovak Republic.

Labor Market and Social Welfare Reforms

In order to foster national and inter-regional convergence, the government should implement labor market reforms that will decrease the disparities in employment and unemployment rates across regions, particularly between Bratislava and the rest of the country. The specific reforms involved are discussed in chapter 1 and chapter 4. They should strive for two main goals: to increase the employment rates in regions outside of Bratislava and to increase the outflow of labor from depressed regions to regions with better employment opportunities. Raising the employment rates in poor regions would decrease the gap in regional output per capita levels, by boosting production in poor regions. Improving labor migration would decrease the regional disparities in unemployment levels and per capita output by decreasing the non-productive population in poor regions.

Fiscal Sustainability

To be viable, this investment strategy will need to fit within the overall fiscal consolidation strategy. In other words, *the utilization of structural funds will need to fit within a declining overall expenditure envelope.* This is the objective the country has set itself in the context of its pre-accession economic program (PEP). The discussion in Chapter 1 highlighted just how central that objective was to the entire development scenario.

The role of this overall budget constraint can hardly be exaggerated. Depending on the assumptions about macroeconomic variables and about the rate of utilization of EU funds, the Slovak Republic could be receiving funding equal to 1.6–1.8 percent of GDP in 2004 (see Table 3.11). Together with cofinancing from the Slovak sources, the structural operations supported by the EU funds may amount to 2.5–2.8 percent of GDP in 2004 and 3.0–3.5 percent in 2006. By that time, if the PEP is to be taken seriously, government expenditure outside of subsidies and transfers should have come down to about 12 percent of GDP. The implication is that, by that time also, *more than one-quarter of the monies spent on government consumption and investment will need to come from EU Structural Funds.* To put it another way, if the government decided to apply Structural Funds to finance investment only, *the entire projected public investment program would need to be financed from that source* to absorb the amounts discussed.

To make this possible, the Slovak government should avoid the temptation of using EU funding on newly created spending programs. On the contrary, what is required is *a massive redirection of existing government programs in such a manner as to meet the eligibility criteria for EU funding* (including the so-called "additionality" criteria). The financial resources from the structural funds should be viewed as additional revenues that should be fully integrated into the existing public investment planning.

Indeed, the government has already taken important steps in this direction by amending the existing laws to allow the EU funds to become a part of the national budget revenues, flowing through the Treasury and managed by the Ministry of Finance. The Slovak government has also adopted a wise decision to assign the function of payment authority for both Cohesion and Structural Funds to the Ministry of Finance. Such an institutional setup will permit a more efficient and transparent conduct of the payment functions.

Furthermore, in order to enhance the country's absorption of Structural Funds, it may be preferable to focus the necessary reprogramming of government expenditure and related capacity

TABLE 3.11: POTENTIAL UTILIZATION FROM COHESION AND STRUCTURAL FUNDS, 2004–06

	2004	2005	2006
EU disbursements			
Total (Euro million)[a]	480	560	710
Per capita	92	107	137
% of GDP	1.6–1.8	1.8–1.9	1.9–2.3
Counterpart financing[b] (% of GDP)	0.9–1.0	1.0–1.1	1.1–1.2
Total (% of GDP)	2.5–2.8	2.8–3.0	3.0–3.5

a/ At 1999 constant prices.
b/ Assuming average EU co-financing of 65 percent.
Source: World Bank estimates.

building efforts on a small number of sectors. At the moment, the government is developing five sectoral operational programs (SOPs) for the utilization of the Structural Funds. Based on what was suggested above, it might be advisable to cut these programs down to two or three—transport infrastructure, the environment, and human capital–and to de-prioritize the proposed SOPs for agriculture, rural development, and fisheries, and for general economic development.

Conclusions

The observation that significant regional differences exist in the Slovak Republic in terms of output per capita should not lead to the wrong policy conclusions. First, these differences reflect similarly large productivity differentials. Second, they have only a limited impact on household income and living standards. Indeed, it is the attempt to equalize living standards (through labor market and social polices) irrespective of productivity differentials that is at the core of the most worrisome form of regional disparity: disparity in unemployment rates. It would be similarly wrong to direct regional development funds away from the regions with the best growth potential on the basis of the assumption that they would already be more productive.

Instead, the experience of the Cohesion countries suggests that, to achieve the most rapid overall convergence possible, the government should target public investment to those areas in which such investment generates the highest returns, even if that involves an initial widening of regional GDP differences.

Three strategic priorities have emerged from the discussions above. The actions they would entail are listed below:

(i) Foster the development of a limited number of growth poles, starting with that of Bratislava, where external effects are highest, focusing public investment, including the EU funds, on *human capital* and *productive public infrastructure,* particularly transport infrastructure.

(ii) Improve *the* functioning of the labor market to facilitate a rapid diffusion of the induced growth.

(iii) Redirect, *rather* than expand, the existing expenditure programs to meet the eligibility criteria for Structural Funds financing.

CHAPTER 4

EXPENDITURE STRATEGIES

S trategies to reduce and redirect public expenditures can help the Slovak Republic achieve its broader strategic objectives of sustained economic recovery, employment growth and macroeconomic stability, not only by contributing directly to fiscal consolidation, but also by supporting growth and employment objectives more effectively.[56] This Chapter discusses how this can be done, beginning in the next section with a broad review of the overall levels, trends and composition of the Slovak Republic's public spending, followed by a more detailed review of the spending programs and reform needs in selected sectors.

Public Expenditure Overview

Table 4.1 provides an overview of the trends in the Slovak Republic's public spending (as a percent of GDP) as seen through the economic and functional classification of its fiscal accounts. Comparative data on spending by the other CEECs are shown in the last column.[57] The table highlights several important aspects of the country's spending:

  (a) The rise in total spending (Table 4.1, line A.2.1) over the past three years (by 1.8 percent of GDP), while revenues dropped by over 3 percent (line A.1), underscores *the need to postpone further revenue reductions until real expenditure reductions have been achieved.*
  (b) *Subsidies (both capital and current transfers) to non-financial enterprises* have grown significantly (by 1.8 percent of GDP) since 1999, and are now, at 6.0 percent of GDP, 40 percent

---

56. In particular by removing distortions resulting from enterprise subsidies; and by reducing some of the barriers to a better-functioning labor market (such as the payroll tax burden in financing health and sickness insurance and possibly pensions); work disincentives in Social Assistance programs; and the disconnect between the education system and labor market (and student) needs.

57. Comparisons drawn from World Bank, *Expenditure Policies toward EU Accession*, (2002). The comparator countries are the Czech Republic, Bulgaria, Estonia, Hungary, Latvia, Lithuania, Poland, Romania, and Slovenia.

TABLE 4.1: EXPENDITURES OF THE CONSOLIDATED GENERAL GOVERNMENT
(percent of GDP)

		1996	1997	1998	1999	2000	2001	Other CEECs 2000
		ECONOMIC CLASSIFICATION						
A.1	**Total Revenue and Grants**	**43.5**	**40.1**	**37.8**	**39.8**	**37.9**	**35.7**	**38.0**
A.2	**Total Expenditure and Net Lending**	**46.7**	**45.0**	**42.9**	**44.0**	**47.0**	**44.2**	**39.6**
A.2.1	**Total Expenditure**	**45.5**	**43.9**	**41.9**	**40.3**	**43.1**	**42.1**	**40.5**
A.3	Current Expenditure	39.0	37.2	36.6	36.4	37.5	36.6	36.3
A.3.1	Exp. on Goods and Services	17.3	17.7	16.4	15.9	15.8	15.9	16.6
A.3.1a	Wages and Salaries	10.1	9.8	9.7	9.4	9.1	8.6	7.1
A.3.1b	Other Goods and Services	7.2	7.9	6.7	6.5	6.8	7.3	9.6
A.3.2	Interest Payments	2.1	1.9	2.8	3.2	3.2	4.0	2.6
A.3.3	Subsidies and Other Curr. Transf.	19.6	17.5	17.4	17.3	18.4	16.7	17.0
A.4	Capital Expenditure	6.5	6.7	5.3	3.9	5.7	5.5	4.2
A.4.1	Investment.	4.4	5.4	3.9	3.2	3.2	3.2	2.7
A.4.2	Capital Transfers	2.1	1.4	1.4	0.7	2.4	2.3	1.4
A.5	Lending minus Repayment	1.2	1.1	0.9	3.8	3.9	2.1	−0.9
	Overall Deficit/Surplus	**−3.2**	**−4.8**	**−5.1**	**−4.3**	**−9.1**	**−8.5**	**−2.5**
	memo item							
	Transfers to Enterprises	**8.0**	**5.3**	**5.1**	**4.2**	**7.3**	**6.0**	**4.3**
		FUNCTIONAL CLASSIFICATION						
A.2.1	**Total Expenditure**	**45.5**	**43.9**	**41.9**	**40.3**	**43.1**	**42.1**	**40.5**
B.1	General Public Services	3.7	3.7	3.1	3.0	3.3	3.7	2.9
B.2	Defense	2.3	2.1	1.9	1.7	1.8	1.6	1.5
B.3	Public Order and Safety	2.3	2.3	2.2	1.6	1.6	1.7	2.0
B.4	Education	4.4	4.2	4.0	3.9	3.8	3.7	5.2
B.5	Health	6.3	6.0	5.5	5.5	5.7	5.7	4.6
B.6	Social Security and Welfare	13.7	13.6	13.6	13.8	13.6	13.1	14.2
B.7	Housing and Communal Services	2.3	1.8	2.1	2.1	1.9	1.7	1.9
B.8	Recreation and Culture	1.1	1.0	1.0	0.8	0.9	0.9	1.1
B.9	Economic Services	7.4	8.0	6.5	5.3	8.3	6.6	4.5
B.9.1	Fuel and Energy	0.8	0.7	0.5	0.2	0.0	0.1	0.1
B.9.2	Agriculture	2.5	2.4	2.0	1.5	2.4	1.8	1.1
B.9.3	Nonfuel Mining and Mineral	0.7	0.5	0.5	0.2	0.6	0.4	0.2
B.9.4	Transport and Communication	1.6	1.4	1.1	0.6	1.9	1.6	2.4
B.9.5	Other Economic Services	1.8	3.0	2.5	2.9	3.5	2.7	0.8
	Interest Payments	2.1	1.9	2.8	3.2	3.2	4.0	2.6
	Miscellaneous	−0.1	−0.7	−0.8	−0.7	−1.1	−0.6	−0.1

Sources: IMF, Government Finance Statistics, Ministry of Finance, Staff Calculations.

higher than the CEEC average (memo item, Table 4.1). A sharp reduction in these subsidies (which are focused mainly on agriculture, railways, energy, and hospitals) would go a long way toward achieving the necessary fiscal consolidation. Spending on *agriculture* and related activities (line B.9.2 in the functional classification), which consists largely of subsidies, has averaged more than 2 percent of GDP since the mid-1990s, about 60 percent higher than in the comparator countries. An approach to reducing the subsidies in agriculture is discussed below.

(c) *Wages and salaries* (line A.3.1a) also claim an unusually high share of public spending in the Slovak Republic. Though slowly declining, this category of spending is still about 1.5 percent of GDP higher than in the comparator countries. This reflects the overstaffing in education and health (discussed further below). It also underscores the need to consolidate steps taken so far in the decentralization process to reduce the risks of an excessive expansion of public employment due to duplication, fragmentation, and loss of economies of scale.

(d) While spending on *social protection* as a share of GDP (line B.6) has not shown a rising trend, and is about average compared with the other CEECs, these aggregate figures mask major problems. As discussed below, urgent reforms are needed to: prevent looming pension system deficits; curb the rising cash assistance payments and correct the disincentives preventing recipients from to working their way out of welfare; reduce the payroll tax burden; and contain spending.

(e) *Health spending* (line B.5) has been rising, and is substantially (more than 20 percent) higher as a share of GDP than in the comparator countries. Deep reforms are needed to contain and rationalize the rising demand pressures, improve the financing mechanism, and reduce high costs of supply that result in large part from overstaffing and excess facilities. These reforms are discussed in some detail below.

(f) Aggregate *spending on education* (line B.4) has declined as a share of GDP, and is more than one percent of GDP lower than in comparator countries. However, in this case the demographic shift has worked to reduce pressure for increased spending, and, as argued below, the scope for reducing excessive numbers of teachers and schools at the primary and secondary levels is only beginning to be tapped. This consolidation needs to be intensified and accompanied by reforms to reorient secondary education and gradually expand the tertiary level to create a better match between system outputs and labor market (and student) needs.

The sections below focus on agriculture, social protection, health, and education, sectors that, together with the enterprise subsidies noted above, accounted for over two-thirds of total public spending in 2001. It is difficult to see how the needed expenditure adjustment could be realized and sustained without dealing with these sectors, and with the regional development spending issues discussed in Chapter 3. Of course, other important areas of spending not discussed in this report (for example, energy, environment, defense, general public services and other economic services) should also be subject to rigorous review as part of an overall strategy to contain spending. The discussions below seek to illustrate the range and complexity of the issues that confront the Slovak Republic's policymakers as they seek to contain public expenditures and make them more effective. While this part of the report proposes both short and medium-term recommendations, it does not pretend to provide a fully detailed, comprehensive reforms blueprint. Rather, it seeks to highlight the difficult issues that need to be confronted, and at the same time reinforce the case for improvements in fiscal management. In each sector, the discussion focuses not on across-the-board cuts, but rather on reform options that can help to reduce or contain spending while improving its effectiveness in supporting the strategic goals of growth, employment, and stability.

It should be stressed that while there are some important measures that can and should be taken in the short term (especially reducing enterprise subsidies and starting to raise the retirement age), most important measures to contain expenditures in a sustainable way will require a thorough, comprehensive review of the overall expenditure program, not as a one-shot exercise, but as a continuous process to identify reforms of the main expenditure programs, including a careful assessment (and subsequent monitoring) of the impact of reform on the poor, especially the Roma. This process will involve choices over time about what the public sector should do, how much it should do, and how it can do it most effectively. Many of these choices will be politically sensitive, so an important part of the effort needs to be to develop an understanding and political consensus for the need for such reforms.

This is why this report emphasizes the critical need for the Slovak Republic to develop the institutions, capacities and processes that will help generate the assessments of program performance and reforms needed to bring about continuous improvements in the effectiveness of the public sector and the efficiency of public expenditure. This would call for the development of analytical capacities in core and line agencies alike, including continued improvements in the measurement and comprehensiveness of budget accounts, the development of a more formal and systematic medium-term approach to fiscal programming in both the Ministry of Finance and in the line ministries, and a move towards a greater performance orientation in budgeting, as well as the establishment of periodic, representative household budget surveys.

Agriculture

As noted in Chapter 2, the Slovak Republic spends an excessive amount on agricultural support to support a policy framework that is condemned to disappear with the imminent accession to the EU's Common Agricultural Policy (CAP). To facilitate the transition, it is now time to prune down and reformat the support programs so that they conform to CAP requirements. This would make it possible to cut back expenditure commitments on agriculture by about 15–20 percent. Upon accession, much of the remaining charges should be transferred to the EU budget, relieving the Slovak budget accordingly of this uncommonly high burden.

Forms and Levels of Agricultural Support

Slovak budget expenditures on agriculture not only exceed the levels observed in all other candidate countries, but they are much higher as a percentage of GDP than those of the EU and of the large OECD economies. In 2000–01, current subsidies to producers (which include price support and direct payments for current measures—excluding capital expenditure) absorbed over 50 percent of the agricultural budget (see Figure 4.1). Most of these amounts are subsidies to crop and livestock production, as well as generous subsidies to farming in less favored areas (each category received over 20 percent of the total). Capital expenditure subsidies (including small credit subsidies for investment loans) account for another 10–15 percent of the total, and the rest is equally divided among subsidies to general services, agri-environmental and rural development subsidies, and tax concessions (about 10 percent each year in each category). A key feature of this system is a bias against small farmers, as most of the farmer-related payments have condi-

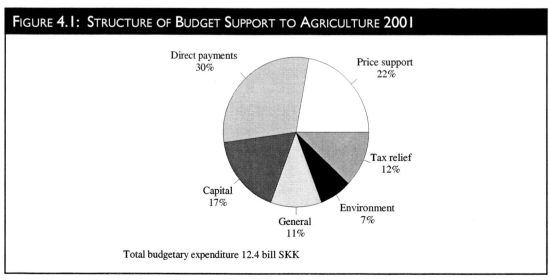

FIGURE 4.1: STRUCTURE OF BUDGET SUPPORT TO AGRICULTURE 2001

Direct payments 30%

Price support 22%

Tax relief 12%

Capital 17%

Environment 7%

General 11%

Total budgetary expenditure 12.4 bill SKK

Source: Ministry of Agriculture and Ministry of Finance.

tions regarding the minimum size of operations (e.g., 5 cows, output values corresponding to 5 ha, etc.).

A Two-Step Approach to CAP Harmonization

The current agricultural support system mixes heavy government intervention with the principles of a market-based agriculture but does not yet correspond to CAP requirements. Efforts should be concentrated on the adaptation of the same policy instruments as in the EU, but without yet applying them at the same level. Although there is pressure to immediately increase support and to converge at EU levels before accession, the level of support and border measures should remain at the current level in order to maintain the pressure to complete reforms and to remain within budgetary constraints and WTO commitments. The level of support would then automatically rise to CAP levels after the accession, but the burden of that expenditure would shift to the EU budget.

Using the Agenda 2000 proposals for the reform of the EU's CAP as a reference, the following adjustments would need to be made promptly.

(a) *Market support* (including border measures as well as direct and indirect intervention in the market) and *direct payments* are provided in the EU at a level of price support higher than that in the Slovak Republic on average. Therefore, little in the way of expenditure reductions can probably be realized here prior to accession. The instruments used, however, need to be adjusted to a transparent, CAP-conforming framework incorporating the potential use of quotas in the case of some products. Changes should be made in the current intervention, which is based on an ex ante system (the intervention is based on short-term forecasts on production and consumption) to an ex post CAP-type intervention mechanism in which market intervention decisions by the private sector are based on the observed evolution of EU market prices. In addition, to be consistent with the principles of the CAP, price support would need to be transferred to the wholesale level instead of the farmgate for most products. As concerns direct payments *stricto sensu,* the generalized area payment scheme outside of the less favored areas could be adapted and fitted into the national envelopes proposed for the dairy and beef sectors under the Agenda 2000.

(b) Expenditures on supporting inputs for irrigation and for the preservation of selected genetically valuable livestock are not provided in the EU and should be eliminated.

(c) *The existing credit guarantee scheme* should be made fully consistent with EU standards, and most credit *subsidies* should be discontinued in their present format. None of the current support measures aiming to improve the access to financing of capital and non-capital expenditures is admissible under the CAP.

(d) *Subsidies for modernization and restructuring* also need to be streamlined in line with EU guidelines.[58] However, no subsidy to agro-processors is admissible in the EU for modernizing and restructuring. These should be eliminated.

(e) *Tax preferences for farmers* are not allowed in the EU and these will have to be eliminated entirely before accession (including the current tax refunds on diesel fuel used for farming purposes).

The potential impact of these measures on budget expenditures on agriculture and food can be seen in Table 4.2. Policy items that can be terminated are highlighted in bold typeface in the table;

---

58. The EU currently allows some grants for structural development measures, but these must meet one or more of the following objectives: reduce production costs; improve product quality; preserve and improve the environment; meet hygiene and animal welfare conditions; encourage diversification in agricultural activities.

TABLE 4.2: STRUCTURE OF BUDGET EXPENDITURE ON AGRICULTURE AND FOOD, 2000–01
(percent)

		2000	2001
1.1	Subsidies To Crop Producers	10.5	9.9
1.2	Subsidies To Livestock Production	9.5	12.4
1.	MARKET PRICE SUPPORT	20.0	22.3
2.1	Subsidies To Farming In Less Favored Areas	22.9	25.7
2.2	**Subsidies For Non-Capital Inputs (Irrigation, Livestock Genetic Pool)**	**2.4**	**3.4**
2.	DIRECT PAYMENTS	25.3	29.1
3.1	Disaster Insurance	0.4	0.6
3.2	Special Drought Payments	12.2	0.0
3.	INCOME STABILIZATION PAYMENTS	12.6	0.6
4.1	*Subsidies For Capital Expenditures To Farmers*	*9.6*	*15.1*
4.2	**Subsidies For Capital Expenditures To Processors**	**0.4**	**0.6**
4.	CAPITAL EXPENDITURE SUBSIDIES	10.1	15.7
5.1	*Investment Credit Subsidies To Farmers*	*1.0*	*1.6*
5.2	**Investment Credit Subsidies To Processors**	**0.2**	**0.1**
5.	INVESTMENT CREDIT SUBSIDIES	1.2	1.7
6.1	Soil Improvement And Reclamation	4.2	2.6
6.2	Agri-Environmental Schemes	6.2	4.2
6.3	Rural Development Schemes	0.2	0.6
6.	SUBSIDIES TO GENERAL SERVICES	10.1	11.1
7.	AGRO-ENVIRONT. AND RURAL DEV. SUBSIDIES	10.6	7.4
8.	**TAX RELIEF**	**10.1**	**12.0**
	TOTAL	100.0	100.0

Source: Ministry of Finance and Ministry of Agriculture.

they add up to 16 percent of the 2001 agricultural budget. Policy items that can be at least partly reduced are highlighted in italics.

Transport
Introduction
The transport sector in the Slovak Republic faces fundamental challenges in the coming years. On one hand, the sector needs to adapt and respond to long-term changes in the underlying patterns of demand. On the other hand the sector needs to correct years of misallocation of scarce resources that have left the basic sector infrastructure under-maintained. In addition, the supply response needs now to make room for additional demands arising from the upcoming integration with the EU.

The sector needs to be transformed to respond to the following problems/demands: (i) the sweeping transition-induced shifts in demand across transport modes, with rail freight dropping by over 25 percent, while road freight grew by about 70 percent (1993–2000, see Table 4.3 and Table 4.4)[59]; (ii) large operating losses and mounting debts and arrears in railways; (iii) the build- up of a large backlog of maintenance in roads, railways and public transport; and (iv) a major program of new transport investments, mainly for the Trans-European Network (TEN) corridors. In addition to resolving these issues, the policy response should also: (a) make room for increased participation by the private sector in transport through privatization and commercialization of existing transport activities;

---

59. Similar changes occurred in passenger transportation with railways dropping by almost 60 percent and road rising by almost 25 percent.

TABLE 4.3: TRENDS IN GOODS AND PASSENGER TRANSPORT
(billions of ton-km or passenger-km)

	1993	2000	% change
Goods Transport			
Rail	14.17	11.23	−26
Road	16.80	28.58	+70
Inland Water	1.60	1.38	−15
Air	0.057	0.022	−59
Oil Pipeline	—	2.08	—
Total	32.63	43.29	+32
Passenger Transport			
Rail	4.57	2.87	−59
Automobile	14.36	24.41	+69
Bus	12.34	8.68	−42
Inland Water	0.006	0.004	−50
Air	4.46	2.51	−77
Total	35.74	38.47	+8
	(Thousand passengers/year)		
Urban Public Transport	649	405	−60

Source: Statistical Yearbooks of the Slovak Republic.

(b) reconsider the use of Public Service Obligations (PSOs) as a vehicle for social policy in light of the leaks to non-targeted population and the price distortions they impose; and (c) make a more intensive use of cost recovery options such as electronic tolls to help finance new investment and maintenance.

The sector response to these needs remains inadequate. As in other Central European Countries, this response is characterized by: (i) an overemphasis on *new motorway construction* (accounting for 82 percent of total road expenditures) and (ii) *excessive rail services*. The bias towards new motorway

TABLE 4.4: TRANSPORT BASIC INDICATORS, 1996–2000

	1990	1996	1997	1998	1999	2000
Road public transport						
Transported passengers, thousands	937,528	699,758	667,427	656,230	621,567	604,249
City transport						
Transported passengers, thousands	574,405	542,389	527,662	509,862	485,472	404,539
Number of employees, persons	6,337[a]	5,667	5,656	5,608	5,582	5,480
Railway transport						
Transported passengers, thousands	119,262	74,294	71,489	70,008	69,431	66,806
Transport of goods, thousand tons	117,237	58,147	59,377	56,569	49,115	54,177
Number of employees, persons	60,074[a]	51,770	49,517	49,427	47,671	46,813
Water transport						
Transport of goods, thousand tons	3,715	1,413	1,378	1,172	1,507	1,607
Cars and motorways						
Number of passenger cars, thousands	837	1,058	1,136	1,196	1,236	1,274
Length of motorways, km	na	215	219	288	295	296

[a]Data for 1991.
Source: Statistical Yearbooks of the Slovak Republic.

TABLE 4.5: CENTRAL GOVERNMENT FUNDS TO AND EXPENDITURES IN THE TRANSPORT SECTOR, 2001
(millions of US Dollars)

	Railways	Roads	Inland Waterways	Aviation	Grand Total
Total Central Government Flows of Funds for Transport Sector					
Constr./Rehab./Maintenance	122.9	102.9	1.4	4.2	231.5
PSO[a]	200.0	—	—	—	200.0
Operating/Labor Costs	—	22.0	11.0	2.6	35.6
Debt Service[b]	39.6	3.1	—	—	42.7
Total	362.5	128.0	12.4	6.8	509.8
as % of 2001 GDP	1.88	0.66	0.06	0.04	2.64
Total Transport Expenditures					
Construction[c]	125.1	175.8	0.6	2.7	304.2
Rehabilitation/Maintenance[c]	131.0	38.6	2.4	6.0	178.0
Operating/Labor Costs	190.4	22.0	11.0	2.6	226.0
Debt Service	42.0	62.0	—	—	104.0
Total	488.5	298.4	14.0	11.3	812.3
as % of 2001 GDP	2.53	1.55	0.07	0.06	4.21

[a]PSO lump-sum payment for 1997–2000.
[b]Interest only.
[c]Including loans to road and railways entities, including government guarantees which are significant contingent liabilities of the government.
Source: Slovak Republic Report to EU on the Accession Progress, Ministry of Finance, MTPC, and staff calculations.

construction contributes to the increasing backlog in road maintenance[60] and delays the necessary upgrading of the existing road network to EU standards; while the oversupply of rail services contributes to boost losses. They all combine to put extra pressures to the already strained fiscal situation in Slovakia.

In dealing with these expenditure pressures, the Slovak Republic will need to concentrate scarce public resources exclusively on those activities where the private sector cannot operate and/or invest effectively. In addition, it needs to reallocate public funding progressively away from decaying subsectors such as railways, into the most dynamic ones, such as roads with due consideration of environmental and social issues. The country needs also to focus on completing the remaining areas for transport commercialization and restructuring (especially in railways) and to balance carefully the urgent needs for repair and maintenance against proposals for new investment.

Transport Expenditures
Total transport spending and amortizations in 2001, amounted to about US$812 million, or some 4.2 percent of GDP; with the Central Government contributing with some US$510 million (2.6 percent of GDP, see Table 4.4) in the forms of transfers and payment for called guarantees. The sections below outline the use of these funds and some of the most important technical and economic issues regarding the two main sub-sectors: road infrastructure and railways.

Road Infrastructure
As in many countries in the region, financial imbalances in the sector translate into *inadequate maintenance* of road infrastructure. In fact, if the backlog in maintenance was to be eliminated

---

60. Only 18 percent of the total expenditure on roads is allocated to maintenance.

within a five-year period, it would require an average US$90 million per year. On top of this, routine and periodic maintenance would require another US$110 per year. The two combine for a total US$200 million per year over the next five years. In contrast, only US$39 million was spent in 2001 in maintenance, further contributing to the rising backlog. Without a detailed analysis, needed capacity increases in the basic national road network (non-motorways) are difficult to estimate. Nevertheless, in light of the EU requirements for expanded axle weight limits in the main corridors, a lower bound estimate could be around US$100 million per year over the next five years. Finally, for *motorways*, the completion of the proposed network would require US$340 million. However, assuming a considerably reduced high standard road program, an amount of about US$200 per year over the next five years seems more realistic and adequate. Therefore, assuming that the correction of the backlog in maintenance, as well as the capacity increases in both, the basic road network and the high standard road network is implemented, the needed expenditures would be about US$500 million per year. This compared to an actual of US$215 million/year, would require a 2.3 fold increase.

The need for extra funding does not necessarily translate into a corresponding increase in state budget allocations for this purpose. In fact, as argued below, a number of alternative source of funding, including the structural and cohesion funds, are becoming increasingly available to the Slovak Republic. These sources could cover up to 75 percent of individual Slovakia TINA (Telecommunications/Informatics Infrastructure New Assistance) projects; which are estimated at Euro 4–7.5 billion—subject to further verification of unit costs and feasibility. Alternatively, the financing of motorways and expressways could be based on the use of electronic tolls, and more generally, on various public-private partnerships. The combination of these alternative sources of funds should reduce the requirements on the state budget.

Decentralization and development of the network. The imminent decentralization of government functions will bring about a radical change in the way roads are administered. It will also become a window of opportunity to implement further needed changes in the sector. However, in parallel to the transfer of the responsibility for road maintenance to the local and regional government, it is necessary to provide these governments with the appropriate funding and technical expertise. So far this transfer has been missing. For the first time in 2002, the Slovak Road Administration (SRA) signed an annual road administration contract with the Ministry of Transport, Posts and Communications (MTPC). Under the current decentralization proposals, about three-quarters of the road network will be transferred from the SRA to the eight new regional governments by 2005. The remaining roads will be transferred to the municipalities, while according to current plans, 4,700 km of motorways, expressways and Class I roads will remain with the SRA. However, up until now, there have been no proposals for the transfer of revenues or technical expertise to regional governments.

Motorways. Although the motorways were not designed as toll roads, it would be feasible to create an open toll road network from them that would generate more net revenue than the present vignette system. Electronic toll systems that could eliminate the need for manned toll stations already exist and are rapidly being introduced in other countries. The EU is now preparing a unified system to be introduced in all member states by 2004. A Motorway Company (MC) would be able to securitize its revenue from the existing toll network for the issuing of bonds to finance its expansion. The Motorway Company could initially be state owned, but once the revenue stream from tolls had been established, it should be concessioned (or sold) on a long-term basis to a private company. The motorway development plan to be undertaken over the period of the concession would be included in the terms of the concession. This plan should cover the network as a whole and not individual roads or parts of them. The preparation of the development plan should take account not only of the revenue earning capacity of each section of the network to be constructed but also overall network finances. It would be the responsibility of the bidders for the concession to propose a construction schedule and financing plan compatible with their estimate of the revenue earning capacity of their development schedule.

Revenues from tolls could provide sufficient funds for the construction of about 100km of motorway per year, allowing completion of the remaining 356 km of the planned 648 km network within about 4 years after the existing debt was paid off. In fact, with an electronic tolling system that would avoid the need for toll plazas, a toll equivalent to about US$0.025 per car km could produce an annual revenue of about US$23 million in 2005 from the existing motorway network. Most of these proceeds would go to amortize the securitized bonds.

Railways

The railways' expenditure for construction and reconstruction in 2001 amounted to about US$ 250 million, which was covered in part by the state budget and in part by EIB loans. In addition, the Public Service Obligations (PSOs)[61] in 2001 amounted to some US$130 million, which the state did not cover. The current situation is unsustainable, with the railways resorting to expensive short term borrowing. On top of the operating expenses, the financing of the restructuring/ modernization of the railways needs to be covered. While the current charges for the use of rail infrastructure appear to be sufficient; a too large rail surface coverage (which is not compensated for by PSO) causes further losses. In addition, operation of lines that are uneconomic due to low of traffic gives the railways companies the excuse/justification not to decrease staffing. Not surprisingly, the staff productivity of Zeleznice Slovenskej Republiky (ZSR) has declined from 340,000 TU (Traffic Unit)[62] per employee in 1995 to 302,000 in 2000. This compares unfavorably with railways systems of similar network size and traffic density.[63]

Railway Restructuring. In the short term, reduction of the government's control of ŽSR through the creation of a separate operating company, Zeleznicna Spolocnost (ZS), coincides with the decentralization of responsibility for funding the PSO for passenger services. This provides an excellent opportunity to reorient the railway. Given its relative small size, it would be inappropriate to divide the infrastructure company, ŽSR, into separate regional railways. However, the large differences between its principal (freight, long distance passenger, and local passenger services) suggests that a separation along business lines would be desirable. Nevertheless, this separation would not deal directly with the infrastructure issue. The EU only requires an accounting separation of infrastructure from operations, so that track charges for other railway users can be determined on an equitable basis. This is what most EU railways have done. The separation of ZS (the railway operator company) into different lines of business while keeping the infrastructure company ZSR integrated, appears to the best approach. Ongoing deliberations suggest that this is the Government's approach.

In light of the ongoing decentralization, it would be desirable to have a stable system of PSO payment by multiple regional governments in place—one that will not have to be changed within a few years- to accommodate the new institutional structure of the railway.

The present restructuring plan for the railways includes a modest proposal for staff reductions. As it is, it does not suffice to improve efficiency to the level of private railways. Experience in much of the world suggests that estimates of minimum staffing made in advance of privatization fall short of the actual reductions attained after a few years of private operation. In fact, once they are stripped of non-essential activities the three railway businesses (freight, intercity and regional passengers) should be able to operate with fewer than 25,000 staff. This could be further reduced if the new regional governments decide they cannot support the current local passenger services. ŽSR could reduce staffing by about 10,000 employees four years ahead of the seven years indicated in the current restructuring plan provided a source of funding is available to cover redundancy costs.

---

61. PSOs are contractual arrangements to subsidy certain type of consumption of public services by qualifying groups.
62. A combined indicator for (freight traffic—ton/km and passenger traffic—passenger/km).
63. The Austrian rail productivity per employee is about 482,000 TU; while the Polish is about 400,000 TU after significant downsizing.

The ministry of Transport, Posts and Communications (MTPC), in co-operation with ŽSR elaborated a concept of fees for use of railway transport infrastructure under which the fees are established on the basis of marginal costs. Fixed costs will be paid by the state. The fixed to marginal cost ratio is within 39–61 percent range. This proportion is based on the EU Directive No. 14/2001 and on the new Slovak legislation in force. It should be gradually implemented in 2002–2005.[64]

Should a local passenger services company be created, it could attract a private operator. However, it might have relatively high fixed infrastructure costs, and be dependent on the new regional governments for a large part of its annual revenue. This has been done in the UK while Sweden and Germany are concessioning their social services through negative concessions.

As the size of the country is more appropriate to motorway-based bus services than to express passenger trains, the long distance rail passenger company would have an uncertain future. Few EU countries can maintain a profitable inter-urban passenger service and most depend on subsidies. Therefore, the chosen scheme, which combines the existing passenger railway assets (provided by the state at a nominal value) with private operation of a strategic operator into a joint venture is commendable. This scheme could attract existing passenger operators in EU countries with close connections to Slovakia. On the other hand, the freight operations of ZS could be a prime candidate for privatization.[65]

Social Protection Programs
Introduction
The Slovak Republic's social protection programs have benefited from recent reforms, but there is still substantial need and scope to improve these programs to contain costs, establish financial sustainability, improve the poverty focus, and reduce disincentives to work.[66] The review highlights the following points:

(a) *The state pension system faces serious financial difficulties given the aging population.* Projections show that the system will run into increasing deficits in the next decade and will become unsustainable, despite the important reforms legislated in May 2002. The government needs to consider deeper reforms of the Pay-As-You-Go (PAYGO) system, including raising the retirement age further to 65, along with other measures to ensure the system's long-term financial viability. It also needs to initiate the technical design work and institutional reforms needed to launch a fully funded *mandatory* second pillar.

(b) *There may be scope to reduce the payroll tax contributions for sickness insurance,* given the sickness insurance fund's recent surpluses. This would be highly desirable in view of the country's high level of payroll taxes and the constraints that such taxes place on employment growth.

(c) *The welfare programs aimed at assisting the poor still lack adequate targeting and also discourage work.* For certain types of households and in certain regions, benefit levels are high relative to average net wages and are likely to be a strong work disincentive. This effect is likely to be stronger in regions where wages are relatively low, hindering labor market adjustment to regional disparities. Benefit structures should be reformed to encourage work, and levels need to be made more modest relative to labor income. The government needs to strengthen its poverty monitoring, and adjust the benefits criteria and categories so that they are better targeted to assist the poor.

---

64. Establishment of the notification and regulation office is under preparation.

65. This was done in the U.K., the Netherlands and Denmark and is being considered in Switzerland.

66. This section draws on "Social Protection" in *The Slovak Republic: Social Sector Expenditure Review* (World Bank, draft, 2002), *Budgeting and Expenditure Management in the Slovak Republic* (World Bank, 2002), and E. Andrews, "The Pension System" and "The Social Welfare System" (draft, 2002).

TABLE 4.6: PUBLIC EXPENDITURE ON SOCIAL PROTECTION PROGRAMS, 1995–2001

SKK billions	1995	1996	1997	1998	1999	2000	2001
Pensions[a,b]	41.9	47.65	53.28	59.20	64.01	70.33	75.74
Sickness and Maternity[c]	5.7	7.4	8.1	9.0	9.5	9.1	8.9
Unemployment Insurance[a,d]	6.1	7.5	8.2	8.9	9.0	9.1	8.5
Social Welfare[e]	22.7	23.6	25.5	28.9	32.5	34.6	36.2
Total (SKK billions)	**76.4**	**86.1**	**95.1**	**106.0**	**115.0**	**123.2**	**129.1**
% of GDP							
Pensions[a,b]	7.36	7.58	7.52	7.64	7.66	7.74	7.66
Sickness and Maternity[c]	1.00	1.17	1.15	1.16	1.14	1.01	0.90
Unemployment Insurance[a,d]	1.07	1.19	1.15	1.15	1.07	1.00	0.86
Social Welfare[e]	3.99	3.75	3.60	3.73	3.89	3.81	3.66
Total (percent of GDP)	**13.44**	**13.69**	**13.42**	**13.67**	**13.76**	**13.55**	**13.07**

a/ Includes administrative expenses after 1995.
b/ Also includes administrative expenses of sickness benefits after 1995.
c/ Mainly covers sick leave and maternity leave.
d/ Includes benefits payable by NLO under Unemployment Insurance, including transfers to SIA and Health Insurance Companies.
e/ Includes Social Assistance, Social Care, and State Social Benefits
Sources: SIA, NLO, MSLAF and MoF.

Overview of Social Protection Programs

The social protection programs in the Slovak Republic consist of (i) social insurance programs based on insurance principles (albeit loosely defined), including state pensions, sickness and maternity benefits, and unemployment benefits; and (ii) non-insurance-based social welfare programs, including Social Assistance and other benefits funded from the state budget. *Social insurance programs* are financed mainly through payroll taxes; and benefits are linked to the individual's wage history, hence to contributions. The combined payroll tax rate to finance these programs plus health insurance is 50.8 percent, one of the highest in the region and in the EU.[67] As emphasized in Chapter 1, this high payroll tax rate poses a heavy tax on labor and is a serious barrier to growth, particularly employment growth. Reducing this burden by shifting the revenue base to more broadly based taxes is thus an important part of a strategy for growth with equity.[68] *Social welfare programs* are financed by general tax revenue; benefit levels and eligibility are linked to a calculated minimum subsistence level (MSL) of income,[69] or to the particular characteristics of the beneficiaries. Overall policy responsibility for social protection programs rests with the Ministry of Labor, Social Affairs, and Family (MoLSAF).

The trends in spending on the main social protection programs are given in Table 4.6.[70] Total spending on these programs has not shown a significant rise as a share of GDP. However, as discussed in detail below, *in pensions major spending pressures are inevitable, while the recent erosion of*

67. The payroll tax rates for the various social insurance programs are: pensions (28 percent), sickness (4.8 percent), unemployment (4 percent), and health (14 percent). The average rate for EU countries is 37 percent of which 23 percent is for pensions.
68. The normal effect of payroll taxes is to reduce employment overall, and/or shift employment into the non-formal sector where tax payment is harder to enforce. See Chapter 1 above.
69. Defined as the income level below which material destitution occurs; levels are calculated for individuals, couples, and children.
70. This table is drawn from administrative program data and may exclude certain programs funded and administered by the local level (estimated at less than 0.05% of GDP in 2001). It also excludes housing allowances, which are to date also relatively small. While not identical to Table 4.1, it shows similar trends.

the revenue base will continue. Other programs also have areas of potential spending pressure or oppor-tunities for cost containment. Further reforms of these programs would help meet the government's need to find additional fiscal space, increase labor market flexibility, and generate greater growth and equity.

Pensions

Background

Compared with that of many other countries in the region, the Slovak Republic's pension system appeared in relatively good shape until the mid-1990s. However, the increase in unemployment in the late 1990s, combined with a rising share of self-employed workers, eroded revenues and pushed the Pension Fund into deficit, placing it on the razor's edge of financial stability. More important, the pension system must contend with the inevitable long-term demographic changes common to all Europe, which will greatly increase the numbers of the elderly (60+) relative those of working age (18–59). The ratio of these two groups, the dependency ratio, is projected to increase from 26 percent today to 39 percent in 2020 and to more than 60 percent in 2040. Put another way, by 2040, there will be half as many working age people to support one retiree as there are today.[71]

The main features of the country's public pension system[72] as it exists today are described in Box 4.1. Pension expenditures have varied within a narrow range of 7.4–7.7 percent of GDP since the mid-1990s. Contributions, however, have not kept pace with expenditures, despite increases in the already high contribution rate in 1996 and 2001, reaching only 6.7 percent of GDP in 2001.[73] Far more serious is that *the inexorable shift in the population's age structure will mean a large increase in expenditures relative to contributions, resulting in unsustainably large deficits, illustrated in Figure 4.2.*[74] Reform is therefore essential to avoid catastrophic deficits and the resulting macro-economic instability.

These issues are well understood by Slovak policymakers and politicians. Since the late 1990s, the Slovak Republic has been committed to fundamental pension reform.[75] The most recent mani-festation of this is *the Social Insurance Act of May 2002.* The act *contains a number of major reforms, with implementation to start during 2003.* The main goals of the reforms are to put the PAYGO system (the *first pillar*) on a much sounder financial footing, to improve the link between a participant's contributions and benefits, and to start to build up a mandatory, fully funded *second pillar* that, combined with the reformed first pillar, would generate adequate retirement income for future generations and would insulate the system from the adverse consequences of the projected demographic changes. The voluntary, private pension program, established in 1996 (discussed further below), would form the *third pillar* of the system.

These reforms will go a long way toward reducing the massive deficits looming in the coming years, but they fall short of achieving financial sustainability. There are options that the government

---

71. I.e., 3.4 working age people per retiree today versus 1.7 in 2040, using base case assumptions (see Annex Table 1); contributors would be about 52 percent of these numbers based on 2001 employment rates.

72. A voluntary, private third pillar (discussed below) was established in 1996 to complement the public pension system.

73. Not including transfers from the state budget or NLO. The Pension Fund was in deficit even includ-ing these transfers.

74. The demographic scenarios include a "pessimistic" case in which fertility rises more slowly, and life expectancy more rapidly, than the base case; and an "optimistic" case, with slower increases in life expectancy than the base case. See Annex Table 1 for details. The deficit peaks at 7% of GDP even under the base case assumptions.

75. The government approved the *Policy of Transformation of the Social Sphere* on December 12, 1995, and the *Policy of Social Insurance Reform* on August 9, 2000.

BOX 4.1: CURRENT PUBLIC PENSION SYSTEM

- The system is a traditional Defined Benefit (DB) PAYGO system, covering old age (63 percent of transfers), disability (21 percent), and survivors/others (16 percent); administered by the Social Insurance Agency (SIA), and governed by a tri-partite board.
- Normal retirement ages are 60 for men, 57 for women.[1]
- Pension indexation has roughly followed wage growth, based on a trigger mechanism.
- The average replacement rate (average net pension as a percent of the average gross wage) is about 42 percent, and is broadly comparable to those of other countries in the region.[2]
- However, the benefit formula, compressed over time by inflation, has become highly redistributive, with virtually no difference between the pension of a person who earned half the average wage and that of a person who earned twice the average wage. For example, a person who worked 35 years and earned twice the average wage throughout would receive the same pension as a person who worked 40 years while earning half the average wage.[3] As a result, the link between benefits and contributions is very weak. Pensions below a socially acceptable minimum are topped up by payments from the state budget.
- Contributions are mandatory for all workers at 28 percent of gross wages. This contribution rate is comparable to those of other transition economies, but much higher than the EU average of 23 percent.[4] The same rate is assessed on one-half of the earnings of the self-employed. While compliance appears high for regular salaried employees, payments by the self-employed appear to be less than half of what they should be.[5]
- The government makes nominal contributions (from the state budget) to the SIA intended to cover the non-contributory periods for certain groups (students, parents of young or disabled children, disabled persons and soldiers). The National Labor Office (NLO) makes similar contributions for those receiving unemployment insurance benefits. Both payments have been very low, have varied widely from year to year, and do not appear related to the additional liability assumed by the pension system.[6]

1/ Retirement ages for women are reduced from 57 to 54 depending on the number of children raised. There are no other general provisions for early retirement, except for some occupational groups considered at high risk.
2/ Differences in methodology complicate cross-country comparisons.
3/ The degree of redistribution is reduced by the ceiling on wages subject to the payroll tax (SKK 32,000 in 2000, about 2.8 times the average wage).
4/ It lies between that of the Czech Republic, at 26 percent, and Hungary, at 30 percent.
5/ Contribution rates calculated from official aggregate wage, employment, and SIA revenue data, and do not include underreported income estimates. While the SIA has faced contribution arrears from some large enterprises, the arrears build-up has not continued to accelerate.
6/ For example, in 2000, the government payment was less than 3 percent of the contribution of the average salaried employee, while the NLO contribution was less than 19 percent. These amounts are set year by year and depend largely on the fiscal situation.

should consider that would ensure greater financial stability and a tighter benefit-contribution link as well as more secure and higher levels of pensions. The following sections review each of the three pillars, highlighting the recently enacted reforms, and the options for further reforms needed to secure the government's objectives.

First Pillar Reforms
May 2002 Reforms: The main improvements embodied in the May 2002 Social Insurance Act are described in Box 4.2. As Figures 4.3a and 4.3b demonstrate, these reforms go a long way in the right direction.[76] The changed indexing method has a particularly powerful effect. How-

---

76.   For ease of presentation, unless otherwise specified, the projections assume base case demographic trends.

FIGURE 4.2: BALANCE OF PAYGO SYSTEM, NO REFORM, ALTERNATIVE DEMOGRAPHIC SCENARIOS

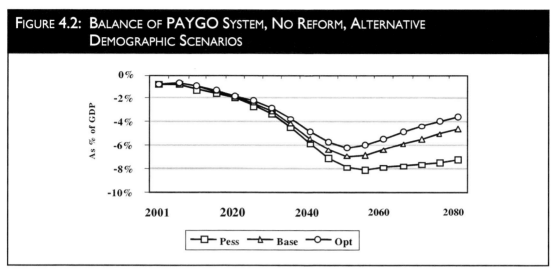

Source: World Bank calculations.

BOX 4.2: MAIN FEATURES OF THE MAY 2002 PENSION REFORMS

▨ Improvements in the pension fund's long term fiscal balance, particularly through:
  • *automatic indexation of pensions by the lower of either prices or wages*[1]
  • gradually *increasing the retirement age for women* to a uniform 60 years, by 2017 for women without children, and by 2026 for women with 4 or more children.
▨ Tighter links between benefits and contributions, particularly through:
  • *a new benefit formula, to be based on individual records* and more closely related to a person's career earnings history, while still maintaining the previous average replacement rate and Defined Benefit (DB) approach;[2]
  • *removal of most preferential pensions* for certain occupations and groups, a measure estimated to reduce costs by 2.5 percent over time;[3]
  • reconfirmation of the principle that "non-systemic" benefits[4] should be paid for by the state budget,[5] rather than cross-subsidized by the contributions of others, and establishment of reduced rates for some of these benefits.[6]
▨ Setting of the broad framework for a fully funded, mandatory second pillar.

1/ This will normally mean indexation in line with the CPI; this is assumed in the projections that follow.
2/ The government's Social Benefits Reform Administration project (SBRA), financed by a World Bank loan, will develop the systems and infrastructure to maintain such individual records. The new formula uses a point system that is based on the ratio of a person's wage to the economy-wide average, adjusted so a person gets full credit for earnings up to 1.25 times the economy-wide average, one-third credit for earnings between 1.25 and 2 times the economy-wide average, and no credit for higher earnings.
3/ Special pension provisions will still be maintained for police and career armed forces, a practice followed in many countries. It is expected that these benefits will be fully paid for through the appropriate budgets and not cross-subsidized by other parts of the economy, but this should be confirmed.
4/ Namely, benefits based on welfare or other policy considerations (such as minimum pensions or credit for non-contributory periods) rather than on actuarially-based insurance principles.
5/ Or from the unemployment insurance fund for those receiving unemployment insurance benefits.
6/ For example, mothers on maternity leave will accrue credit of one-half of a full point, while students and conscripts accrue 0.3 of a point.

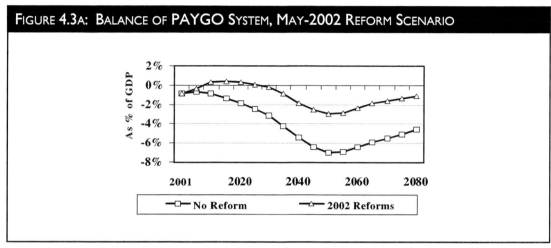

FIGURE 4.3A: BALANCE OF PAYGO SYSTEM, MAY-2002 REFORM SCENARIO

Source: World Bank calculations.

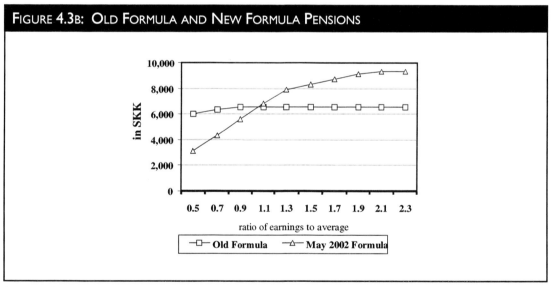

FIGURE 4.3B: OLD FORMULA AND NEW FORMULA PENSIONS

Source: World Bank calculations.

ever, more far-reaching reforms are needed to give the system the kind of financial stability it (and the economy) needs, and to establish the tighter link between benefits and contributions needed to increase support for, and compliance with, the system. In particular, while the reformed system's deficits are much lower (peaking at 2.9 percent of GDP in the base case, rather than at 7 percent without the reforms), *the reformed system's cumulative deficits are still too large to be sustainable.*

Further reforms should also be considered for *the benefit formula, which remains highly redistributive.* While the new formula clearly establishes a closer link between pensions, contributions, and earnings, the link is still rather weak, as are the incentives for compliance. Those earning more than twice the average wage cannot increase their pension and have no incentive to report any higher income. At the other end of the income distribution, those earning less than the average wage will receive lower pensions. Although the initial impact will be mitigated by transition

FIGURE 4.4: BALANCE OF PAYGO SYSTEM, THREE MONO-PILLAR REFORM SCENARIOS

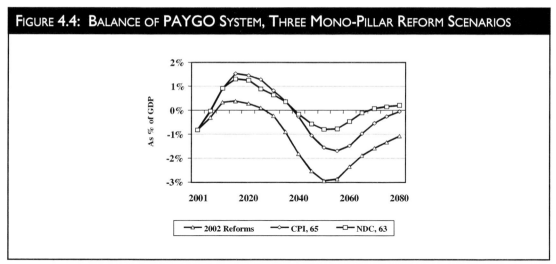

Source: World Bank calculations.

arrangements (a three-year phase-in period, in which new retirees can elect to use the old formula), this group needs to be closely monitored.[77]

Finally, the May 2002 legislation introduced *one new measure that seems to run counter to the overall reform strategy: it reduces the contribution rate for parents by 0.5 percent per child.*[78] This measure will reduce the link between benefits and contributions and is expected to reduce revenues by some SKK 750 million (about 1 percent) per year. *The rationale for this measure is unclear.* It is unlikely to raise the birth rate (presumably one reason for its provision), and there are already adequate, even overly generous, provisions in place for families with children through (i) income tax deductions, (ii) child allowances, and (iii) Social Assistance for low-income families.

Additional First Pillar Reform Required: The May 2002 reform will not be sufficient to bring the public pension system into balance. For that purpose, it will need to be supplemented by a further *increase in the retirement age to 65,* bringing it into line with most EU and OECD countries.[79] This would result in a much lower cumulative system deficit (peaking at 1.7 percent of GDP versus 2.9 percent under the May 2002 reforms: see the "CPI, 65" line in Figure 4.4). Moreover, this option generates substantial surpluses in the early years, making it much easier subsequently to finance the deficit arising from a transition to a fully funded second pillar. Developing a political consensus behind such a measure will be difficult, but it could be possible based on a well-designed public information campaign and combined with a second-pillar reform to generate higher replacement rates.[80]

---

77. It is possible that the new formula could result in a need for significantly higher spending on pension increments to top up very low pensions to the social minimum level. These increments are part of state social benefits (discussed below), funded from the state budget. For the time being, because most workers have long years of service, it does not appear that large numbers will need increments.

78. It is unclear whether this deduction can be claimed by both parents or how it will be administered. It is also unclear if there is an offsetting reduction in pension credit.

79. The projections presented below assume that the retirement age would increase by 6 months per year, starting in 2003.

80. The information campaign could stress how the demographic transition makes such a policy unavoidable if benefit levels are to be maintained close to current replacement rates. Otherwise either benefits will have to be cut or deficits will rise, resulting in inflation and an erosion of the real value of the benefits. Analysis of the key trade-offs involved might also be helpful in reaching consensus.

Several other measures should be considered to complement this reform, including:

(a) Make further changes in the still highly-redistributive benefit formula, by tightening the link between benefits and contributions. This is also likely to improve system finances by increasing compliance.[81]

(b) Make accurate and transparent calculations of the transfers to cover "non-systemic" benefits and ensure that they are fully financed from the state budget.[82] The recent legislation should be amended to require this. Once the costs are transparent, a careful analysis should be conducted to determine if the benefits are worth the costs, particularly regarding the accrual of pension rights by students, and the duration of non-contributory periods for maternity leave.[83] If the explicit transfer of "non-systemic" benefits to the state budget results in significant cost savings to the SIA, these savings should be passed on to the participants by reducing contribution rates.[84]

(c) Establish the instruments needed to monitor the impact of the pension reforms, especially on low-income groups.[85]

(d) Take steps to improve contribution compliance, especially by the self-employed. The steps to reduce contribution rates and tighten the benefit-contribution link will help but should be complemented by improved monitoring and investigation.[86]

(e) Remove the recently adopted provision to reduce parents' pension contributions by 0.5 percent per child. To the extent that there is fiscal space for reducing the contribution rate, make an even reduction for all participants.

Introducing the Second Pillar

This set of reforms to the first pillar will do little to improve the currently low replacement rate of 42 percent. To achieve this would require shifting part of the old-age security system toward a funded system. With that in mind, the May 2002 legislation has established a framework for the introduction of a second, mandatory, fully funded pillar. While the details are still being developed based on additional technical work and analysis, *the current plans*[87] *center on the following features:*

---

81. One option would be to *modify the Defined Benefit formula to allow higher pensions for those earning more than twice the average wage.* This would require either (i) somewhat lower pensions for those who had earned less than twice the average wage, or (ii) somewhat higher system deficits, or some combination of the two. This approach would be more manageable when combined with the increase in the retirement age to 65. A second option, *adopting a Notional Defined Contribution (NDC) framework,* would result in a much tighter benefit-contribution link (and better financial outcomes). Under this approach, contributions are recorded in individual notional accounts, are easily tracked by participants, and benefits are determined by the amount in the account. This approach results in significant cost savings, leading to improved financial balances. As Figure 4.4 illustrates, an NDC reform, combined with a retirement age increase only to 63 (see "NDC, 63" line), produces better financial results than the current DB formula, combined with a retirement age increase to 65 ("CPI, 65" line). Moreover, since the NDC approach adjusts automatically to demographic changes, it produces much more stable results than the DB approach. While the DB approach produces fixed replacement rates, the NDC system gradually adjusts replacement rates either up or down in response to changes in life expectancy and population growth. In the long run, the NDC system will be fiscally stable, while the DB approach will run deficits or surpluses, depending on demographic developments. While the NDC framework results initially in lower replacement rates in these projections, the differences in replacement rates are much less when the NDC is combined with the introduction of a fully funded second pillar (see Figure 4.6b below)

82. Or, in the case of transfers for recipients of unemployment insurance, from the NLO's employment fund.

83. These benefits seem questionable in terms of work incentives and should be reassessed. More "work-friendly" alternatives (such as child care support for working mothers) should be considered.

84. Compensating revenue measures in general taxation may be required.

85. A periodic, nationally representative household budget survey is an essential tool for this purpose.

86. The SBRA project will support improved monitoring and analysis.

87. It should be noted that these "current plans" represent proposals under discussion rather than an agreed policy.

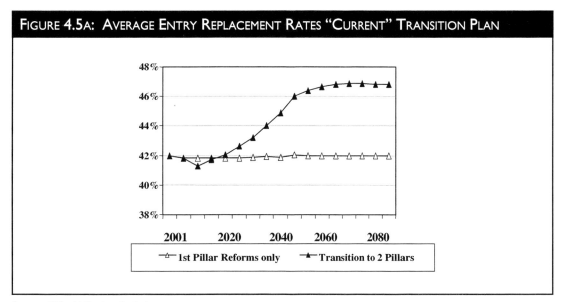

FIGURE 4.5A: AVERAGE ENTRY REPLACEMENT RATES "CURRENT" TRANSITION PLAN

Source: World Bank calculations.

the retirement age and benefit formula would be as defined in the May 2002 first pillar reforms; initially 3.5 percent (and eventually 6 percent) of the 28 percent payroll contribution rate would be redirected to fund the second pillar;[88] and the new system would start in 2004 and be mandatory for all participants under age 50.[89] SKK 65 billion in privatization revenues (about 6.5 percent of GDP) has been set aside to help finance the transitional deficit.

The introduction of the second pillar would create *the opportunity for higher pension benefits.* This would result because the rates of return on the funds in the second pillar are expected to be higher than the GDP, growth rate, the implicit rate of return to a PAYGO system. This assumption is based on the analysis of capital market returns over long periods of time in market economies. Figure 4.5a shows the difference between the replacement rates (average net pension as a percent of average gross wage) with the May 2002 reforms applied only to the first pillar ("first pillar reforms only") compared with those reforms combined with a "transition to two pillars" in the "current proposal" described above. *Replacement rates rise as the second pillar grows, eventually reaching about 47 percent, 5 percentage points higher than with the single pillar reform only.* These projections assume a 2 percent difference between GDP growth and capital market returns. Of course, to the extent that capital market returns approach GDP growth, the difference in the replacement rate from a two-pillar and a mono-pillar system would diminish.

However, *the transition to the second pillar also generates substantial costs over the next four decades,* resulting in substantially worse financial balances than the scenario with the May 2002 reforms applied to the first pillar only. These "transition costs" arise because the contributions to the funded second pillar accounts are not available any longer to meet the continuing liabilities of

---

88. The first pillar PAYGO benefits accrued under the new system would be proportionately reduced to account for the lower contribution rate provided to the PAYGO system. Details of this proportionate reduction must take into account the fact that part of the 28 percent payroll tax will still fund disability and survivors insurance which to date would continue to be part of the first pillar.

89. The introduction could be postponed. The SBRA project establishing a system of individual accounts would need to be in place for the first contributors as all proposals currently in consideration for the administration of the second pillar anticipate that collection be done by the SIA (as is done in Sweden), rather than by individual pension funds (as in Chile, for example).

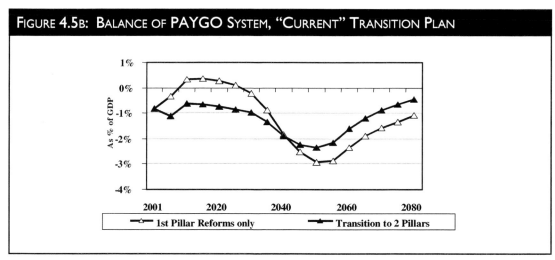

FIGURE 4.5B: BALANCE OF PAYGO SYSTEM, "CURRENT" TRANSITION PLAN

Source: World Bank calculations.

the first pillar; the costs continue until all participants are fully covered by the new system.[90] As an illustration, the size and phasing of these transition costs can be seen in Figure 4.5b as the differences between the system balances (i) under a May 2002 "first pillar reforms only" scenario, and (ii) under a scenario combining those reforms with a "transition to two pillars" as described in the "current plans" above. The transitional scenario increases the system deficit by about one percent of GDP per year for more than 20 years, with the cumulative deficit through 2040 (the year when the deficits of both systems are about equal) on the order of 30–35 percent of GDP. This is clearly much larger than the 6.5 percent of GDP in privatization revenues so far set aside to finance the transition. While the transitional deficit is smaller than that faced by some other countries, and could conceivably be financed through government bonds, *the long-run deficits in the post transition period are dangerously high,* threatening macroeconomic stability and indicating the need for the deeper first pillar reforms discussed above. Indeed, unless the first pillar reforms are deep enough to put the system on a sustainable footing, the transition to a second pillar will only make the system less sustainable.

Additional Reform Options: By modifying the features of the second pillar as currently proposed, and combining this with the stronger first pillar reforms discussed earlier, more attractive reform options can be developed that reduce the transitional deficit to more manageable levels and produce higher replacement rates. Two alternatives are considered below: (i) an increase to a retirement age of 65 years, combined with a requirement that all participants under age 40 (instead of 50) switch to the new system,[91] and an immediate 6 percent contribution to the second pillar (instead of 3.5 percent rising to 6 later),[92] and (ii) an increase to a retirement age of 63 years, combined with an NDC system, a switching age of 40, and a 6 percent second pillar contribution. Figures 4.6a and b

---

90. The costs depend mainly on the retirement age, the size of the second pillar, and the switching strategy through which participants are phased into the new system.

91. Although a fixed cut-off age for participation in the new system is assumed here, it is not necessarily the best policy option, as experience has shown that workers in mid-career may act more favorably toward the reform if they can choose whether to join the new system or remain in the PAYGO plan. These choices can be modeled to assist the government in forecasting the potential fiscal needs of the reform.

92. The alternatives present an immediate increase to the 6 percent contribution rate rather than the phase-in provided in plans under discussion. The reason for this is that the ultimate contribution rate is less likely to be reached with a phase-in. This is already the experience in Hungary. It is likely to be easier to build consensus on a plan that starts with a higher contribution rate and allows choice for middle-aged workers (say between 40 and 50) depending on their preference. However, as discussed below, this also needs to take into account the timing of the country's accession to the EU.

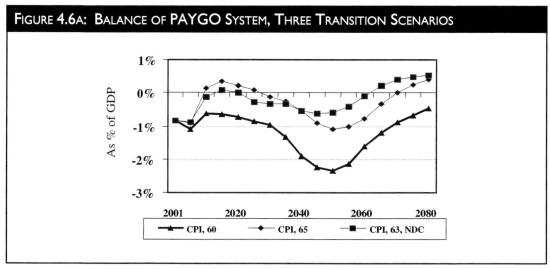

FIGURE 4.6A: BALANCE OF PAYGO SYSTEM, THREE TRANSITION SCENARIOS

Source: World Bank estimates.

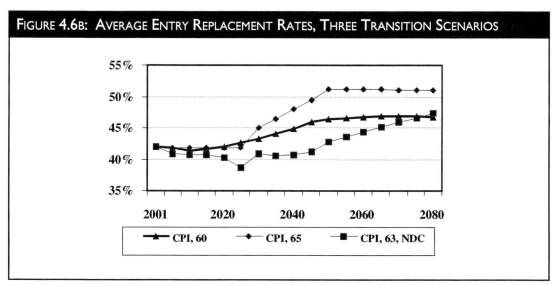

FIGURE 4.6B: AVERAGE ENTRY REPLACEMENT RATES, THREE TRANSITION SCENARIOS

Source: World Bank estimates.

compare the financial balances and replacement rates of these scenarios with those generated by the "transition to two pillars, current plan" scenario in Figures 4.5a and b (here designated as "CPI, 60"). The reduction in the mandatory age for switching to the new system from 50 years to 40 years results in a smaller proportion of contributions being directed toward the new funded system, and hence a smaller initial transitional deficit. Higher retirement ages, of course, reduce the near-term costs of the old PAYGO system even more. While the increased contribution to the new system increases initial transition costs, it also provides the higher rate of return anticipated for the funded system and hence higher pensions for future pensioners. These three parameters can all be changed and all influence the equity, adequacy, and financial stability of the pension system.

The alternative proposals lead to much lower transitional deficits: the "CPI, 65" scenario transition deficit averages 0.2 percent of GDP before it becomes less than the corresponding mono-pillar reform; and the "CPI, 63, NDC" transition deficit averages 0.4 percent. Given the tight fiscal constraints facing the Slovak Republic as it prepares to enter the EU, these alternatives merit serious consideration.

Under each alternative in Figure 4.6b, average replacement rates (and hence pensions) are higher over most of the period than the 42 percent replacement rate under the mono-pillar system.[93] The option that combines the transition to a second pillar with a retirement at age 65, and the DB formula as reformed in May 2002, generates a gradual rise in the average replacement rate to 51 percent of pre-retirement earnings under the base case scenario.

The Third Pillar
The third pillar of private, voluntary, supplementary pensions was introduced in 1996. While it has a substantial number of participants,[94] its asset base in 2002 was only about 0.6 percent of GDP, and distributed pensions are to date miniscule compared with amounts paid out by the public system. Nevertheless, the *third pillar has an important potential role to play, particularly for higher-income workers who want higher replacement rates in retirement, and for those who wish to retire early* (such as groups formerly eligible for privileged pensions[95]). As the May 2002 reforms are further developed and implemented, *it would be useful to review the third pillar's legislative and regulatory framework* to ensure that: (i) the financial management of the funds is adequately supervised; (ii) the tax structure is appropriate;[96] (iii) administrative costs do not become excessive (e.g., through non-transparent subcontracting arrangements by the private companies); and (iv), more generally, the third pillar is well-integrated with the second mandatory pillar so that the multi-pillar system reaches its potential for all participants.

Time Frame
The timing for expanding the funded components of the pension system will need to be judged carefully in the light of capital market developments. As things currently stand, capital markets are not sufficiently developed to absorb a major injection of savings. Central government debt is modest. The nominal value outstanding at the end of 2001 was SKK 366 billion or a modest 37 percent of GDP. The two Slovak securities exchanges, the BSE and the SEE, currently have a rather low level of activity that is likely to continue. The growth in financing of Slovak companies by issuing shares or bonds is likely to be modest. Of the country's larger companies (those most likely to raise funds in the market), an increasing number are foreign-owned. These companies can generally obtain financing from or through their head offices on better terms than in the local market. Nevertheless, as income and household and corporate wealth grow in the Slovak Republic, the demand for stocks and bonds will also grow. However, the desire for portfolio diversification and the ready access to regional, European, and world markets, is likely to limit demand for specifically Slovak instruments significantly. The country's entry into the euro zone, by removing any exchange rate risk within the EU, will compound these effects.

The prospects are for only modest growth in the supply and demand for Slovak market investment instruments and modest trading values for Slovak stocks and bonds. Assuming (realistically) that only Slovak instruments would be listed and traded on the Slovak Republic's exchanges implies low volumes and high trading costs. High trading costs will further reduce the demand for Slovak instruments relative to foreign instruments at the main European exchanges. Similar conditions and factors throughout the region are encouraging the merger of major European exchanges and the development of regional exchanges. The Slovak Republic's imminent admission to the EU

---

93. The NDC plan simulation includes a retirement age of 63. If the retirement age were increased to 65 years, the replacement rate for NDC would be even higher.

94. There were about 320,000 third pillar participants in 2002, but only about 2000 pensions distributed in CY2000.

95. These groups were in occupations considered risky.

96. Normally, with contributions made before tax, accruals tax-free, and taxes paid as pensions are distributed.

and freer access to Europe's exchanges are likely to bring the viability of a separate Slovak exchange, much less two of them, into question.

In the circumstances, it would seem preferable to *time any major shift toward funded schemes with the country's accession to the integrated capital markets of the EU, or even better with the adoption of the euro.*

Administrative and Institutional Issues

The pension reform will require many fundamental changes in the way pensions are administered at all levels. *Getting the appropriate administrative and institutional arrangements in place is as important as getting the right policy framework*, for without adequate management no policies, no matter how sound, can realize their potential. The SBRA project can provide the framework and the technical and financial resources needed to complete the design and implementation of the reforms, including the necessary systems and infrastructure.[97] The administrative arrangements for the *integration of disability pensions*, which appear slated to continue on a PAYGO basis, also need to be considered. Most important, the *management of the second pillar funds* raises significant questions of administrative responsibility for collection, selection of investments and investors, and regulation of pension funds.[98] *It will be essential to strengthen the capacity to regulate and supervise both the second and the third pillar funds, including through measures to develop the Financial Markets Authority.* For example, it will be very important to ensure that the pension fund regulators are expert in the financial operations of pension plans. These administrative underpinnings are still in an early stage of development and steps need to be taken now to ensure these arrangements and a sound regulatory structure are in place as soon as possible.

Pension reform is a process, not a one-time event. Actual outcomes can easily deviate from projections, especially over long time periods. For example, labor market behaviors could change over time in ways that result in fewer workers with long, continuous periods of formal employment. As a result, the share of the population not qualifying for adequate pensions could rise, resulting in an increased need for pension increments funded from the budget. Consequently, *continual monitoring, evaluation, research, and policy development is needed* as circumstances change. Ongoing economic and social developments need to be assessed by the MoLSAF, the SIA, and/or other regulatory agencies on a continuing basis with a professional actuarial office and continuing research and evaluation.[99] *A periodic, nationally representative household survey of income and expenditure would be an essential tool for this analysis* for the MoLSAF, the MoF, other policymakers, and stakeholders, not only for pensions and other social protection programs but also for health, education and many other dimensions of economic and social policy.

Other Social Insurance Programs

The two other main social insurance programs are sickness insurance (SI), administered by SIA, and unemployment insurance (UI), administered by the National Labor Office (NLO), under a tripartite governing board, with overall policy guidance from the MoLSAF. Both of these programs grew significantly in the mid-1990s, but have since stabilized (see Table 4.6). By 2001, spending on both programs was lower as a share of GDP than in 1995. *In SI, however, there appear to be policy options that could improve program effectiveness and/or reduce costs. In particular, there may be opportunities to reduce the payroll tax burden of SI.*

---

97. It can also lay the groundwork for consolidating the collection of contributions for health insurance as well as for the SIA and NLO.

98. In the Slovak Republic's situation, it would seem appropriate that the SIA act as a clearinghouse for contributions, but that fund management be subcontracted to private asset managers or pension funds operating in a sound regulatory framework.

99. The SBRA project also provides assistance in the areas of monitoring, evaluation, and projections.

Sickness and Maternity Leave

The SI program, funded by a 4.8 percent payroll tax, insures mainly against income lost while on sick leave (82 percent of SI spending) and on maternity leave (14 percent).[100] *The SI fund has been running high surpluses* (equivalent to over 40 percent of revenues) in recent years. Until 2002, effective replacement rates were quite high for low income workers,[101] but were subject to a low daily ceiling (equivalent to about two-thirds of the average wage), making them very low for higher income workers.[102] The May 2002 Social Insurance Act introduced several important changes, particularly in the benefit structure: the sick leave benefit is now 55 percent of the assessment base for SI contributions and the assessment base has been raised from SKK 4,400 to 32,000 per month. This should go a long way to correct the previous imbalance in the benefit structure.[103]

The following policy options could be considered for the SI program:

(a) Shifting the burden for financing the first few days of sick leave to employers, thereby giving employers a stronger incentive to monitor sick leave use.[104]

(b) Monitoring SI use by the self-employed with particular care, given the substantial scope for fraud and abuse. Consider withdrawing participation by the self-employed if use is abnormally high.

(c) Returning current and prospective SI fund surpluses to participants by reducing the payroll tax. Preliminary calculations suggest that the tax could be reduced from 4.8 percent to 2.0 percent.[105]

Unemployment Insurance and Employment Programs

The NLO administers both passive UI benefits (including not only payments directly to the insured unemployed, but also contributions that the NLO makes on behalf of UI recipients for pensions,[106] sickness and health insurance), and active labor market programs (ALMPs, including job-matching services, assessment of worker skills, training support, and administration of temporary job creation programs targeted for the unemployed). These programs are financed by a 4 percent payroll tax and, increasingly in recent years, by state budget transfers for ALMPs.

The sharp rise in unemployment toward the end of the 1990s directly affected large numbers of insured workers, leading to a rapid increase in passive UI benefits (from SKK 2.2 billion in 1995 to SKK 7.3 billion in 1999). This was funded in part by drawing on reserves, and in part by cutting back sharply on ALMP spending (which dropped from a peak of SKK 4.3 billion in 1996, to a low of SKK 0.5 billion in 1999). UI benefits peaked in 1999, and subsequently declined, reflecting both a change in labor market dynamics[107] and a tightening of benefits.[108] This, combined with

---

100. Other benefits include limited provisions for care for other family members and certain costs of pregnancy.

101. Seventy percent for the first three days; 90 percent for an unlimited period thereafter.

102. Anecdotal reports suggest that this policy created incentives for low-wage workers to call in sick, but for higher-income workers to use paid holiday leave when ill, rather than sick leave.

103. It is not clear, however, that the increase in the assessment base is adequate to cover the potentially higher payments.

104. This should help contain costs, making the proposed reduction in the payroll tax less risky.

105. In 2001, the surplus was nearly 42 percent of contributions. This is equivalent to 2 percent of payroll. Before reducing the payroll tax, there is a need to ensure that the new benefit policy does not reduce this surplus, and that offsetting revenue adjustments, if necessary, can be made. See also *2002 Annual Review-Slovak Republic*, OECD, para 118, which makes a similar recommendation.

106. See OECD, *op.cit*, para 80, which argues that such pension contributions should be discontinued.

107. Since the mid-1990s, an increasing share of the unemployed have either exhausted their UI benefits (by remaining unemployed for more than 6 months) and have become eligible for Social Assistance (see below), or are new entrants to the labor force who have not yet qualified for UI. Thus, UI payments have declined, despite high continuing unemployment rates.

108. The benefit levels (replacement rates) were reduced in 1999, as was the duration of benefits for some workers.

substantial state budget transfers specifically for ALMPs, has permitted a major recovery in spending for such programs, though not to the earlier levels.[109] Spending on these programs should be carefully monitored and based on rigorous assessment of program effectiveness. While such programs are often popular, their real results are as often in question. Moreover, a previous World Bank analysis suggested that ALMPs were not as well targeted as other programs.[110] Opportunities for coordination with Social Assistance should be explored.

Following amendments in 1999, *UI eligibility provisions, benefit levels, and duration are generally reasonable and are not overly generous* compared with those of other countries. With longer spells of unemployment, a larger proportion of the Slovak Republic's unemployed exhausted their UI benefits, so that by 2000 fewer than one in four unemployed were UI beneficiaries. Most unemployed workers ineligible for UI benefits, however, receive payments from the Social Assistance program, subject to a means test. It is this program that is likely to create work disincentives (discussed below in the section on Social Assistance).

During 2000, the NLO was charged with administering another program, the *guarantee fund*, which was established to compensate workers dislocated by plant closings and downsizing for wage arrears. This was reportedly a requirement to bring the country's programs into harmony with those of the EU. The fund is financed in equal parts by a 0.25 percent payroll tax and funding from the state budget. The financing rules are unclear as there is no experience with which to determine the appropriate tax rate or the design of the compensation package.

Policy options for the employment programs could focus on the following:

(a) *Continued assessment of ALMPs*, to concentrate spending on the most effective, well-targeted programs.[111]
(b) The development of transparent procedures for using the guarantee fund to facilitate restructuring in a non-distortionary way.
(c) *Close monitoring of the unemployed*, including recipients of both UI and Social Assistance to ensure that the programs are well coordinated.

Social Welfare Programs

The main social welfare programs fall into two groups: State Social Benefits, including mainly child and parent allowances and pension increments; and Social Assistance and social care, including cash and in-kind benefits for the poor and disabled. There is also a housing assistance program, whose expenditures are relatively insignificant to date. All of these programs are financed from the state budget. *Spending on the welfare programs as a group is substantial, and has risen from SKK 22.7 billion in 1995 to SKK 36.2 billion in 2001 (see Table 4.6). As a share of GDP, however, welfare program spending has been relatively stable, ranging between 3.6 and 4.0 percent of GDP since 1995,* with a gradual decline in State Social Benefits as a percent of GDP (by about 1 percent), offset by a rise in Social Assistance. *These programs play a significant role in reducing poverty in the Slovak Republic: an earlier World Bank study found that without these programs the poverty rate in 1996 would have been 18.6 percent instead of the actual 10.1 percent.* However, the study also found that the non-poor receive a significant share of social transfers, while some 20 percent of the poor receive no benefits.[112] Moreover, the study found that *the programs significantly reduced incentives to work, creating a major risk of trapping recipients in poverty.*[113] For these reasons, combined with the fact these programs use a substantial amount of

---

109. Spending on ALMPs was SKK 2.2 billion in 2001.

110. "Social Protection," in *The Slovak Republic: Social Sector Expenditure Review*, World Bank, 2002.

111. Possibly in coordination with activity testing for Social Assistance (see below).

112. World Bank, *Slovak Republic: Living Standards, Employment, and Labor Market Study* (2001), p.16–17.

113. *Ibid.*, pp. 69–98.

TABLE 4.7: STATE SOCIAL BENEFITS
(SKK billions)

	1995	1996	1997	1998	1999	2000	2001
Main Components							
Child Allowances	10.0	10.0	9.1	9.9	9.2	8.7	8.4
Parent Benefits	2.5	2.8	4.1	4.5	4.4	4.3	4.2
Social and Wives' Pension	0.3	0.3	0.3	0.3	0.3	0.3	0.3
Pension Increments	1.1	1.3	1.2	1.3	1.3	1.3	1.5
Birth and Death Grants	0.2	0.2	0.3	0.3	0.3	0.3	0.0
Spa Care	0.9	1.1	1.3	1.3	1.3	1.0	0.9
Total Spending (SKK billion)	**15.1**	**15.7**	**16.3**	**17.6**	**16.8**	**16.0**	**15.2**
Total as % of GDP	**2.65**	**2.50**	**2.30**	**2.27**	**2.01**	**1.76**	**1.54**

Source: SIA and MoF.

the country's scarce budget resources, these programs deserve careful analysis to identify ways to contain their costs, improve their targeting and effectiveness in helping the poor, and ensure they provide adequate work incentives. In this way the programs could better support a sustainable strategy for growth with equity.

State Social Benefits
Table 4.7 shows the main components of State Social Benefits. *The overall level of spending has been fairly stable,* in part reflecting the impact of declining birth rates on the largest spending component, child allowances. *However, this could change:* recent changes making the child allowances available to all parents, and the changes in the pension formula (discussed above), could cause spending on child allowances and pension increments to rise.

The recent decision to make *child allowances*[114] available to all parents seems problematic for several reasons. First, *the allowances do nothing to help the very poor, as their social assistance benefits are reduced by the amount of the allowances, leaving their net income unchanged.* Second, while there could be a justification to provide assistance to a segment of low income families who earn too much to benefit from Social Assistance (as the previous policy did), *there is no clear reason to pay subsidies to the upper quintile of the population* (as the new policy does), since these families can care adequately for their children without such support. Third, the decision appears to have been taken without a careful analysis of its impact on costs, or an analysis of how the resources could be used more effectively to help the poor.[115] *The new policy could raise costs significantly, while doing nothing for the poor.*[116]

---

114. Child allowances had been paid to families with incomes below twice the MSL that had children under 15 (the compulsory school attendance age), full-time students up to age 28, or severely handicapped children up to 18.

115. An earlier version of the new policy that was not adopted would have restricted the allowance to a maximum of 3 children. This could have had very negative consequences, especially for low income families not eligible for Social Assistance, since families with more than three children are far more likely to be needy than smaller families. They are also much more likely to be Roma as Roma families are much larger than the national average. An analysis of the 1996 Microcensus found that while families with three or more children represented only 6.3 percent of the population, they accounted for 18.1 percent of the poor (World Bank, . . . *Labor Market Study*, p.14). The children in such families are most in need of assistance if they are to break out of a cycle of poverty.

116. This is another issue for which an up-to-date household budget survey would be an indispensable analytical tool.

TABLE 4.8: SOCIAL ASSISTANCE AND SOCIAL CARE
(SKK billions)

	1995	1996	1997	1998	1999	2000	2001
Main Components							
Cash Assistance	4.8	4.5	4.6	6.4	9.6	11.6	12.3
for Unemployed	4.1	3.9	4.2	5.8	8.8	10.5	11.2
Other	0.7	0.6	0.5	0.6	0.8	1.1	1.1
Support for Disabilities	0.7	1.1	1.3	1.6	2.1	2.9	3.6
Institutional Care	2.1	2.3	3.1	3.1	3.5	4.1	5.1
Total Spending (in SKK billion)	**7.6**	**7.9**	**9.2**	**11.3**	**15.7**	**18.6**	**21.0**
Total as % of GDP	**1.34**	**1.26**	**1.30**	**1.46**	**1.88**	**2.05**	**2.12**

Source: MLSAF and MoF.

A thorough review of State Social Benefits appears warranted, possibly focusing on the following issues:

(a) *Child allowances: Consideration should be given to restoring the income test for this benefit.* This could be followed with an analysis of *alternative payment options* that could reduce costs or improve poverty focus (e.g., ending the student benefit after the completion of secondary school;[117] and/or reducing the benefit per child as numbers of children rise (recognizing the economies of scale in larger families)). If, instead, a universal child allowance is retained, additional options should be identified to contain costs (e.g., limiting the benefit only to younger children; or reducing the benefit levels for older children). In this case, child allowances should be made subject to the income tax, to reduce this policy's negative impact on income distribution.

(b) *Parent allowances* should continue to be subject to an income test; it would also be useful to explore alternatives that might encourage a return to work, such as an option to convert this allowance into a targeted child day-care subsidy.

(c) *Pension increments:* The forthcoming pension reforms and labor market trends should be monitored and analyzed to assess their impact on the size and distribution of pension increments, and to identify policy responses as needed.

(d) *Spa Care:* The objectives of this benefit should be carefully and its impact on poverty should be carefully reassessed to determine if there are other, more effective uses of scarce public resources (e.g., to fund a tapered withdrawal of Social Assistance benefits as discussed below).

Social Assistance and Social Care
Social Assistance and social care programs provide the most vulnerable members of Slovak society with cash benefits and a range of in-kind services. Social Assistance is paid to families deemed to be in material need. Many persons with disabilities receive in-kind services, while those with the most severe handicaps receive care in institutional settings. Financial assistance is paid through the budget and administered at the local level through the administrative arm of the Ministry of the Interior. MoLSAF sets policy. Table 4.8 shows the overall growth and changing composition of expenditures: *total spending has grown sharply, from SKK 7.5 billion (or 1.3 percent of GDP) in 1995 to SKK 21 billion (or 2.1 percent of GDP) in 2001;* spending on *disabilities* has jumped more

---

117. Instead, as proposed in the education section, a system of scholarships and loans is likely to be a more effective way to finance higher education.

than 400 percent, increasing its share in these programs from less than 10 percent to more than 17 percent; and *cash assistance for the unemployed,* by far the largest program component, has grown by nearly 30 percent per year since 1995.

The sharp rise in spending to assist those with *disabilities* is particularly startling since the underlying population of severely handicapped persons does not change much over short periods. Among the various categories of spending to assist the disabled, spending on motor vehicles (purchases, upkeep, repair, and use) has shown the most rapid growth. *A detailed analysis of spending, especially on motor vehicles, is likely to identify ways to reduce excess spending for these services.*

The rapid increase in *cash assistance for the unemployed* is more understandable: this category of Social Assistance continues to carry the main fiscal burden of assistance for the unemployed following the rapid increase in unemployment since the mid-1990s. This includes both workers who have exhausted their UI benefits (after 6 months for most workers), as well as new entrants to the labor force (a population age group that is still growing, and which has the highest unemployment rates). Between 1995 and 2000, *almost all (93 percent) of the 80 percent growth in cash assistance recipients was due to unemployed recipients,* and consisted almost entirely (90 percent) of individuals or couples without dependent children. In 2000, the total number of Social Assistance recipients was 313,000; including their dependants, the total number of beneficiaries was 611,000, or about 12 percent of the population.

Cash assistance benefit levels are set in reference to the Minimum Subsistence Level (MSL),[118] with fixed amounts specified for an individual/head of household, for a second adult, and for each dependent child.[119] Cash assistance is intended to close the gap between these amounts and the family's actual income. If the family/individual needs assistance for "objective" reasons (i.e., is involuntarily unemployed and unable to find work despite search efforts), the benefits are based on the full amounts specified. After receiving assistance for 24 months for "objective" reasons, the amount specified for the household head is reduced by half,[120] with other amounts remaining the same, and continues indefinitely. If the reasons are "subjective" (i.e., voluntarily leaving a job and/or not accepting job offers), the amount specified for the household head is reduced by half from the start, with other amounts remaining unchanged. Until the start of 2001, unemployed school leavers had been granted full cash assistance benefits; since then, however, they have been deemed in "subjective" need and their benefit levels reduced by half.

As noted earlier, in some ways this system, in concert with other social benefits, has served the country well, helping it to reduce poverty significantly and to deal with a rapid rise in unemployment. However, *the system has an unintended effect of reducing incentives to work, owing to both the level and the structure of benefits. This creates a serious risk of a "poverty trap" and the development of a long-term culture of poverty that could be very difficult to rectify.* On the *benefit levels,* several analyses[121] have noted that the benefits are high relative to the average wage, and especially so for larger families. To cite a recent OECD report:

> "High benefit levels raise the reservation wage for the unemployed. In particular, specialized workers displaced by industrial restructuring are unlikely to accept lower wages in low-skill occupations. . . . families with two or more children that have no income receive cash benefits (which are not taxed) exceeding the average production worker's net wage. For a family with four children, benefits are 37 percent higher than the average net wage."[122]

---

118. The link between the MSL and benefit levels may have been reduced lately, as benefit levels have remained constant since 2000, while the MSL has risen in line with prices.

119. The amount for a given family increases by a fixed amount per child, with no upper limit.

120. Reportedly, three months of employment in public works is sufficient to re-entitle such persons to full benefits.

121. See in particular OECD, 2002 Annual Review–Slovak Republic, Chapter III, and World Bank, *Slovak Republic: Living Standards, Employment, and Labor Market Study* (2001), Chapter 3.

122. OECD, *op. cit.,* p. 46.

Moreover, the *benefit levels are uniform for the country, and thus do not take into account the considerable cost of living variations* across different regions. It is quite possible this makes work incentives the weakest in the poorest parts of the country.

Since the *benefit structure* provides benefits net of other income, *any income earned by the family is effectively taxed away by reductions in benefits,* until earned income exceeds the initial benefit level. Since the earned income is subject to the income tax, families receiving Social Assistance can be subject to a marginal tax rate in excess of 100 percent.[123] This combination of high benefit levels and high marginal tax on earnings from work substantially undermines work incentives.

Given the important role that these programs play in reducing poverty, policy reforms in this area should be approached with care and based on careful analysis. In some cases a balance may need to be struck between short-term, static effects which might raise poverty (or program expenditures) in the short run, and longer run dynamic benefits in moving families out of dependence on welfare and into productive employment. Policymakers should look for reform options that will help "make work pay" and will help reduce the numbers of welfare recipients over time.[124] If such reforms are not undertaken, there is a serious risk that a culture of poverty and welfare dependence will emerge and become increasingly difficult to correct.

Policy options to consider include the following:

(a) *Measures to adjust the benefit level* and widen the distance to the average wage,[125] in particular: (i) either *adjusting the benefit level to reflect the regional cost of living differences,* or calculating the benefit level excluding Bratislava;[126] (ii) *reducing the per child allowance as the numbers of children increase* (to reflect the economies of scale in larger families); and (iii) *adjusting benefit levels for individuals for consumption shared with their families* (for example, by treating housing provided by families to adult children as implicit income, and reducing the child's benefits concomitantly).

(b) Measures to adjust the benefit structure to "make employment pay," including: (i) allowing recipients to keep a portion of earned income by tapering the reduction in benefits;[127] (ii) ensuring that *the* program's activity tests are strictly enforced and, if they are not met, reducing benefits accordingly; (iii) identifying and adopting more effective approaches to activity testing as cited by OECD;[128] (iv) using AMLP funds to reduce work-related costs (e.g., targeted subsidies for child care); and, (v) engaging Social Assistance offices more actively in assisting clients, especially Roma clients, with job searches, interviews, and training.[129]

(c) Measures to restrict *access* to benefits for groups not in evident need, in particular, reassessing the need for benefits to school leavers.

---

123. Moreover, if both adults work, the household loses its child allowances. World Bank, *op. cit.,* pp. 121.

124. *Ibid.,* pp. 96–97

125. Attempting to widen this differential by such measures as raising the minimum wage would be counterproductive, as this would introduce an additional rigidity into the labor market, artificially putting upward pressure on wages, thus reducing employment. OECD, *op. cit.,* pp. 56.

126. Standards of living and prices for all goods are considerably higher in Bratislava than elsewhere. In fact, studies indicate that living standards in the capital are equivalent to those in Western Europe.

127. In the short run, this would raise program costs; over time it should lower them by reducing numbers of recipients. The short run costs could be financed from savings in other areas (e.g., spa care, or some of the proposed reductions in benefit levels).

128. OECD, *op. cit.,* pp. 47–48. The report cites in particular successful programs in Australia and the United States. Another option to consider is making the allocation per child conditional on full time school attendance.

129. This could require a reorientation of social workers to work more effectively with Roma clients. Relationships between Roma and Social Assistance workers were found to be more contentious than relations with other social service providers. World Bank, *et. al., Poverty and Welfare of Roma in the Slovak Republic* (Bratislava, 2002), pp. 44.

Housing Subsidy Program

The housing subsidy program[130] should be carefully reviewed and possibly phased out. Begun in 2000 and intended to help low-income consumers meet rent and utility costs, it has grown slowly, reaching only 52,000 households in 2001, and involving relatively low levels of spending to date (about SKK 0.7 billion in 2001). However, this could change rapidly as utility rates move toward market levels in 2003 to 2005, and as the calculated minimum housing costs used to determine benefits are revised.[131] There is thus a substantial risk that *the program could become a significant drain on public resources.*

A second problem is that *it is unclear that this program benefits many of the poor.* Since benefits from the program are netted out of Social Assistance benefits, there appears to be no net gain for recipients of Social Assistance. Moreover, the documentation requirements are too difficult for many low-income households, and especially the Roma, to meet.[132] *A third problem is the program's potential impact on the housing market:* it could set an effective floor, raising prices at the low end of the market as landlords learn the available benefit levels. This could have an adverse effect on Social Assistance recipients and, by putting upward pressure on real estate prices generally, on others as well.

The country's extensive and well-developed Social Assistance system should be adequate to cope with increases in housing (and other) costs, and it would appear to make more sense to use the mechanisms in that system to adjust for the price changes.[133] Then the current housing subsidy could be phased out. *Given the importance of the Roma housing problem, and its links to their integration into the country's broader economic and social life,[134]* consideration should be given to targeting any housing subsidies for use as part of a broader strategy to encourage the Roma to move into integrated communities, better linked to job markets and social services.

Main Recommendations

This review of the Slovak Republic's social protection system highlights its comprehensive and complex nature, and its importance both in terms of using public resources and in terms of reducing poverty and securing the welfare of the people. In considering the reform of such a system, it is important that reforms be based on sound technical analysis within a holistic view of the relationships among the programs and their impact on the people, especially the poor. This review cannot provide that analysis; rather, it points to what appear to be the main problem areas and options for significant reforms.

The first item in developing the reform agenda is designating a highly qualified team responsible for conducting the technical analysis and consensus building essential to an effective reform strategy. In some areas, for example pension reform, much work has already been done, though more effort is needed to work out detailed provisions and implementation plans and operating procedures. Almost all areas of policy reform would benefit greatly from the kinds of information that could be provided by a well-designed, nationally representative household budget survey, carried out at regular intervals. Establishing a routine system for monitoring program impacts, and for assessing these against program spending, could develop into an ongoing process of developing reforms to improve program effectiveness and rebalance spending allocations so as to make the best use of public resources. The SBRA project can provide the resources for strengthening these systems and capacities. The program-specific priorities for social protection reform that emerge from this review are outlined below.

---

130. This section draws extensively on NERA, *Alleviation of Social Impacts of Energy Tariff Rationalization in the Slovak Republic*, (June 2002).

131. Reportedly, these needed to be raised by 24 percent already in 2002 to reflect cost increases. *Ibid.*

132. Includes deed or lease and records that utility payments are up-to-date. *Ibid.*, pp. 26–27.

133. While keeping or increasing the differential with average wages. If this approach proves insufficiently flexible, some of the alternatives in the NERA report (notably a targeted lifeline electricity tariff and natural gas benefit for low-income customers) should be considered as interim measures.

134. World Bank, *Slovak Republic: Living Standards, Employment, and Labor Market Study,* pp. 105 and 108–9.

In pension reform, the important start made in the May 2002 Social Insurance Act needs to be maintained and pushed further. Of the various possible reforms, none would have greater impact, or be harder to achieve, than *raising the pension age to 65.* The impact that this reform would have on increasing the fiscal security of the country's pension system (and macro economy) is clear in the figures presented here and cannot be overestimated. Combining this with an NDC approach would further enhance the stability of the system by reducing its exposure to shocks, and would tighten the link between benefits and contributions. Combining these reforms with *a transition to a second pillar* would allow a gradual rise in replacement rates.

Other pension reform measures to consider include: (i) accurately and *transparently accounting for "non-systemic" benefits, and funding them fully from the state budget (while rigorously assessing their cost effectiveness, and reducing them where warranted);* (ii) *closely monitoring contribution compliance, especially by the self-employed;* (iii) *reversing the recent policy that allows parents to reduce their pension contribution by 0.5 percent per child;* and (iv) *passing any savings from these measures on to participants in the form of a reduction in the payroll tax.*

Options related to the current plans for the *second pillar* include: (i) *moving immediately to the ultimate second pillar contribution rate of 6 percent,* instead of raising it in stages; and/or (ii) *lowering the age for switching to the new system from the currently proposed 50 to 40* (and possibly allowing workers between certain ages a choice of system).

The key areas to consider for *adapting administrative and institutional arrangements to the new system* include: (i) *integrating the disability pensions;* (ii) strengthening the *regulatory system* for managing the funds in the second and third pillars; and (iii) reinforcing the *capacity for ongoing program monitoring and policy analysis.*

For **sickness insurance,** the main options to consider are to return the surplus currently being generated in this fund to participants by *reducing the payroll tax (possibly by as much as 2 percent);* and to contain the pressure on spending by having employers (instead of the fund) pay for the first few days of sick leave.

For **unemployment insurance,** the option to consider is *keeping active labor market programs under close review and assessment to ensure their cost effectiveness* and to identify ways in which they can *work in tandem with Social Assistance* to move people off the welfare rolls.

For **state social benefits,** the major option to consider is *reversing the recent changes in the child allowance,* by making the allowance available for more than 3 children and subjecting recipients again to an income test. Various options for modifying the level and structure of the benefit could also be considered. If the universal child allowance is retained, it should be subject to the income tax. Spending to subsidize *spa care* could be reassessed to determine if there are not more effective uses of funds to improve social protection (e.g., to fund tapering withdrawal of Social Assistance benefits as recipients earn income).

For **Social Assistance and social care,** reforms should focus on *cash assistance for the unemployed.* The main areas for consideration are (i) *reductions in the benefit levels* (to widen the gap between benefits and average wages); and (ii) adjustments in the benefit structure to "make employment pay" (mainly by *reducing the rate of withdrawal of benefits* as recipients earn income; strictly *enforcing activity tests,* and developing more effective ones, possibly linked to ALMPs). *Strengthening the capacity of Social Assistance staff to conduct activity testing and to work effectively with the Roma could also be important.* It would make sense to analyze the rapid increase in *spending for disabilities,* particularly for motor vehicles, given the unusually large increase in this spending category.

For **housing subsidies,** the main option to consider is *terminating the program,* relying on Social Assistance (or specific energy-related benefits targeted for low income consumers) to meet the needs of the poor in this area. However, it may make sense to develop a subsidized housing program as part of a larger *strategy to integrate the Roma more effectively in the economic and social life of the country.*

In all of these areas, *close attention needs to be paid to the impact of reforms on the poor in general and the Roma in particular.* This highlights the need for systematic household budget surveys and for fieldwork by social workers to understand the evolving issues facing their clients.

Health

Despite more than a decade of frequent and continuing reforms, and despite some improvements in the Slovak Republic's health indicators, health care remains beset by serious problems.[135] *First, the health care system does not appear to be financially sustainable.* Demands on the system have risen rapidly, bringing public spending to levels that are high relative to the country's income level. The payroll tax rate for health (14 percent) is the highest in the region, yet the system runs persistent deficits, reflecting a very broad benefit package, unconstrained demands, inadequate revenue growth, and inefficiencies in the provision of care. Efforts to contain public spending have resulted in a rise in formal and informal private payments, as well as in large and growing payment arrears throughout the system. Substantial infusions of extrabudgetary privatization revenues have been used to reduce the levels of debt from time to time, but the underlying imbalances that caused them remain, with system-wide arrears approaching 2 percent of GDP by March 2002. The country's multiple Health Insurance Companies (HICs) may only add to the problems by increasing administrative costs and fragmentation.

Second, *the existing health infrastructure continues to rely heavily on relatively costly, input-intensive approaches,* with too much emphasis on costly in-patient care and specialist physicians. Little progress has been made in realizing the substantial scope for improved effectiveness and efficiency through less intensive input use and a shift toward more cost-effective preventive and out-patient approaches. The incentives in the system do not appear adequate to reduce overstaffing and excess numbers of hospital beds and facilities. *Unsurprisingly, there appears to be widespread dissatisfaction with the health care system both among patients and among health care providers,* with concerns ranging from declining quality, denial of service, and rising informal payments, to low salaries for medical personnel. Surveys have shown that *more than half of households and public officials viewed the health care system as having "very widespread" corruption,* the highest level of perceived corruption of any public sector activity.

The fact that many other countries share these symptoms does not make them easier to diagnose and cure. Without substantial reform, these problems are only likely to get worse: demands on the system will rise as incomes rise, yet resources will become more constrained as the numbers of employees, the system's main contributors, decline relative to the elderly, whose health care costs are much higher (some 2.5 times) than those of the rest of the population. Over time, these problems are likely to compromise the quality of health care, particularly in the vitally important and cost-effective areas of disease prevention and health promotion, and to result in an erosion of the health of the population. While there are no ready-made solutions, the most productive areas for short- and medium-term action and reforms appear to include the following:

(a) *Containing the excess demand inherent in the system* by narrowing the scope of the benefit package, tightening the link between contributions and benefits, and increasing cost sharing by consumers, with safeguards for those with low incomes.

(b) *Reforming the health financing mechanism,* to make it more efficient, to improve collection compliance, and to broaden its revenue base.

(c) *Further developing provider payment mechanisms and other health system incentives* to encourage more efficient resource use and more effective treatment approaches.

(d) Ensuring that the system has adequate incentives and funding for essential public health functions, including cost effective programs to prevent sickness and promote good health practices.

(e) *Protecting* access *and equity* for all groups in the country.

---

135. This section draws heavily on "The Health Sector" in *The Slovak Republic: Social Sector Expenditure Review,* mimeo, World Bank 2002. For concise reviews of past health reforms and outstanding issues, see also R. Kovac and S. Hlavacka. "Transformation of Health Care," *The Slovak Republic- Decade of Independence* (conference at the University of Ottawa, June 6, 2002), and P. Pazitny and R. Zajac, *Strategia reformy zdravotnictva—realnej reformy pre obcana,* (MESA 10, Bratislava, 2001).

Sectoral Overview and Issues

For more than a decade, the Slovak Republic has sought to transform a highly centralized, Soviet-style health system, funded and operated by the state, into a more pluralistic approach with a mix of public and private providers and more diverse financing sources, based on a Western European model of mandatory social insurance embodying strong solidarity principles. Virtually all payments for patient care take place through the multiple Health Insurance Companies (HICs), which receive contributions from salaried employees, from the self-employed, and from the government (on behalf of the rest of the population).[136] The premiums collected by the HICs are pooled and then redistributed among the HICs based on the number and age composition of their clients.[137] The government, through the Ministry of Health (MoH), retains broad powers over the health care system. On the expenditure side, through negotiations with providers, it defines the annual volume and most prices of reimbursed services and drugs, as well as the provider payment mechanisms and pay scales for medical personnel. On the contribution side, it sets payroll tax rates for contributions, its own level of contributions on behalf of the economically non-active, and the redistribution of contributions among the HICs. *The transformation of the health system is thus far from complete, and the transitional system faces serious problems.* These problems are most evident in the areas of the financing and efficiency of individual health care.

Unconstrained Demand

In its simplest terms, the basic problem confronting policymakers is how to provide an appropriate level of health care services to the population within the available resource envelope. The Constitution and the associated legislation guarantees a very broad range of health services at no, or very little, direct cost to patients.[138] Patients thus have had little incentive to limit their use of health services. Not surprisingly, this has led to a very rapid increase in demands on the system, with hospital admission rates and per capita outpatient visits rising by about 18 and 20 percent, respectively, between 1990 and 1999. Reflecting these rising demands, spending increased rapidly (Figures 4.7 and 4.8), rising by one-third as a percentage of GDP between 1991 and 1999. Public spending on health averaged about 5.8 percent of GDP in the second half of the 1990s—more than 1 percent of GDP higher than the average for other CEECs,[139] and more than 2.5 percent of GDP higher than the average for upper middle income countries.

Faced with this relentless growth in health spending, the government has actively tried to contain rising costs and to achieve a better balance between spending and contributions, by making various changes in provider payment mechanisms and by raising contribution rates. To date, however, these changes have not produced the sustained results desired. Changes in the provider payment mechanism in 1996, for example, placed ceilings on the per treatment day payments to hospitals. While this (along with other measures) led to a pause in public expenditure growth in 1997 and 1998, the pressures for increased health services spilled over into arrears to and from providers, and into a growth in informal private payments to ensure service delivery. From 1998 to 2001, growth in public spending on health accelerated to over 10 percent per annum, as the

---

136. There are now 5 HICs (down from 12 in 1996), dominated by the state-owned General Health Insurance Corporation (GHIC) which covers about 70 percent of the market. Government transfers referred to here include those transfers from the NLO for the unemployed receiving unemployment insurance benefits as well as state budget transfers.

137. The redistribution formula is intended to equalize each company's revenues per risk-weighted enrollee. It implies a large cross-subsidy between the HICs that have a younger, employed clientele and the HICs that have an older, economically non-active clientele.

138. Exceptions include dentistry, which involves significant co-payments, some types of elective surgery, and a relatively small portion (about 6–10 percent) of drug costs.

139. Data from "Expenditure Policies towards EU Accession," World Bank (Technical Paper, forthcoming). While these data and those in Figure 4.8 are somewhat different from the WHO data in Figure 4.7 (in order to reflect differences in data consolidation methods and to be consistent across countries), they show very similar trends.

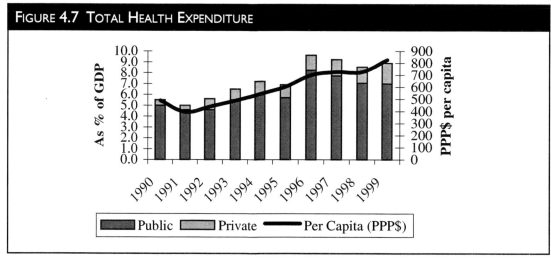

FIGURE 4.7 TOTAL HEALTH EXPENDITURE

Source: WHO and WDI.

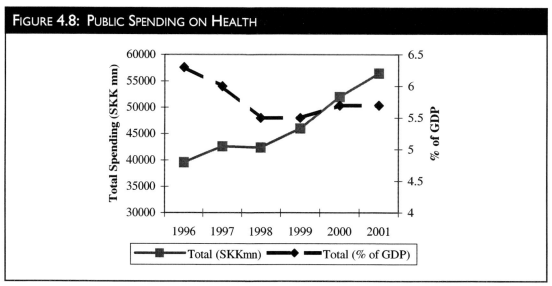

FIGURE 4.8: PUBLIC SPENDING ON HEALTH

Source: MoF.

ceilings were relaxed and large pay increases for medical personnel worked their way through the system.

Problematic Financing System

This rapid growth in spending has placed severe strains on health finances, as shown in Figures 4.9 and 4.10.[140] As a result, extrabudgetary contributions have grown rapidly from almost nothing to

---

140. Figure 4.9 shows the growth in total health spending by major source. The bulk (about 85 percent) of public spending, and most of its increase, was from HICs, and represents transfers to providers for individual health care. Direct State Budget spending was less than 7 percent of public health spending, and has not contributed much to total spending growth. Most of this (over 70 percent) pays for capital investments in state-owned hospitals, leaving less than 2 percent of public spending on health available for all other MoH functions, including public health activities.

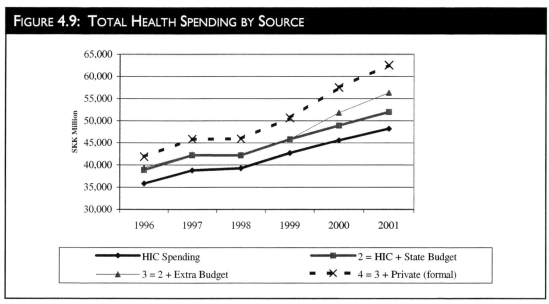

FIGURE 4.9: TOTAL HEALTH SPENDING BY SOURCE

Source: MoH & MoF.

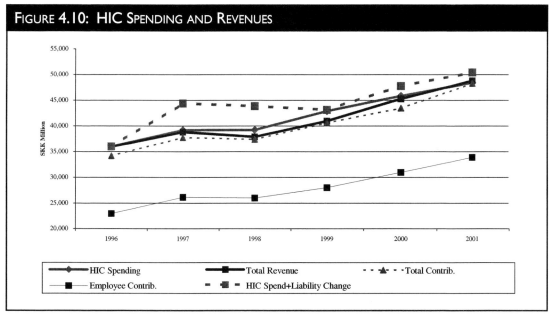

FIGURE 4.10: HIC SPENDING AND REVENUES

Source: MoF & MoH.

over 7 percent of health spending in 2001. These extrabudgetary contributions appear mainly to be transfers of privatization receipts from the National Property Fund to pay down health system arrears and liabilities. *This use of non-recurring revenues to fund what appear to be recurring expenditures, combined with the continuing growth of health system arrears, is a clear indication of the weakness of health system finances.*[141]

---

141. By March, 2002, the arrears of health care providers had risen to SKK 18.9 billion, nearly 2 percent of GDP.

Figure 4.9 also illustrates another important development in the financing of the country's health system: *private payments have risen rapidly,* from less than 6 percent of total health spending in 1996 to over 10 percent in 2001. Moreover, these data capture only the *formal* private payments (for legally mandated co-payments) recorded in government statistics. It is likely that *total* private spending, including *informal* quasi-legal payments, is two to three times this amount.[142] *In addition to being a symptom of excess demand for health care, the growth in informal private payments raises questions about the equity of the system and its accessibility for the poor, and appears to be one of the major sources of dissatisfaction with the system.*

A closer analysis of the finances of the HICs highlights some additional aspects of the underlying financial problems. First, *HIC spending has been greater than revenues, resulting in substantial cash deficits in some years* (see Figure 4.10). These deficits become even larger on an accrual basis once changes in HIC liabilities are added in (top line in Figure 4.10).

Second, employee contributions, which generate nearly 70 percent of HIC revenues (from some 36 percent of the population),[143] have not narrowed their gap with expenditures, despite the increase in the mandatory payroll contribution rate to 14 percent in 2001.[144] The reasons for this are sharply different for the salaried workers and the self-employed. *The contributions of salaried workers, who make up about 28 percent of the population, appear roughly in line with their mandated contribution rate.*[145] *The picture is quite different for the self-employed, whose implied contribution rates average about 3.6 percent, suggesting a very large element of non-compliance by the self-employed, involving annual revenue losses on the order of SKK 2–3 billion.*[146] This problem is all the more serious since the self-employed are a growing share of the labor force. *Incentives for the HICs to improve collection from either the self-employed or delinquent firms, however, are blunted by the redistribution of HIC revenues described above.* Moreover, the self-employed have little incentive to keep their contributions current either, since there are no systematic checks of patient contribution records or sanctions for delinquent payment.

For this and other reasons, *the current multiplicity of HICs does not appear to play a useful role at this stage in the evolution of the country's health system.* HIC functions are limited to the collection of contributions and to payments to providers as specified by the MoH. They inevitably duplicate each other, collecting in the same firms for different clients, and making payments to the same providers for their MoH-determined share of services.

Third, government payments on behalf of the more than 60 percent of the population that is unemployed or not economically active generate less than 30 percent of HIC revenues.[147] *This indicates a*

---

142. WHO estimates of total private spending, shown in Figure 4.7, suggest that total private spending was 20% of all health spending in 1999. From a policy and poverty analysis perspective, the lack of accurate and timely data on the level and incidence of private health spending is an important gap and underscores the need for regular, systematic household budget surveys.

143. In this discussion, and in Figure 4.10, "employee contributions" include those made by salaried workers and the self-employed, while "total contributions" in Figure 4.10 also include payments from the state budget for the economically non-active and from the NLO for the unemployed (as well as some minor unclassified contributions). "Total revenue" includes other unspecified non-tax revenue.

144. The payroll tax is notionally split between employers (10 percent) and employees (4 percent), and is assessed only on salaries below a ceiling (SKK 24,000 per month in 2000, about twice the average wage), and on half of the income of the self-employed.

145. I.e., in the 12–13.6% range in years when the contribution rate was 13.7%. Sluggishness in the growth of this revenue component appears related mainly to the general economic downturn and rapid increase in unemployment in the latter half of the 1990s. In addition to substantial worker layoffs, a number of firms in financial distress were in arrears in paying their share of the payroll tax. Looking forward, the demographic shift can be expected to reduce the share of workers in the total population.

146. This rough calculation is based on aggregate data and should be verified. It takes into account that the assessment base for the self-employed is half of their income. However, since it does not include unrecorded income, it probably overstates the actual contribution rate of the self-employed.

147. These payments cover mainly pensioners and children, whose medical costs are substantially higher than those of the working population. Yet the government payment averaged less than SKK 300 per person per month in 2000, compared to the more than SKK 1,600 per month paid by the average salaried worker (and the less than SKK 200 paid by the average self-employed worker).

FIGURE 4.11: INPATIENT COSTS AS % OF TOTAL HIC SPENDING

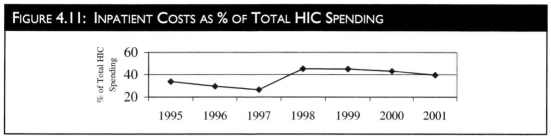

Source: MoF.

massive cross-subsidy between salaried workers and the rest of the population. The health contribution combines with other social insurance contributions to make the Slovak Republic's labor force one of the most highly taxed in the world.

Cost-effectiveness and Supply-side Incentives

On the supply side, on the other hand, there has not yet been much sign of a shift from more expensive curative approaches, involving mainly in-patient services and a high use of physical inputs and medical personnel, towards greater emphasis on preventive approaches and out-patient care. As Figure 4.11 indicates, there is no sign of a decline in spending on in-patient treatment as a share of total HIC reimbursements. In input use, while the number of hospital beds per capita has shown some welcome decline, it remains high. Combined with the continued low occupancy rates, this suggests that excess hospital capacity persists. Moreover, the average length of hospital stay remains high. The number of physicians, while already high, continues to increase. Drug costs are a large and rapidly growing component of total costs, increasing by more than 60 percent between 1996 and 2000, and shifting in composition to more expensive medicines.

The incentive framework, although revised frequently in response to different problems, has not helped to generate a major transformation in the way health care is provided. First, until recently, at least,[148] money has not followed the patient. Instead, most payments to providers have been based on contracts pre-negotiated by the MoH. For example, primary outpatient providers, paid mostly on a capitation basis, have had strong incentives to pass patients up the line to more expensive providers, as well as to provide more drugs, and more expensive drugs, in line with patient preferences. In-patient providers (hospitals) have been paid mainly on the basis of their previous year's costs. In neither case is there a clear incentive to provide the most cost-effective treatment for the particular mix of patients and cases presented. Nor is there any incentive to check on patients' payment records.

Reform Priorities

The issues facing the country's health system are complex and will take time to resolve, and this is all the more reason to act now to design and implement coherent reforms. This is underscored by the fact that the demographic shift under way in the country will mean that in the future the group contributing the lion's share of health revenues (salaried workers) will be smaller, while the group with the largest health costs (the elderly) will be much larger. The fundamental need is to put in place reforms that will strike a better balance between the demands on the health system and the system's ability to meet those demands at an affordable cost. The following paragraphs highlight some of the major areas and options for productive reforms.

---

148. There were changes in the provider payment mechanism in January 2002 that were intended to improve the structure of incentives. It has not been possible to analyze their impact for this report. For primary providers, a fee-for-service payment was added to the capitation amount for the provision of preventive care. The incentive effect would depend on the relative size and structure of the fee. There were also changes for inpatient providers.

Containing Excess Demand

On the demand side, there is at present little to contain the high levels of consumption of health services and medicines, since consumers face very little direct cost for a very generous package of benefits. Probably the most straightforward and effective way to contain and rationalize demand would be to increase the scope for consumer cost sharing (e.g., co-payments). This would give all consumers at least some incentive to contain costs, and would reduce the moral hazard in the current system. While such a policy will probably meet with formidable political resistance, no other policy measure is likely to have as strong an effect in containing costs and in reinforcing the other policies under consideration to put the health system on a more sustainable path.[149] *The authorities are encouraged to identify ways to expand the scope of consumer cost sharing.* To reduce the potential adverse impact on the poor, this measure could be accompanied by a system of refunds of co-payments, for example, for those on Social Assistance. Other complementary measures that could be considered to make higher co-payments more politically acceptable include: (i) an appropriately calibrated reduction in the payroll contribution rate for employed workers, who now bear a high share of the system's costs; and (ii) a well-publicized policy that makes acceptance of informal payments illegal.

In addition to introducing increased consumer cost-sharing, *the authorities should also identify ways of defining the basic benefit package in a more limited and feasible manner.* This is also likely to be an unpopular move, but the current situation is not working as intended (see for example, the rise in informal payments) and only reinforces unrealistic expectations. In addition to helping realign expectations and demand, narrowing the scope of the basic benefit package would create an opportunity for the development of private supplemental insurance. Presently, there is almost no scope for such insurance since the basic package covers virtually all of the important services.

Aligning Supply-Side Incentives

Ensuring that supply-side incentives consistently support the most cost-effective types and levels of health care calls for parallel reforms that: (i) improve the design of the provider payment mechanism; (ii) give providers the operational autonomy and incentives to respond efficiently to the signals from the reformed payment mechanism, within a regulatory framework that safeguards patient access to the appropriate type and level of care; (iii) guide the development of a more efficient network of provider facilities; and (iv) encourage a better balance in the numbers and types of medical personnel.

The ongoing reform effort should continue to identify improvements in the way providers are paid for services.[150] International experience suggests that, *if they are well designed and well implemented, mixed provider payment mechanisms appear to help control costs without compromising quality and access. Approaches to be considered include global budgeting with performance targets using block contracts, case-mix payment systems such as those based on Diagnosis Related Groups, and general practitioner (GP) fund-holding systems.* As a starting point for designing such mechanisms (and eventually for operating them) it is important to establish information systems to generate and analyze up-to-date production and delivery cost data for specific health service interventions on a comprehensive and regular basis. *Reforms should also seek to incorporate an approach in which "money follows the patient," with payments to providers based on the actual delivery of services.* This should strengthen the role of consumer choice in the process as well as reinforcing providers' incentives to

---

149. Higher co-payments would reinforce, and should be combined with, changes in the provider payment mechanism to reduce demand-inflating incentives, for example, to pass patients unnecessarily on to higher levels of more costly service, or to over-prescribe drugs, especially non-generics. Patient pressures can often encourage such behaviors, especially when cost sharing is low.

150. The provider payment mechanisms were modified in January 2002, with the intention of improving the incentives for treatment at the primary outpatient stage and for more efficient inpatient care. It has not been possible in this report to assess the impact of these changes, or their consistency with the overall level of resources available. There were reports early in 2002 that the higher prices established would necessitate a substantial (20 percent) reduction in the volume of services purchased by the HICs.

treat and to rationalize their services. *A system for checking patient contribution records should be established at the point of service to ensure eligibility, and protocols should be established on how to treat delinquent patients.*[151] Finally, *reforms of the payment mechanism should consider ways of reinforcing the role of general practitioners as gatekeepers, ensuring that their incentives and protocols encourage adequate emphasis on health promotion and preventive services and avoid excessive referrals and excessive prescription of drugs, especially the more expensive branded drugs.*

Merely changing the ways in which providers are paid will not have a sufficient effect unless providers and managers have the flexibility and tools to manage their resources actively and to redirect their use in response to the changes. The payment mechanism must also function in such a way that providers are able to capture at least part of the cost savings that they achieve, and that such savings are not immediately translated into lower prices. *For the system to work well, it is essential that providers have an appropriate balance between autonomy and accountability and the management skills and tools needed to operate effectively in a more decentralized environment.* Steps are already under way to transform many of the existing hospitals into "public non-state organizations governed at the regional or municipal levels."[152] It is not clear, however, whether this form of organization will provide the autonomy and flexibility needed. Nor is it clear whether the regulatory framework has been developed that will provide the safeguards needed. In the circumstance, *suggestions to decentralize the regulation of providers to the regional or municipal level seem premature.*

In addition to the provider payment mechanisms, there is scope for the MoH to use its position as owner of and main source of capital for the hospitals to rationalize hospital size and structure and help hospitals develop the management capacities they need to operate more autonomously. Efforts by the MoH to reduce the number of hospital beds reflect this approach. These efforts could be intensified, given the extent of the remaining excess hospital capacity. *There is a need to develop a Hospital Master Plan to guide decisions on which facilities to shut down and on where conversion to clinics or downsizing would make sense.* This could be based on such factors as the capacities of the existing facilities, the size and the demographic and disease profiles of the population in the catchment area, utilization, access, equity, and cost-effectiveness. Implementation would involve a number of political, administrative, technical, and legal steps, and would take time, and could be accompanied by steps to build up the management capacity of the facilities as well as investments to restructure facilities where necessary. MoH transfers to providers for investment or the settlement of arrears should be granted only if the facility fits into the Master Plan and restructures itself to ensure financial viability. *It would seem logical to delay further devolution of specific facilities until it is clear that they would continue to operate in the smaller, rationalized network.*

Improving the Financing System
The efficiency and effectiveness of the health financing system could be improved by consolidating the multiple insurance companies, improving collection performance, and broadening the revenue base. The administrative costs of the current system of multiple HICs run about 4% of benefit payments, which appears high given the HICs' very limited role. The multiple HICs increase administrative costs in the areas of: (i) duplicate staff and infrastructure; (ii) fragmented and duplicative revenue collection efforts in different organizations; (iii) burdens on hospitals and other providers from managing separate contracts and relationships with several HICs; and (iv) management of the complex mechanism for redistributing revenues to equalize risk across the different HICs. *Consolidating the HICs into a single collection and payment agency would eliminate much of this cost. The costs could be further reduced and the process of collecting contributions further streamlined by piggybacking the collection of health insurance contributions on the existing system for collecting contribu-*

---

151. For example, elective services could be deferred until eligibility was restored, and urgent services provided in the lowest cost facility appropriate and costs billed to the patient.

152. R. Kovac and S. Hlavacka, *Op. cit.,* p. 7, and Pre-accession Economic Program, pp 50–51.

tions for pensions and other social insurance benefits.[153] Since currently there is no scope for competition among the HICs, there is no basis for concern that their consolidation would cause any offsetting efficiency loss.

Such a *consolidation is also likely to facilitate a broader effort to improve contribution compliance,* since (i) a single agency would have stronger incentives to improve collections, as it would no longer be necessary to maintain the redistribution mechanism; (ii) a single agency could maintain contribution records and other patient data more systematically, allowing a more systematic approach to auditing compliance; and (iii) it would be possible to cross-check client records with other social insurance and social assistance records, and to coordinate efforts to improve collections with other agencies.[154]

Careful consideration should be given to measures that would broaden the revenue base for health care financing, reducing the its current heavy reliance on payroll contributions and reducing its highly redistributive structure. As noted above, nearly 70 percent of HIC revenues come from the less than 30 percent of the population who are salaried workers. The 14 percent contribution rate that they pay is the highest in the region. It combines with other social insurance contributions to produce a total payroll tax of 50.8 percent, which significantly raises labor costs, discouraging growth, especially employment growth.[155] *Drawing a larger share of health care revenues from a broader, more neutral revenue base (such as the VAT, or the personal income tax) would create room for an offsetting reduction in the payroll tax rate, which should boost Slovakia's growth and employment prospects.*[156] Moreover, given the demographic shift underway, the working age population, the group on which the system largely depends for revenues, will decline as a share of the total population, making this revenue source unstable in the longer run. In addition, payroll tax revenues are highly cyclical, declining sharply during recessions, making system revenues unstable in the short run. *Greater diversification of the financing sources, by shifting a larger share of system finance from the payroll tax to a broader based tax, should lead to a more stable revenue stream.* Finally, reducing the current reliance on payroll taxation would reduce the degree of redistribution from salaried workers to the rest of the population, since a larger part of the redistribution in the system would be funded by the broader tax base, reducing the redistribution from the payroll. This could have two beneficial effects. First, it would result in a closer link than now exists between payroll contributions and the insurance benefits received, which should improve compliance incentives. Second, the current redistribution may produce unintended regressive results for some groups, especially for low-income salaried workers, who may be subsidizing those who are better off than they. In addition, since the 14 percent contribution rate is levied only on wages below a ceiling,[157] workers with incomes above the ceiling pay a lower effective rate. Reducing the payroll tax rate would lessen the scope for such a regressive effects.

In short, *a shift in the source of health care financing towards a broader, more neutral base while keeping the total system revenues constant, could create room for a reduction in the payroll tax rate, reducing the system's dependence on this revenue source. This could have several beneficial effects in terms of promoting growth and employment, improving the long and short term stability of revenues, tightening the link between contributions and benefits, and possibly even improving the system's distrib-*

---

153. Slovakia's Social Benefits Reform Administration project, financed with assistance from the World Bank, is designed so that the platform being developed for managing social insurance contributions could also be used for health insurance, if it were so decided.

154. Consolidation could also facilitate the development and maintenance of more systematic patient records and other operational data, enabling analysis and monitoring of health service costs and risks. Among other things, this could generate the empirical data needed to design and implement improved provider payment mechanisms that encourage appropriate, cost-effective levels of care.

155. See Chapter 1 for a discussion of the macroeconomic and labor market implications of high payroll taxes.

156. Poland, for example, finances its health care system largely from a 7.75% tax on personal income.

157. In 2000, the ceiling was SKK 24,000 (571 Euro) per month (roughly twice the average wage).

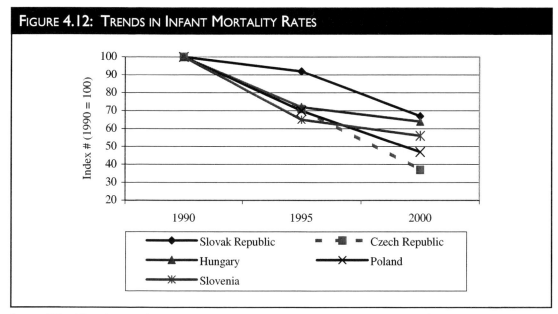

FIGURE 4.12: TRENDS IN INFANT MORTALITY RATES

Source: Word Development Indicators (World Bank) and TRANMONEE database (UNICEF).

utional equity. Adopting such an approach would call for careful prior analysis to determine the best alternative revenue source and structure, to verify the anticipated distributional improvements, and to calibrate the size of the decrease in the payroll tax so that it matches the increase in revenue from the alternative source, as well as to determine what possible compensating adjustments in worker take-home pay might be warranted.[158]

Public Health
While the topics above are the main focus of current policy debate in the Slovak Republic, *it is also critically important that the government ensure that essential public health functions, including health promotion activities and disease surveillance, prevention, and control, are given adequate funding and managerial attention.* These programs usually have large payoffs in terms of health outcomes, and do not usually involve high costs. But since they have high externalities, there is a danger that they will be under-funded relative to individual health care. Consequently, the public sector has an important role to play in setting priorities, funding levels, and incentive structures to ensure adequate action in these areas.

While some indicators (the relatively low incidence of TB, high immunization rates, declining IMR) suggest that a number of these functions have been carried out effectively, there are no grounds for complacency. As Figure 4.12 indicates, several other transition economies have achieved more rapid improvements. It may be some years before the full effects of a decline in performance become evident, and by that time these effects may be difficult to reverse. Moreover, important opportunities to reduce the health risks of the population (e.g., programs to reduce smoking) may be being missed. Budget allocations for these important activities have been constant in nominal terms since the mid-1990s and amount to less than 0.1 percent of GDP. *These factors suggest that, as part of its reform effort, the Slovak Republic should keep its public health activities under diligent review to ensure an adequate focus and adequate levels of support.*

---

158. It would also be important to consider other changes, such as including social benefits in taxable income, to broaden the base of other revenue sources.

Equity and Access Issues
An important part of the reform agenda should be ensuring that all citizens have equal access to an adequate level of health care. As things currently stand, the health status of the Roma is generally worse than the rest of the population, with outbreaks of communicable diseases that are linked to very poor living conditions (unsafe water, overcrowding, lack of waste disposal) and of non-communicable diseases and disabilities that are related to poor diet, smoking, and untreated injuries. Access to health services is very uneven. In many cases the isolation of Roma settlements from urban areas (where most of the health facilities are) sharply limits access. In addition, language barriers between the Roma and the health workers, and also discrimination, were cited as problems. *This suggests that health care reforms should contain measures to better serve such communities.* Possible areas to consider include: the implications of the location and access problems of these communities for plans to rationalize the provider network, special training programs to help health workers treat the Roma, and information programs to assist the Roma in dealing with health providers.[159]

Establishing the Capacities to Reform and Manage the Health System
The complexity of the issues involved in health care makes it likely that their resolution will involve a reform process over a number of years, followed by the ongoing requirements of managing the reformed system and adapting it further to changing conditions. This suggests the need to build up different types of capacities in different parts of the system. *First, at the national level, information systems need to be reinforced to ensure the timely availability of different types of data,* including: (i) an analysis of accurate sources and uses of funds to permit better budget monitoring, an analysis of health system expenditures and program effectiveness, and the development of National Health Accounts;[160] (ii) a detailed analysis of the costs of providing different services and carrying out different protocols, as well as the incidence of different types of cases, to permit further improvements in the provider payment mechanism (such as a move toward a Diagnostic Related Group approach) and better risk assessment; (iii) regular, systematic household budget surveys, to determine the incidence of private and public health care expenditures on different income groups, as well as the health status and access to health care of these groups; and (iv) a system of feedback or consumer report cards from clients, to identify problems and develop solutions. In addition, as providers gain increased autonomy and as the health care system becomes increasingly decentralized, the MoH's direct links with providers are likely to decrease, but it will need to ensure that its capacity and systems for policy analysis and formulation and for the regulation and monitoring of the system are designed to work effectively in the new environment. In particular, the MoH will need to *ensure that the nation's supervisory and regulatory system, including hospital accreditation and provider licensing, is well designed so that that standards of quality and access are maintained.* The decentralization of regulatory functions would thus seem to be premature at this stage.

Second, at the HIC level, the HICs (possibly consolidated into one entity) could usefully *develop a patient database,* keeping an accurate record of client contributions (to aid efforts to improve compliance) and patient reimbursements (to analyze risks and costs). *Third, at the local government level, capacities and systems of accountability could be put in place to ensure that the decentralization of responsibilities and facilities supports improvements in quality, access, and efficiency.* At present, it is not clear to what extent local governments are in a position to take on the tasks that are being devolved to them. It would be logical to assess the impact of the decentraliza-

---

159. *Poverty and Welfare of Roma in the Slovak Republic,* World Bank, Foundation S.P.A.C.E., et al., Bratislava, April 2002, pp. 22, 40–41; and *Slovak Republic: Living Standards, Employment, and Labor Market Study,* World Bank, Report No. 22351-SK, August 2001, pp 107, 118.

160. These should become important inputs into a systematic review of program effectiveness, and how to improve it, in the context of annual budget reviews within a medium-term expenditure framework. Additional work is needed to clarify public expenditure accounts and place them in a consistent framework. At present, they are prepared by different sources, at different times, for different purposes, using different concepts.

tion that has already taken place and to build on that experience to put in place appropriate regulatory systems that will ensure accountability. It would also be logical to develop plans to rationalize the provider network before decentralizing it.

Fourth, at the provider level, the development of a hospital management capacity to operate in a more autonomous, decentralized system is likely to be a high priority, together with the development of management capacity for clinics and other provider organizations. *Medical training may need to place more emphasis on producing an appropriate generalist/specialist mix* and on strengthening the capacities of general practitioners both as primary care providers and as gatekeepers. *Professional medical associations could develop the capacity to design cost-effective protocols,* such as guidelines for prescribing antibiotics and other drugs, and to guide the MoH in specifying standards for quality and access. *Finally, at the patient level,* it would be an important part of the reforms to *ensure that patients have a good understanding of their rights and responsibilities, as well as of the standards of service that they should expect.* A clearer, more realistic definition of the benefit package, a strict policy of limiting non-formal payments and setting co-payments, clarification of the patient's responsibility to be current in contributions, guidelines on the expected quality and service standards, and a mechanism for feedback on the lines of a consumer report card, would all be important parts of this effort.

Main Recommendations

The reform of the health sector will require a sustained effort over time. While this reform may not produce significant short-term savings, it remains indispensable to start taking measures now and to put health care on a sustainable footing in the medium term.

The *first priority is to provide a focal point for the reform effort by designating a health sector reform team.* This team can then take on the task of defining more precisely the reform priorities and sequencing, making adjustments as needed as the reform process unfolds.[161] As a second short-term step, *it is important to strengthen or put in place the information systems needed to design reforms and to better manage the health system.* This information system would include a broad range of data for different purposes: consistent data on health system expenditures and finances; detailed data on the costs of service provision; client contribution records; household survey data on health status and private expenditures on health; etc. As a third step, *the existing mechanisms for supervising and regulating the health system, including hospital accreditation and provider licensing, should be thoroughly reviewed and strengthened where necessary to ensure that providers are held accountable for the appropriate standards of quality and access.* Introducing a system of contracting only with providers that meet agreed standards of quality, access and cost control, would give providers strong incentives to meet those standards. A fourth area for action is *to rationalize and contain demand by defining a more limited and feasible benefit package, and by broadening the scope for consumer cost sharing, together with providing a system of rebates for low-income patients.* A fifth area is to take steps to *consolidate the HICs, and to piggyback the collection of contributions on the system used for other social insurance payments.* As this would permit better records of client contributions, a system of checks on payment records should be introduced by service providers. A sixth area would include *taking steps to reduce the dependence of the system on the payroll tax and could be introduced in the medium term,* possibly in stages (first to offset the revenues from increased co-payments, and second as part of a larger shifting of part of the burden to a broader based tax). As a seventh area, *steps should be taken to improve the efficiency of the provider network, including improving payment mechanisms based on the principle that "money follows the patient," developing a Hospital Master Plan to rationalize the network, and increasing autonomy for providers, within a regulatory system that focuses on accountability for transparent standards of quality and access and that maintains a hard budget constraint.* An eighth area of short-term action would be to *review*

---

161. The proposed Health System Modernization Project, currently under preparation for possible World Bank financing, is intended to support the design and implementation of the Slovak Republic's health reform effort.

public health functions to ensure that they are properly focused and adequately funded. Finally, initial steps in the area of access and equity could include: *designing specific interventions to improve the health status of the Roma and their access to care; using household survey data to analyze the health status of the poor, their access to health services, and the incidence of formal and informal payments for health services on the poor; and introducing a system of rebates for co-payments by low income patients, once co-payments are expanded.*

Education

The sweeping changes brought about by the transition are having a major impact on the education system in the Slovak Republic, but the system has not adapted fast enough or far enough to meet the needs of a modern market economy. As a result, the system needs to be reoriented to increase its focus on the more general, higher-level skills that the economy needs, by reorienting secondary education and by expanding access to tertiary education.[162] There are good reasons to believe that this can be done while keeping public spending on education at its current level of under 4 percent of GDP for some time to come, by taking advantage of the sharp drop in the school age population, the substantial potential for efficiency gains in the present system, and the scope for generating additional resources from tuition at the tertiary level.[163] But it is important to act quickly and aggressively, or the opportunities will slip away. The key elements of the proposed approach, most of which have been considered in the country's ongoing education reform efforts,[164] include the following:

(a) Consolidation and reduction in numbers of primary and secondary schools and teachers
(b) Acceleration of the shift already under way in secondary school enrollments from narrowly specialized vocational/technical programs toward more general academic training in "learning how to learn"
(c) Phased expansion of enrollment in higher education institutes (HEIs) based mainly on a more intense use of the existing facilities and faculty.
(d) Implementation of decentralization in ways that ensure accountability for achieving agreed outcomes, that reduce disparities in outcomes across and within regions, and that permit savings from consolidation and reorientation at the primary and secondary levels to be realized and to be used to expand the tertiary level and to improve quality at all levels.
(e) Intensification of efforts to ensure equal education opportunities for all children, especially for Roma minority children.

Sectoral Overview and Issues

Transition and the Education System
The transition has placed new demands on the education system, but it has also brought other changes, creating some scope to meet these demands without major increases in total public spending. Sweeping, economy-wide changes in the structure of employment have occurred, and there is a demand for more general, higher-level skills associated with a shift from traditional manufacturing, mining and agriculture to services, finance, and public administration. At the same time, there has been a rapid increase in the market valuation of education, with widening salary differen-

---

162. "Expenditure Management in Education," in *Budgeting and Expenditure Management in the Slovak Republic,* World Bank, 2002.

163. Over a longer period, particularly after the school age population stops declining, education spending is likely to grow as a share of GDP, but an increase in the share of private spending could account for much of this.

164. See, for example, M. Beblavy and M. Kubanova, *National Report on Education Policy,* Bratislava, December, 2001 (hereinafter referred to as NREP).

tials between workers with different education levels that suggest greater scope for charging tuition, especially for the higher levels of education.[165]

Two significant differences between the Slovak Republic's labor force and that of other OECD countries suggest the need for significant changes in the output of the education system to align it with those of other modern market economies: (i) a relatively small proportion of workers has completed tertiary education (10 percent versus an OECD average of 23 percent)[166]; and (ii) a high percentage of upper secondary school students is enrolled in traditional vocational programs as opposed to more general academic programs (79.6 percent in vocational programs versus 47.0 percent for OECD countries).

There has also been a dramatic decline in fertility, resulting in much smaller numbers of school age children and excess school capacity at the primary and secondary levels. The primary school-aged population shrank by nearly 18 percent over the past decade; it is projected to fall by another 25.5 percent by 2010, and to continue falling through 2020. As this smaller cohort ages, the secondary school cohort, which declined by about 2 percent over the past decade, will shrink by 23 percent by 2010 and by another 22 percent by 2020. The tertiary level cohort, which grew by over 24 percent during the past decade, will decline by 16 percent by 2010, and by nearly 29 percent by 2020.[167]

The Slovak education system has begun to respond to these changes, as is reflected in the enrollment trends over the last decade (shown in Table 4.9).

(a) Enrollment in the 9 years of *primary education* (which is free in state schools, compulsory, and nearly universal—outside of the Roma minority) declined significantly (9.7 percent) in the 1990s, reflecting the decline in the school age population. A sharper decline (13.3 percent) in state schools was partly offset by an increase in private enrollment.

(b) Total *secondary school* enrollments declined slightly (by 1.6 percent), in line with the age cohort, but the composition shifted dramatically: *general academic* enrollments rose by nearly 45 percent (22 percent in state schools), while *vocational/technical* enrollments fell by 13 percent (16 percent in state schools), resulting in a rising share of general academic schools in secondary enrollments. Secondary education in state schools is free of tuition.[168]

(c) At the *tertiary level,* enrollments have risen sharply, with full-time "internal" students increasing by 71.7 percent, and "external" students growing by 367.8 percent.[169]

Part of this response reflects the growth in private provision of education at all levels. The expansion has been particularly remarkable in general academic secondary education, where private enrollment grew from less than 0.3 percent of the total in 1990 to over 16 percent in 2000.[170]

Public Expenditure Trends
The composition of spending has not changed to reflect the major changes under way in the structure of the education system. Total public spending on education has fallen somewhat as a share of GDP (see Figure 4.13),[171] along with the decline in the school age population and numbers of students

---

165. NREP, p. 20, Table I.8.
166. NREP, p. 92.
167. Sources: M. Hrabinska, Institute of Information and Prognoses of Education (IIPE), Bratislava, 1996, as cited in M. Canning, *Education Policy Priorities in the Slovak Republic: a Discussion Paper,* World Bank, 2001.
168. State schools can and do charge for some related expenses, such as catering.
169. "Internal students" are full-time day students admitted with full scholarships; "external" students are usually part-time, and until recently were charged tuition fees.
170. Private schools include religious schools. They are allowed to charge tuition and also receive a state subsidy based on their enrollment and a fraction of the per student expenditure in state schools.
171. The spending data used excludes revenues from fees that would add another 0.2–0.3 percent of GDP.

TABLE 4.9: SCHOOL ENROLLMENT TRENDS, 1990–2000
(number of students)

	1990	1991	1995	1999	2000	% Change[a]
Pre-primary: Total	216,336	188,821	161,697	161,818	154,232	−28.71
State	216,336	188,821	161,268	161,128	153,456	−29.07
Private	n.a.	n.a.	429	690	776	1,093.85
Primary: Total	721,687	716,416	661,082	671,706	650,966	−9.70
State	720,920	707,032	635,135	645,384	625,265	−13.27
Private	767	9,384	25,947	26,322	25,701	3,250.85
Secondary General: Total	55,644	59,172	76,380	76,662	80,615	44.88
State	55,482	57,847	67,648	64,224	67,487	21.64
Private	162	1,325	8,732	12,438	13,128	8,003.70
Secondary VoTech: Total	224,584	224,262	248,892	192,064	195,016	−13.17
State	224,584	223,492	242,581	185,296	188,590	−16.03
Private	n.a.	770	6,311	6,768	6,426	734.55
Secondary: Total	280,228	283,434	325,272	268,726	275,631	−1.64
Tertiary: Total[b]	62,103	59,737	82,982	117,432	135,392	118.01
State (internal)	52,669	52,430	72,525	88,192	90,446	71.73
State (external)	9,434	7,307	10,457	29,240	44,129	367.77
Private	n.a.	n.a.	n.a.	n.a.	817	n.a.

a/ From 1990 (or earliest available year) to 2000.
b/ Includes "external" students.
Sources: Institute of Information and Prognoses for Education, as citied in NREP, Annex tables 1a and 1b.

(Table 4.6), resulting in a virtually unchanged level of spending per student when measured in constant prices. However, as Figure 4.14 indicates, the shares of state budget spending on education have not moved in line with the overall structural changes under way in the system shown in Table 4.6. In particular, the shares of spending for the rapidly expanding general secondary level declined slightly, while those in the declining vocational-technical stream rose.

The disconnect between these broad expenditure trends and the structural changes in education is also reflected in physical and staffing developments in the state schools:

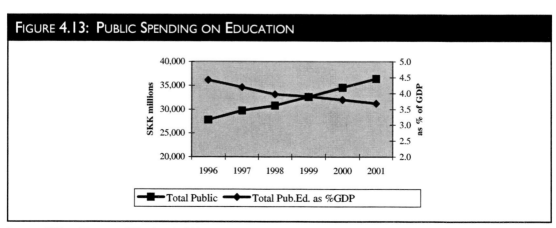

FIGURE 4.13: PUBLIC SPENDING ON EDUCATION

Source: IIPE and Statistical Yearbook, 2001.

FIGURE 4.14: SHARES IN STATE EDUCATION BUDGET BY LEVEL

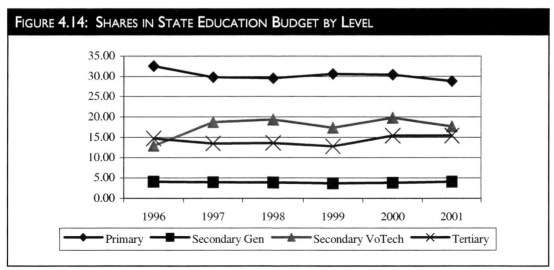

Source: IIPE and Statistical Yearbook, 2001.

(a) In *state vocational and technical schools,* while enrollments fell by 16.0 percent between 1990 and 2000, the number of teachers rose by 19.8 percent, and (more inexplicably) the number of schools rose by over 44 percent.

(b) In *state primary schools,* while enrollments fell by 13.3 percent (or 95,000 students), the number of teachers (including part-time staff) rose by over 8 percent, and the number of schools declined by only 6 (or 0.2 percent). Student-teacher ratios, already low at the beginning of the decade, are below OECD levels and far below the average for upper-middle income countries.

(c) At all levels, except the tertiary level, the numbers of teaching staff rose more rapidly than the number of students. Moreover, the physical plant, with its related heating and maintenance costs, remained the same or grew over the decade. Given that the amount spent per student remained roughly constant in real terms over this period, this increasing staff- and building-intensive delivery system had two consequences: (i) sizable arrears developed at the school level, especially for heating bills; and (ii) spending on items particularly important for raising school quality and effectiveness, such as learning materials, training, etc., was severely squeezed.

Reform Options and Sequencing

The dramatic and continuing fall in the school age population, combined with the expansion in the numbers of teachers and schools over the past decade, has resulted in a large and growing excess capacity at the primary and secondary levels. As a result, the country's student-teacher ratios are lower than the OECD averages and far lower than the average for upper-middle income countries, and the numbers and sizes of schools far exceed the needs. This provides an opportunity for significant cost savings, which should be used as a source of much needed fiscal space, allowing scope for the use of freed-up resources to improve the quality of education and to expand tertiary education.

Consolidating Primary and Secondary Schools

It will therefore be important for the government *to continue and intensify the rationalization program* begun in 2001.[172] This will require a detailed effort at the school and community level to

---

172. As of September 2001, only 79 proposals to drop schools from the network had been considered, of which 69 were agreed. NREP, p.30.

develop a higher quality school network. The fact that substantial numbers of teachers are at or beyond retirement age, combined with natural attrition, should make it easier to reduce the numbers of teachers. It will also be important that the school funding mechanism be reformed on the lines suggested below, so that it reinforces the consolidation process. The MoE will need to take the lead in ensuring that the savings generated are used effectively to raise quality at all levels and to help fund phased expansion at the tertiary level. Finally, there will be a *need to coordinate this process with the reorientation of the secondary level,* including the possibilities of converting vocational schools into general secondary schools, or converting them into comprehensive schools with both general and vocational streams, or closing them down.

Reorienting Secondary Education

While the quality of human capital in the Slovak Republic is reasonably high, there are clear indications that there is a need for more general, flexible, and higher level skills, which would enable workers to learn and to adapt throughout their careers. This type of learning is best provided in general academic high schools rather than vocational schools with large numbers of highly specialized programs that lead to a specific, narrowly defined occupation. Students who enroll in vocational programs commit themselves at an early age to a specific occupation. They are unlikely to be able to shift easily to radically different occupations as labor market conditions change. In a dynamic labor market, where an individual can be expected to hold several different jobs over his or her lifetime, it is important that students learn "how to learn," rather than learning specific skills. This suggests that (i) the ongoing shift in enrollments towards academic schools should be encouraged, and (ii) the vocational stream should be scaled back and fundamentally reformed. The reform of the vocational program should consider both its content (e.g., placing more emphasis on general learning skills, problem-solving, communications, and teamwork, than on occupation-specific skills) and its structure (e.g., consolidating of programs and schools, and, where conditions warrant, converting the schools into general secondary schools or comprehensive schools with both general and vocational tracks).

These reforms at the secondary level should be *coordinated with efforts to increase quality and relevance at the primary level,* so that those graduating from primary schools will be prepared for the changing orientation at the secondary level. Apparently, such coordination is not strong at present,[173] and the division of responsibilities for primary and secondary schooling between the municipal and regional levels could make a coordinated approach even more difficult. As with the rationalization program, reorientation of the secondary level so that a higher proportion of students is in the general stream, should result in substantial cost savings, since the cost per student in the general stream is about 40 percent less than in the vocational stream.[174] These cost savings, like those from rationalization, can be used for quality improvements at all levels and for phased capacity expansion at the tertiary level.

Gradual Expansion of Tertiary Education

In light of the excess demand for workers with tertiary education, the relatively small proportion of the labor force with such education, and the excess student demand for higher education, the *expansion of capacity at the tertiary level appears justified.* However, this raises *issues of basic public finance,* as well as the issue of an efficient strategy for meeting this demand. In terms of public finance, since education is an investment in students' future labor market success, and since students clearly draw large private benefits from this, particularly at the tertiary level, it is entirely appropriate that they pay at least a substantial part of the costs involved. Moreover, tuition could also provide a market-based signal to regulate excess demand. Finally, the need for very tight fiscal

---

173. NREP, pp. 119.

174. Data for 1999 are from IIPE, as cited in "Expenditure Management in Education," in *Budgeting and Expenditure Management in the Slovak Republic,* World Bank, 2002.

restraint both now and in the future argues against keeping higher education tuition-free. For these reasons, the recent decision to abandon tuition payments for external students should be reconsidered.

In addition, *the strategy for tertiary expansion needs to be carefully developed and phased*. The excess apparent demand may quickly evaporate once tuition is introduced more widely and as the economy's backlog of demand for workers with tertiary education is reduced. The sharp drop projected in the size of the 18–23 year age cohort is also likely to take much of the steam out of demand growth. While this age cohort rose by 24 percent over the 1990s, it is projected to fall by 40 percent between 2000 and 2020. As a result, merely maintaining the current number of full-time students will raise enrollment rates from 24 percent in 2000 to over 40 percent by 2020, a rate higher than that in many high-income countries. Moreover, it will be important to ensure that tertiary institutions have the critical mass needed to provide quality education. The existing HEIs now have very low student-faculty ratios, but their libraries, laboratories, and other facilities are reportedly under stress. The fixed costs of establishing new tertiary institutions are extremely high; therefore, the expansion of existing HEIs may be the most efficient approach. If, as a part of this strategy, it appears desirable to establish new tertiary institutions, measures to reduce start-up costs by using surplus buildings, or by basing them on existing institutions, should be explored. Institutionally, HEIs will need the autonomy and management skills to make sound resource allocation decisions and will need to face accountability mechanisms, such as an effective accreditation process, that hold them accountable for achieving agreed outcomes and service delivery standards within hard budget constraints.

Improving Funding Mechanisms
These efforts should be supported by a *fundamental reform in the way in which funds are allocated to and utilized by schools*. In particular, it would seem most transparent and efficient to allocate the bulk of a school's budget as a capitation payment (a fixed, standard amount per enrolled student[175]), with school management having sufficient autonomy (within standards) to use the funds in the most effective way (such as reducing staff numbers to free up resources for teaching materials, or higher allowances to a smaller number of teachers, or investments to reduce heating costs). The money would "follow the student" in the sense that schools with increasing enrollments would have a proportional growth in their budgets. The recently adopted Schools Financing Act is an attempt to move in this direction, but the financing norm is still too flexible, as it is based not only on numbers of students but also on numbers of "classes or groups, lessons taught per week, and teaching load," with a low minimum class size threshold. The norms also guarantee the costs of utilities and rent. As a result they will tend to lock in the school's current staffing levels and plant size, and will provide no incentive to reduce these costs.[176] In addition, schools would need the managerial skills and the autonomy to make such adjustments, as well as the accountability to meet service delivery standards, within a hard budget constraint. Further reforms in these areas could reinforce incentives for efficiency and consolidation and could encourage the expansion of general secondary education and expenditure on quality-enhancing materials.

In addition to promoting efficiency, quality, and transparency, *a capitation approach could also play an important role in improving equity across different parts of the country*. Analysis of per student expenditures across regions and districts suggests little variation at the regional level but

---

175. In its purest form, the amount would be standard for all schools at a given grade level. Some adjustments will be necessary, but they need to be carefully designed. If too many adjustments are built in, or if they are too large, they would undercut the incentive to move to the most efficient and effective mode of instruction (e.g., if the capitation grant fully adjusts for the higher unit cost of vocational education, it blunts the incentive to convert to the lower cost general stream).

176. NREP, pp. 110–111 (note: this does not apply to capital costs, whose allocation is less transparent).

massive variations at the district level.[177] For example, in the Presov region expenditures per student in 1999 ranged from SKK 2,000 in a district with a 44.1 percent minority population, to SKK 43,000 in a district with a less than 7 percent minority population. In Košice, the range is from SKK 5000 to 40,000, and in Banská Bystrica, from SKK 11,000 to 39,000. It is difficult to understand differences of this magnitude, especially since it might be expected that per capita expenditures in areas with concentrations of minorities would, if anything, be higher, owing to the need for additional remedial and language programs. A uniform capitation approach could also reduce concerns that the decentralization process could lead to the country's substantial geographic disparities being replicated in the classroom.

Another issue related to the mechanisms for funding schools relates to *state support for private (including religious) schools.* According to the new Schools Financing Act, a private school is meant to receive a per student grant equivalent to 100 percent (or 70 percent if it charges tuition) of the per student current expenditure in an equivalent state school. Since the state budget allocation is usually not adequate to fully cover this grant, only a fraction of this amount (estimated at about 80 percent for religious schools and 37 percent for private schools) is actually disbursed. There is a wide variation by region and type of school, with amounts being particularly low (below 19 percent) for general secondary schools. It would be preferable to make such grants more uniform and predictable.

The role of private finance in education should be carefully reviewed, particularly (i) the level and structure of formal and informal fees and contributions *at the primary and secondary levels,* and (ii) the lack of tuition fees at the tertiary level. Comprehensive data on the levels and incidence of the private financing of education are not available, and this hampers the development of coherent policies.[178] However, several ad hoc surveys have confirmed that, in addition to paying tuition fees at private schools, many parents (78 percent) make voluntary contributions (including to state schools) in addition to paying various school-related costs (school books and supplies, commuting, school meals).[179] While many of these costs may be appropriate for families to bear, they should be reviewed to see if compensating policies are needed to ensure: (i) that their proceeds actually accrue to the schools; (ii) that they do not prevent lower-income students from continuing school beyond the compulsory tenth year; and (iii) that they do not generate large disparities between richer areas and poorer areas in the quality of schools.

At the tertiary level, the recent decision to abandon tuition payments for external (part-time) students seems to be a backward step, and one that will leave the HEIs without an important source of finance. It would be appropriate to reexamine this issue, particularly regarding an earlier proposal to charge tuition for both internal and external students. Since only a relatively small part of the population can benefit from tertiary education, and since those with a tertiary education generally earn substantially higher incomes, it makes sense from an equity standpoint that the beneficiaries pay a larger share of the costs than they currently pay. Combined with other stipends and social allowances (including the building up of pension credits), tuition-free higher education could provide an excessively attractive alternative to finding a job in a tough labor market and could lead to rapidly rising demands on the budget. A tuition charge would also help to ration demand, which is currently well in excess of capacity, by requiring students to make a more careful calculation of the costs and benefits of tertiary education. Moreover, tuition would provide HEIs with the resources needed to maintain quality and respond to the demand. This report recommends that *tuition payments* covering a substantial part of tertiary education costs be intro-

---

177. Data are from 1999 from the District and Regional Offices of the MoE and from the Slovak Republic Statistical Office, as cited in World Bank, "Expenditure Management in Education," in "*Budgeting and Expenditure Management in the Slovak Republic,* (2002)."

178. A comprehensive, regular household expenditure survey would be very valuable in providing the information needed in this area (and many others).

179. As cited in NREP, pp. 11–13.

duced *for both internal and external students* to support a phased expansion of opportunities for tertiary education. This step should be combined with an appropriate *loan program* to enable repayment to be made out of the future increased income resulting from attending university, and also with a *scholarship program* to ensure access for otherwise qualified students from low-income families.

For such an approach to work well, several other parallel reforms are needed. School (and HEI) management will require both the autonomy and the skills needed to make sound decisions on the resource reallocation that is necessary to improve quality and efficiency.[180] This is likely to call for training for school headmasters and managers, as well as for initial assistance. At the same time, schools should be accountable for achieving the required results and service standards within a hard budget constraint. The system of and standards for school inspection, complemented by a national student and school assessment system, and improvements in the accreditation process for HEIs, need to be geared up for this task, and the results should be publicly available, especially to parents and school managers.

Making Decentralization Work
The funding and accountability mechanisms proposed above would be powerful tools to ensure that decentralization reinforces national education goals, rather than placing them at risk. In particular, the *proposed funding mechanism* would do much to reduce concerns that decentralization could increase disparities in education funding and in learning achievements between rich and poor areas. The *proposed accountability mechanisms* are also vitally important for measuring performance against agreed standards, and ensuring that decentralized, local education objectives are aligned with national objectives. A system of national assessments of educational outcomes will be an essential tool for monitoring the differences in results both among and within the regions and identifying areas for corrective action.

Other critical steps needed to ensure that decentralization works well include: (i) clarifying the lines of responsibility for a school's performance in the new, decentralized setting (a critical point that remains to be resolved);[181] (ii) ensuring that headmasters and others responsible for school management have the skills and tools needed to operate effectively, with greater auton-omy, within a tighter framework of accountability; and (iii) ensuring good coordination of the programs to rationalize and reorient the system, including coordination between the primary and secondary levels.

Access and Equity
The most pressing problems of access and equity in the education system are those facing Roma children. Data from the 1991 census provide a bleak, though dated, picture: only 77 percent of Roma had completed primary education, 8 percent had completed vocational training, and less than 2 percent had completed academic secondary or university education.[182] A qualitative survey conducted in 2000–01 found a similar situation among Roma adults, along with high levels of unemployment and dependence on Social Assistance. It also found that few Roma children from segregated settlements had completed a vocational stream. While many Roma children from inte-grated areas fared better, attending a special kind of vocational school offering some forms of sub-

---

180. For example, schools need to be able to decide, within agreed norms, whether to allocate savings from a smaller teaching staff to additional allowances for the remaining teachers (to compensate for increased work-loads and attract a higher quality teacher in a competitive market), or for teaching materials or other uses.

181. As stated in NREP, pp. 139–40: "Relations between mayors and municipal authorities and the heads of regional and district offices and regional authorities, school boards, head teachers, students, and parents are very complicated, so they may disguise who is actually responsible for a particular school's results."

182. Data from a 1990 survey found that only 44 percent of Roma men and 41 percent of women had completed grade 8 (WB, Report No.22351-SK, p.108).

sequent education, the survey found no Roma children from any area who had attended a general secondary school, let alone a university. Without greater access to a better quality of education, the coming generation of Roma will, like their parents, be caught in a poverty trap of low incomes, high unemployment, and high welfare dependence. Consequently, programs that will improve Roma access to a better quality and higher levels of education and will increase their chances of success, should be given high priority in the country's education strategy. Experience suggests that the chances for success are much higher in integrated conditions; therefore, creating a desegregated school environment should be a major policy objective.[183] The rationalization program for the consolidation of schools could be used as one vehicle for desegregation in selected areas, while the reorientation program would improve the relevance and quality of the content of education for all children, including the Roma. Other measures, specifically targeted to Roma children, could include: (i) providing free textbooks and other materials to reduce the private costs of education to Roma parents; (ii) providing extra funds to schools, based on the number of Roma students, to cover the extra costs of remedial, language, and head-start programs and to provide an incentive for integration; (iii) expanding pre-school head-start programs, which have already shown success even in segregated communities;[184] and (iv) providing programs that will raise parent's awareness of and demand for education for their children.

While problems of equity and access are less severe for the population at large, they do exist, and policies should be designed to reduce these problems. First, there is the issue of the extremely wide differences in spending per student across different parts of the country. The recommended change in the funding mechanism could do much to correct this. Second, the private costs of even state education could pose a disincentive for low-income parents to continue their children's education beyond the compulsory tenth year. Consideration could be given to making the child allowance conditional on the child's full time enrollment in school through the secondary level. Third, the selection process at the secondary and tertiary levels has important flaws.

At the secondary level, the current process allows students to apply to only one school, often forcing them to apply to a "second choice" school, because they fear ending up in a third choice school (or worse) if they are not admitted to their highly competitive first choice. At the tertiary level, each HEI generally has its own admissions examination, which is used in addition to the standard nation-wide school leaving examination as a basis for admitting candidates. At both levels there are serious concerns of corruption. One survey undertaken with World Bank support indicated that 12 percent of students admitted to bribery to gain access and improve grades at the secondary level, and 22 percent admitted to the same at the university level.[185]

Reforms are needed in both the content and the process to make selection more transparent and merit-based, and to better reflect student/parent preferences. Better designed examinations could be one element of these reforms. Finally, the authorities should introduce a regular, periodic, nationally representative integrated household budget survey as an indispensable tool with which policymakers could monitor these (and other) issues and design appropriate policy responses—not only in education but also in other critical areas of economic and social policy.

Raising Quality
The *reforms proposed above should be seen as important opportunities for enhancing quality.* Indeed, most of the proposed reforms would strengthen features of the Slovak Republic's education system

---

183. More broadly, there should be a major effort to integrate the segregated communities, in which about a quarter of the Roma live, into the mainstream of the Slovak Republic's society and economy. See also NREP, p. 139.
184. NREP, pp. 139.
185. As cited in NREP, pp. 16.

that cross-country analysis has shown to explain higher country performance in standardized international science and mathematics exams, specifically: central exams; centralized curriculum and budget control mechanisms; school autonomy in process and personnel decisions; incentives for teachers to select proper teaching methods; encouragement of parents' interest; and competition from private providers.[186] The reorientation of emphasis on the secondary level should lead to a more relevant, focused, and flexible curriculum at both the primary and secondary levels. The savings generated by *consolidation and reorientation* should free up resources for quality improvements, as would tuition at the tertiary level. The proposed *funding mechanism*, combined with appropriate school-level autonomy, should give schools more flexibility to use resources to raise quality. Among other features, it could enable them to deal with one of the most difficult concerns affecting quality: low teacher pay and morale.[187] The country's experience suggests that *private schools* have helped enhance quality, particularly in focusing on "learning how to learn." Operating in a semi-competitive environment with public schools, private schools are likely to help raise performance throughout the system, and thus have a dynamic, qualitative role to play, well beyond their weight in total enrollments. The *stronger accountability mechanisms* proposed would ensure that greater school-level autonomy is not misused, by evaluating both state and private schools and HEIs against standards of service delivery and student achievement (as measured through national assessment examination), within a hard budget constraint. The results could be combined with systematic parent/student feedback on school performance and could then be made widely available to parents and other stakeholders in the form of a school report card focused on school quality. This could not only inform parent decisions, but could also identify problems and areas for improvement.

Capacities to Reform and Manage the System
To design and manage an education reform strategy, including the issues outlined above, and to manage the system subsequently, it will be important to ensure that critical systems and capacities are in place at various levels. The critical institutional capacities and systems needed include: (i) designating a highly qualified team to take the lead in coordinating the design and implementation of an education system reform strategy, with the skills and resources needed for the analytical and consensus-building work involved; (ii) strengthening the supervisory, accreditation and accountability mechanisms to ensure that schools and HEIs meet expected standards within hard budget constraints; (iii) establishing systems of national student assessments and a periodic, nationally-representative household budget survey; (iv) improving capacities for expenditure monitoring and program assessment and budgeting; and (v) building management capacities and tools needed for schools and HEIs to operate effectively with greater autonomy in a more decentralized environment.

Main Recommendations
Reorienting the education system to the needs of the Slovak Republic's modern market economy calls for an increasing focus on the more general, higher level, skills that the economy needs, as well as expanding access to tertiary education. There is a good chance that this reorientation can be accomplished while keeping public spending on education at its current level of around 4 percent of GDP, and enhancing equal opportunity in education. This could be done by taking advantage of the sharply declining numbers of school age children, the small size of classes and low teacher workloads, and the growth of private sector schools, in order to consolidate at the primary and

186. Woessmann (2001) and Korda (2002), as cited in *Lifelong Learning in the Global Knowledge Economy*, mimeo, World Bank 2002.
187. For example, schools could reallocate part of the savings from a reduction in the number of surplus teachers to pay bonuses to a smaller number of higher quality teachers carrying a larger workload.

secondary levels and shift resources to the tertiary level, while expanding the use of tuition payment to recover costs and contain the prevailing excess demand for higher education.

In *the short run*, the main priorities are to:

(a) Establish a specialist team to take the lead in coordinating the design and implementation of an education sector reform strategy.

(b) Intensify and expand the "rationalization program" to consolidate primary and secondary schools, capitalizing on the sharp drop in the school age population to generate savings.

(c) Initiate plans to reorient the secondary level, along with coordinated curriculum reforms at the primary level.

(d) Introduce tuition at the tertiary level, both to contain excess demand and to finance the expansion of enrollment and quality improvements needed at existing institutions.

(e) Intensify efforts to ensure equal opportunities for Roma children at the primary and secondary levels and for all students at the tertiary level. Student loans and need-based scholarships will become increasingly important as the use of tuition expands at the tertiary level.

(f) Initiate steps to establish a system of national assessments of student learning achievements and a system of periodic, nationally representative, household budget surveys.

(g) Strengthen accountability mechanisms, including the accreditation process for HEIs.

The priorities for a *medium-term strategy* include:

(a) Developing a mechanism to enable part of the savings at the primary and secondary school level to be used by the central government to support demand-driven gradual expansion at the tertiary level, including the program of need-based scholarships.

(b) Reforming the school funding mechanisms to reinforce such sector policy objectives as more efficient use of resources, including more rapid school consolidation, and equity throughout the country.

(c) Encouraging the reorientation of the secondary level, so that most students learn the general academic skills needed for lifetime learning, by expanding enrollment in general secondary schools, and by reforming the technical and vocational school curriculum to increase the general academic content.

(d) Implementing the program of quantitative national educational assessments to monitor progress in meeting education objectives nationally, and across and within regions, and holding schools accountable for meeting standards.

(e) Ensuring that the education system works well for all regions and socioeconomic groups in the newly decentralized setting, by implementing improved accountability mechanisms, aligning national and local objectives, specifying accountabilities, and monitoring outcomes.

Conclusions

The discussions above on agriculture, social protection, health and education confirm that there is substantial scope for the government to restructure public expenditure programs to *achieve* its strategic objectives of growth, productive employment, and stability. The main options to consider in the short run include:

(a) *Curtailing subsidies* to non-financial enterprises, especially by pruning down all agricultural support not compliant with CAP, and reducing railway subsidies;

(b) *Raising the retirement age to 65* to avoid the massive pension system deficits that the demographic transition will otherwise bring.

Other key measures on which on which work should start now as part of a longer-term effort include:

(a) *Initiating a program of well-designed, periodic, representative household budget surveys,* as a tool for analyzing the impact of, and designing reforms for, programs and policies across a wide range of sectors.

(b) Raising pension replacement rates over time *by gradually shifting towards a mandatory fully funded second pillar* (but at a lower age for mandatory switching to the new system than currently envisaged) and *adopting* complementary *reforms to tighten the link between benefits and contributions and (possibly) to reduce the burden of the payroll tax.*

(c) Restricting eligibility to sickness benefits and turning the surplus now generated in the for Sickness Insurance fund to participants *by reducing the payroll tax, perhaps by as much as 2 percent;*

(d) *Curbing the rising cash assistance payments under Social Assistance,* and correcting the disincentives that are preventing recipients from working their way off the welfare rolls, by *adjusting benefits* to observed minimum subsistence levels outside of Bratislava, *reducing the rate of withdrawal of benefits* as recipients earn income, strictly enforcing *activity tests,* and developing more effective ones.

(e) *Containing excess demand for health care* (through more narrowly defined benefits and greater cost sharing); making the financing mechanism more efficient and equitable (by merging health insurance companies, integrating collections with other social contributions, improving compliance, and broadening the revenue base by shifting responsibility for funding a larger share of the non-contributing participants from the payroll tax to general taxation); increasing provider efficiency (through better-designed payment mechanisms, a provider network rationalization plan that reduces overstaffing and excessive hospital beds, a strong mechanism to hold providers accountable to quality and service delivery standards, and development of management skills at the facility level); ensuring adequate support and focus for public health functions; and protecting access to health services for all, especially the Roma.

(f) *Consolidating education* facilities and staff at the primary and secondary level with the support of a new funding mechanism based largely on capitation payments; reorienting secondary education to meet labor market demand better (by increasing both general academic enrollments and the general academic content of vocational streams); using the cost savings from consolidation and reorientation to improve quality at all levels and fund, along with tuition, gradual expansion at the tertiary level; establishing stronger mechanisms, including a system of national student assessments, to hold schools and HEIs accountable; and ensuring equal education opportunities, especially for the Roma.

Implementation of these approaches would contribute to the Government's strategic objectives not only by directly supporting fiscal consolidation but also by helping these programs support growth and employment more effectively. For example, *the options proposed offer several opportunities for significant reductions in the payroll tax* (to offset the surplus in sickness insurance; to shift the burden of providing health insurance coverage to non-contributors from the payroll tax to general taxation; and, if some suggested areas of cost saving or revenue enhancement materialize, it may be possible to reduce the payroll tax for pensions). While in some cases, other measures to raise general tax revenues would be needed to offset the revenue loss, the net effect on growth, especially employment growth should be quite positive. *The proposed reforms in Social Assistance would also reduce labor market rigidities,* by improving the incentives for cash assistance recipients to work, while *the reforms proposed in education should make the education system more responsive to the needs of the economy, resulting in a more productive labor force with the skills needed by a dynamic market economy.*

The sector discussions above place considerable *emphasis on building the institutions and capacities needed to design reforms and manage them once in place.* This will be an important determinant of the success and sustainability of this *effort.* Especially since so many of the programs reviewed have an important impact on the lives of the poor, it will *be essential to analyze reform alternatives in terms of their impact on the poor, and to monitor that impact subsequently* to determine if modifications are needed. As stressed repeatedly, a well designed, up-to-date household budget survey is one essential tool for assessing program impacts on the poor (and all others). *Improving the tools of fiscal management and program assessment is also critically important.* Transforming the medium term budgeting and program budgeting frameworks into effective fiscal planning tools, improving the quality of underlying financial and performance information, and enhancing the systems' integrity are thus all important goals. It is especially important to ensure that the basic fiscal accounts are accurate, timely, and maintained in ways that are consistent and well understood across line and core agencies. Finally, it will also be important to *consolidate the recent decentralization to ensure that capacities and accountability mechanisms are in place before moving to the next phase of devolution.* As highlighted in the sectoral discussions, this will be essential to ensure that the quality and effectiveness of the delivery of basic public services are maintained and improved, and that duplication and fragmentation do not result in rapidly rising public employment and wage bills. These and other institutional and governance issues are discussed in more detail in the next Chapter.

CHAPTER 5

GOVERNANCE

A s is clearly evident, the ultimate success of the policy reforms outlined in the previous chapters will depend to a great extent on the government's capacity to strengthen the *institutional framework* in which those policies are conceived, decided upon, and executed. The year and a half that separates the Slovak Republic from EU Accession offers a window of opportunity also in this regard. In fact, the drive to meet the obligations of membership should provide the incentives and the compromise not only to implement the right policies but also to make it in the most effective way. The benefits of those policies will arise from *their actual implementation, not from pro forma legislation.* In other words, only if the government has the institutional capacity to carry.

The need for institutional strengthening and development is true in such diverse areas as agriculture, trade, financial sector development, energy, regional development, and government financial control. While the need to improve the working of existing institutions is true also for many accession countries, the case is stark in the Slovak Republic. The results of a recent perception survey (reported in Table 5.1) indicate on one hand that the Slovak Republic has come a long way in improving the effectiveness of its administration and the quality of the governance framework more generally. On the other hand, the survey also reflects that the country still rates among the lowest on most counts among acceding countries, indicating the urgent need to step up efforts. In addition, many of the country's institutions have fairly recently been elevated from the sub-national to the national level. While this, *per-se*, posses extra challenges; their first steps in this new role have been marred by cronyism and corruption. Therefore, a double handicap needs to be overcome.

This chapter focuses on three issues: (i) the reform of public expenditure management systems and practices needed to support a growth-oriented fiscal consolidation; (ii) the consolidation of local and regional self-government which is now a prerequisite for further advances toward decentralization; and (iii) the long-needed overhaul of the judiciary system.

TABLE 5.1: PERCEIVED QUALITY OF GOVERNANCE IN THE CEECs, 1997/98–2000/01								
	Government Effectiveness		Regulatory Quality		Rule of Law		Control of Corruption	
	1997/98	2000/01	1997/98	2000/01	1997/98	2000/01	1997/98	2000/01
Acceding countries								
Czech Republic	0.59	0.58	0.57	0.54	0.54	0.64	0.38	0.31
Estonia	0.26	0.86	0.74	1.09	0.51	0.78	0.59	0.73
Hungary	0.61	0.60	0.85	0.88	0.71	0.76	0.61	0.65
Lithuania	0.13	0.26	0.09	0.30	0.18	0.29	0.03	0.20
Latvia	0.07	0.22	0.51	0.30	0.15	0.36	−0.26	−0.03
Poland	0.67	0.27	0.56	0.41	0.54	0.55	0.49	0.43
Slovak Republic	−0.03	0.23	0.17	0.27	0.13	0.36	0.03	0.23
Slovenia	0.57	0.70	0.53	0.52	0.83	0.89	1.02	1.09
Other EU candidates								
Bulgaria	−0.81	−0.26	0.52	0.16	−0.15	0.01	−0.56	−0.16
Romania	−0.57	−0.54	0.20	−0.28	−0.09	−0.02	−0.46	−0.51

Note: The range is between −1.5 (worst) to +1.5 (best).
Source: WDI.

Public Expenditure Management

The previous chapters have described the magnitude of the fiscal challenge facing the Slovak Republic. Obtaining sustainable public finances is not simply a question of having the political will to impose expenditure cuts or raise revenues. Sustainable public finances can only be the result of the workings of a system of institutions, including relationships between the government, Parliament, the Ministry of Finance, the line ministries, and individual ministers. Effective management of public finances depends on a contract or understanding among policymakers in all spheres (ministers, parliamentarians, and officials) that policies are constrained by the available resources and that there should be mechanisms that oblige policymakers to confront the resulting fiscal choices openly.

Where public finance institutions can help is by providing a framework in which (i) meaningful choices can be made (for example, there should be information structures that illuminate, rather than obfuscate, the nature of the policy choices at hand and their implications and a timeframe should exist in which such choices can be effected); (ii) coordination can be established and consensus reached among interested parties; and (iii) reliable feedback is generated on the actual implementation of the policy and financial decisions made, as well as on the outcomes of those choices (financial and otherwise), including the ability to permit corrective action where needed. This section deals with the types of reforms necessary to establish these institutions and mechanisms.

The following three fundamental arguments relating to this discussion are:

(a) While changes to legal structures (such as the Act on Budgetary Rules or the act establishing the State Treasury) can assist the process of reform, legislation does not in itself constitute reform.

(b) The best intentioned reforms will remain ineffective if the people involved are not clearly aware of their new responsibilities and relationships in the reformed system, or if they do not see how the reforms would help them.

(c) While technology can be of considerable help, it cannot by itself change working practices or political relationships; thus, to rely on new systems alone to promote change will inevitably result in disappointment.

First Reform Steps

The idea that public expenditure management systems are unequal to the task of fiscal consolidation is not new. Historically, the budgeting process in the Slovak Republic was driven by "budgetary incrementalism," whereby each spending agency applies for funding based on its own assessment of financial needs for existing personnel and facilities and on established spending norms. Moreover, the focus of budgeting was on an extremely short time horizon and on a narrow state budget that excluded numerous extrabudgetary activities. This narrow budget fell far short of the standard definition of general government and did not provide an effective indicator of the impact of public finances on the overall economy. Equally, budget preparation was not embedded in a sound and consistent macroeconomic framework.

Frustrated with this state of affairs, the government in 1999 launched an ambitious program of public finance reform aimed at: (i) the use of a medium-term fiscal framework; (ii) improvements in budget coverage and classification; (iii) the gradual adoption of program budgeting; (iv) a major overhaul of budgetary legislation; and (v) the creation of a State Treasury and of a Debt and Liquidity Management Agency.

While the overall direction of reform remains appropriate, it is now necessary to increase the pace of reform and to focus less on paper measures and more on actual changes in areas critical to the success of the fiscal consolidation effort. This would involve: (i) articulating a binding medium-term budget strategy to bring down the overall fiscal deficit in government policy statements; (ii) transforming program budgeting into a living reality; (iii) generating reliable feedback on financial and program performances; and (iv) strengthening the integrity of budget execution systems.

Role and Authority of the Medium-Term Budgetary Framework (MTBF)

A fundamental step toward fiscal consolidation is to achieve consistency between policy decisions and resources. This necessitates a view of the fiscal impacts of all current and likely future policy commitments on public resources. Such a view is not possible if the focus is only on the current or the next fiscal year's expenditures. This is the point of a medium-term budgetary framework (MTBF): to set out the policy targets for budget expenditures and revenues under which ministries whose policies and plans have been included in the MTBF can be reasonably sure of their funding levels over the following years. This objective is based on the notion that the policy decisions made by government should be disciplined by the resource realities over the medium-term, and that the most effective way for countries to restructure their spending so that policy decisions reflect resource availability is by taking a medium-term perspective.

The MTBF is not simply a forecast or a wish. It is easy to show in a macroeconomic policy document a forecast of revenues, targets for the deficit, and the corresponding levels of expenditure. However, this is not an MTBF. A true MTBF must be a political commitment on incomes and expenditures, driven by known or expected policy changes and changes in the overall economic environment that influence these choices. To be effective, the resource constraint embodied in the macroeconomic framework must have an unquestioned authority for all involved in the budgetary process.

While a formal commitment has been made to medium-term budgeting (most recently in the new Act on Budgetary Rules), the actual move toward multi-year budgeting, as just defined, has only begun. An important first step was the publication from 2000 by the Institute for Financial Policy (IFP) of the Ministry of Finance of three-year projections of aggregate revenues and expenditures. The latter are now serving as a basis for the annual pre-accession economic program (PEP) that the country presents to the EU.

It is recognized that in practice the said forecasts do not have a strong impact on the budget, and at present they are a peripheral activity to budget preparation and execution. One illustration of this phenomenon is the wide gap between the target presented in the 2001 PEP for general government expenditure in 2002 and the current official projection (37 percent of GDP versus 40.6 percent of GDP, respectively, excluding interest on bank restructuring bonds).

Strengthening communication and the institutional relationship between the IFP and the Budget Section of the Ministry of Finance (responsible for budget preparation), and improving the techniques and methodology for making macroeconomic forecasts including revenue forecasts, would enhance the authority of the medium-term programming exercise. These steps should be taken, but they are likely to prove insufficient without formal institutionalization of the MTBF and of the macroeconomic strategy that underpins it.

To achieve that institutionalization, a growing number of governments are finding it useful to bind themselves at the most senior level and in the most public fashion to medium-term budget rules.[188] The experience suggests that such rules should be best expressed in terms of expenditure targets. Recently, Poland adopted the now famous "CPI+1" rule to guide its expenditure containment efforts. It might be still better to set such rules in nominal terms and in conjunction with the country's inflation objectives. Apart from providing a framework for monetary and fiscal policy coordination, the key advantage of this method is its simplicity. The comparative ease with which compliance can be monitored, including by the public at large, makes it easier to enlist the public's support for the government's fiscal strategy . . . and to call on it when the time comes for painful fiscal choices.

Comprehensiveness of the Budget

The budgetary exercise would be of limited use if it encompassed only parts of government operations, while other parts operated irrespective of the government's overall financial constraints and strategic priorities. Considerable progress has been made in this respect with the elimination of extrabudgetary funds and the integration of their finances into the state budget. These funds, in particular the Road Fund, had accumulated large debts and their expenditures systematically exceeded their revenues. The state budget spent on average 1 percent of GDP per year to "subsidize" them. All extrabudgetary funds except the Agricultural Market Regulation Fund (transformed into an Agency), the Nuclear Fund (which accumulates revenues for the decommissioning of the power plant), and the Housing Development Fund (which will be abolished in January 2003) were abolished in January 2002 and their finances integrated into the budget.

However, challenges still remain. It is notable that the recently approved Act on Budgetary Rules distinguishes between budgetary and semi-budgetary organizations. Semi-budgetary organizations may be units of ministries or quasi-state enterprises with their own sources of revenue. The legislation suggests that the revenues of semi-budgetary organizations belong to these organizations and are not included in the overall budgeting process—nor are they included as public revenues. Potentially, this means that the semi-budgetary organizations could function as extrabudgetary funds. It will be necessary to avoid such an outcome.

A further potential danger is that extrabudgetary funds would be allowed to borrow commercially without prior permission as long as they have sufficient own income to service the debt. The Act explicitly precludes the issues of government guarantees for such borrowing, but it is difficult to imagine that such borrowing will not constitute an implicit liability for the government. It would appear necessary to at least ensure that the revenues of semi-budgetary organizations are included as part of general public revenues and the Treasury system and that their borrowing powers are limited, or should at least require permission from the Ministry of Finance.

Toward Program Budgeting

Expenditure rationalization would also be easier if the budget process generated a better sense not only of where public monies are spent but of what is being delivered and achieved with public monies. Such information would also make it easier to evaluate the trade-offs which fiscal consolidation makes unavoidable.

---

188. See Feldman, Robert, and C. Maxwell Watson, *Into the EU: Policy Frameworks in Central Europe*, International Monetary Fund, Washington, D.C., 2002.

A number of important steps have been taken toward such greater performance orientation, and the introduction of program budgeting appears to be proceeding in a well-structured manner. First, a functional classification of government operations (COFOG) in accordance with international standards was adopted starting with the 2002 budget. Second, four budgetary chapters of the 2002 budget (Education, Supreme Court, Constitutional Court, and Academy of Sciences) have been presented in a program format. Program structures have been prepared for six more chapters in the 2003 budget and the budget will be in a complete program structure for 2004.

Nevertheless, concerns have been raised as to whether units in the line ministries fully understand the changes implied by program budgeting, or whether they simply see it as a set of forms and information requirements imposed from outside. Program budgeting will successfully assist resource allocation only where *its goals* are well understood, so that government operations can be assessed (or at least challenged) in terms of their cost as well as their conformity with stated policies; and where *its means* are embedded in the daily operational routines of line agencies. One of the implications of this is that progress in budget methodologies needs to rest firmly on the strengthening of analytical capacities within line ministries.

The most difficult part of implementation may be the follow-up and review process of the performance of programs and sub-programs. This will require strong institutional mechanisms to feed information back to the management of the ministries so that priorities can be reassessed and spending reallocated according to performance. It is also necessary to have mechanisms that allow the government as a whole to assess the effectiveness of spending and judge how far it corresponds to previously established priorities.

Execution and Information Systems

The possibility of making such productive use of the program budgeting framework will therefore depend critically on the quality and reliability of the underlying financial and information systems. Unfortunately, fiscal information coming from spending units arrives late and in an inconvenient form for fiscal analysis (with problems of classification, data recording, and data consolidation and reporting). The lack of an integrated financial information system to bring together the Ministry of Finance, the line ministries, the spending units, the National Bank of Slovakia (NBS) and the NKU creates problems of untimely, unshared, and inaccurate information. The lack of data on expected spending and expected revenues makes reliable forecasting, and therefore cash management, difficult. This is compounded by the lack of commitment accounting.

The main justification and focus of the proposed Treasury reform ought to be to remedy these deficiencies. The project to set up a State Treasury has been functioning since 1999. However, its focus appears to be on the acquisition of Treasury systems (hardware and software) rather than on serving the needs of the Ministry of Finance and, perhaps more important, the needs of the line ministries[189] for the efficient execution of the budget together with timely and relevant reports to serve in expenditure management.

The reasons for wanting to transfer payment functions away from the Central Bank as envisaged in the Treasury Act[190] are less clear, and prima facie, less urgent with regard to the fiscal

189. Treasury systems should be designed not so much as a command-and-control mechanism than as a service to spending ministries and units, so that they derive distinct advantages from it, such as (i) improved budget formulation because of the availability of better tools; (ii) easier consolidation of budget proposals; (iii) more convenient "flexing" of budget proposals; (iv) improved accounting (more accurate and timely records; closer monitoring of each stage of a transaction; more convenient consolidation of data); (v) better reporting (more timely, more complete, less costly); and (vi) direct on-line communication of data with other participants in the budget and accounting processes.
190. The law setting up the State Treasury was approved in June 2002. In the law an initial deadline for the transfer of functions from the Central Bank to the State Treasury was set for 1 January 2003. However, this could be postponed until 1 January 2004, during which period the Central Bank would retain responsibility for government payments.

consolidation priorities outlined above. Budgetary control is strong in the current NBS-dominated system. The main weakness was actually never in the system of control itself but in the fact that some state institutions were operating outside of the NBS net. The responsibility for accounting and financial management is currently correctly located at the level of the spending units. Finally the Treasury's Single Account at the NBS ensures consolidated cash management (to the extent that state institutions are obliged to use it). In practice, however, little preparation has been made for the mandated transfer of payment operations from the NBS.

The legislation setting up the Treasury as well as the Debt and Liquidity Agency are indicative of a general tendency of hastily enacted legislation, often driven by the EU accession process, to include unrealistic deadlines, or to fail to consider the institutional changes required to implement the legislation. In the case of the Debt and Liquidity Agency there would appear to be no transitional provisions, so that in principle it should have assumed operational independence for debt management from the moment the Treasury Act came into force in June of 2002. However, in practice the Ministry of Finance together with the Central Bank continues to manage the debt, despite having no legal basis for doing so, since the new debt agency currently has neither staff nor operational rules.[191] A similar fate appears to await the new Treasury.

There is therefore an urgent need to (i) recalibrate and prioritize Treasury reform objectives to serve the requirements of the government's overall fiscal strategy; and (ii) clarify the responsibilities (transitional responsibilities, if need be) so that debt management and possible Treasury operations do not proceed in a legal vacuum.

Systems Integrity
As regards the integrity of budget execution systems, the main problems appear to arise from weaknesses in procurement and audit rather than from Treasury operations per se. Weak points in the public financial accountability system are: (i) defective procurement practices; (ii) the fact that the Supreme Audit Office (NKU) does not give an audit opinion on the reliability of the government's annual financial statements; (iii) weak follow-up and remedial action on significant audit findings; (iv) weak accountability arrangements for local government units; and (xv) an administrative culture that tolerates corrupt acts.

Procurement
The Slovak Republic was the first country in Central and Eastern Europe to pass a Public Procurement Act (1994), and to establish a procurement system based on the principles of transparency, competition, economy, and efficiency. The current Public Procurement Act (PPA) was passed in September 1999 (with a view mainly to fulfilling the requirements of the country's candidacy for the EU) and amended in November 2001. The PPA provides for four procurement methods: open tendering, restricted tendering, negotiated tendering with prior notification, and negotiated tendering without prior notification. In addition, in 2001 an independent Public Procurement Office (UVO) was created.

As experience has shown, procurement remains vulnerable to corruption and abuse. An audit report from the NKU identifies disregard of procurement rules as the most frequent violation of the public finance laws.[192] One reason for this is that the law itself is vague and formalistic, and lacks secondary legislation; in addition, a series of amendments has made it more confusing. Moreover, the law is unevenly applied and leaves considerable discretion to state institutions as to its

---

191. Although one of the driving forces for the establishment of the Agency was to allow the recruitment of highly qualified professional managers, the government amended the legislation establishing the Agency to stipulate that its personnel would be paid according to civil service pay scales. There would therefore appear to be little possibility of recruiting well-qualified personnel to the Agency in the near future.

192. In July 2002, an NKU investigation showed uneconomical use of finance at UVO, which included 100 percent down payments and was in contradiction to budgetary law (source: NKU website).

interpretation. While provisions on open tendering include transparent procedures conducive to competitive and economic procurement, the PPA does not include appropriate criteria for the use of restricted tendering, such as the availability of a limited number of suppliers, response to natural disasters, etc. Similarly, the negotiated procurement with prior notification method lacks transparency and gives excessive discretion to the contracting authority. Among the factors contributing to this poor record on procurement are: lack of guidelines on the use of various non-public tendering procedures; lack of separate standard bidding documents and contract formats for goods, works, and consultant services; poor and unclear technical specifications; ambiguous and subjective evaluation systems; lack of expertise among the evaluation commissions; and poorly written contracts. The ratio of direct purchases is too high, as is the number of cancelled public tenders (13.6 percent of total).[193]

A blueprint was recently submitted to the government drawing recommendations on how to improve the transparency and efficiency of procurement.[194] Key next steps should include: (i) establishing permanent procurement committees within contracting authorities that are responsible for decision making and for providing oversight and evaluation committees to deal with the bidding process; (ii) developing a formal code of ethics for government employees to improve their accountability in procurement; and (iii) completing procurement guidelines to cover non-public tendering procedures as well as procurement of consultants and updating of standard bidding documents. It is also recommended that the role of the NKU in conducting procurement audits of contracting authorities at regular intervals be enhanced and its reports made public.

Audit

At present, the existing audit (carried out by the NKU and the Ministry of Finance) is essentially external in nature and directed primarily at fault-finding rather than at assessing the adequacy of systems. Modern concepts of financial control, which have not made much headway in the Slovak public sector, locate the prime responsibility for financial control with the management of the entity concerned. If the country wishes to achieve strong public financial management it has to locate the essential controls at the entity level. The job of supervisory control or external audit then becomes an evaluation of whether the internal control systems established by management are adequate and are working properly.

Furthermore, although external audit was recently strengthened, a number of practical difficulties continue to limit its effectiveness. Amendments to the Supreme Audit Office Act,[195] adopted in November 2001, have: (i) expanded the responsibilities and competences of the NKU to include the Cabinet and ministries, other central authorities of state administration and their subordinated bodies, municipalities and regions, state funds, the National Property Fund, and public institutions; and (ii) enhanced its independence by extending the term of its officials and eliminating the control competences of the Ministry of Finance with respect to the budgetary chapter of the NKU.

The key remaining weaknesses involve: (i) the absence of a mandatory requirement for the Ministry of Finance to follow up with line ministries on defects identified at audit and to report to the legislature on the status of remedial actions taken; and (ii) the lack of a legal requirement for the NKU to report to the Slovak people on significant findings and matters arising from audits. Until such issues are resolved, the value of NKU audits (stemming losses, ending bad practices, and stamping out illegal actions) will remain largely unrealized, with a consequent loss of public resources and economic opportunities.

---

193. From information on public procurement statistics in 2001, government session of June 12, 2002.

194. Government Office, Blueprint of Measures for Increased Transparency in Public Procurement, document submitted to the government on September 9, 2002, and not yet discussed.

195. Reflecting the amended provisions of the Slovak Constitution, the requirements and principles of the INTOSAI Lima Declaration on independent financial control, and EU standards in the area of control.

Conclusions

Substantial progress has been made in the Slovak Republic in the reform of public finances. However, some of the changes are apparent only in the legal frameworks and not in the institutional relationships being developed. The most important challenges over the next few years are: (i) to give institutional authority to the multi-year fiscal framework as a basis for budgeting; (ii) to ensure that program budgeting is well understood and fully adopted by all involved; (iii) to develop a realistic implementation schedule for the Treasury system and to ensure that the needs of all clients (line ministries, Ministry of Finance) for improved budget execution information receive priority attention; and (iv) to enhance the security and probity of budget execution systems.

All of these challenges require leadership from the highest levels of the government. They cannot take place simply as a result of technical and legal changes. Perhaps the most fundamental reform will be needed at the highest level of government and will involve a commitment to be bound by budgeting rules that ensure that resources are allocated realistically according to the government's priorities and that the arbiter will necessarily be the Ministry of Finance.

Consolidating Local and Regional Governments

To complicate matters, the Slovak Republic is currently in the midst of a major decentralization process. While in theory this process may help with expenditure restructuring, the reverse is more likely to be the case in practice. There is little empirical evidence that fledgling decentralized authorities would have the needed administrative capacity or political mettle, nor that they would operate in an accountability framework that would definitely maximize the public good. On the contrary, the resulting greater fragmentation of public services might make it all the more difficult to realize the existing potentials for economies of scale. In the face of hard budget constraints, what is more likely to be weakened is the quality and accessibility of services for large segments of the population. This is not to deny the benefits that decentralization could ultimately provide. Rather, what is suggested is that the comprehensive devolution of expenditure responsibilities contemplated by the decentralization law should follow, rather than precede, the expenditure reform called for in this report, and that it should proceed only on the basis of considerably enhanced implementation capacities, service standards, and oversight and accountability frameworks.

Thus, the order of the day is to consolidate the recent advances before planning (or executing) new measures. The immediate priorities are: (i) to clarify the new "rules of the game;" (ii) to maintain the continuity and coordination of public interventions at the regional level; and (iii) to overcome the disadvantages posed by the current fragmentation of municipal authorities.

Decentralization Framework

The Slovak Republic has two tiers of local self-government: municipalities and regions. Local government was first introduced in 1990 (in the then-Czechoslovakia) at the municipal level.[196] Following the 2000 revision of the Constitution, Parliament adopted in September and October 2001, a set of fundamental laws creating Higher Territorial Units (*Vyššie Uzemne Celky*, known as VUCs, also called regions), amending the Act on Municipalities, defining the new competencies, transferring state property (such as schools and public buildings) to these local (i.e., municipal) and regional bodies, and amending the Act on Budgetary Rules accordingly. All in all, about 4.5 percent of GDP in new responsibilities would be transferred to municipalities and regions (see Table 5.2).

The responsibilities of municipalities were initially limited (under Act No. 369/1990) to the provision of basic services such as waste disposal, safe drinking water, public lighting, and maintenance of public roads, (on which municipalities spent about 2.8 percent of GDP).

---

196. The Act of the Slovak National Council No. 369/1990 on Municipalities defines their competencies and governance arrangements, sets the framework for financial management and budgeting, and defines the property of municipalities.

TABLE 5.2: EXPENDITURES TO BE TRANSFERRED TO REGIONAL AND LOCAL GOVERNMENTS
(1999 execution & 2000 budget, SKK thousands)

Sector	1999	2000
Health Care	34,904	32,160
Social Assistance	14,318,437	14,410,830
Fire Protection	600,492	627,002
Civil Protection	51,835	53,902
Local Road Maintenance	1,000,000	1,200,000
Education–Total	25,773,725	25,055,517
Of which:		
Preschool education	3,145,331	2,959,661
Elementary schools	9,731,006	10,053,182
High schools	1,230,256	1,148,173
Vocational high schools	2,214,535	1,986,882
Apprentice high schools	3,745,627	3,482,104
Church schools and facilities	629,127	663,943
Private schools and facilities	102,482	104,355
Other schools	3,623,746	3,406,543
Culture—Total	934,180	921,311
Total (SKK thousands)	**42,713,573**	**42,300,722**

Source: Budgeting and Expenditure Management in Slovakia, Bratislava, May, 16, 2002.

This initial set of responsibilities was greatly expanded under the 2001 decentralization[197] to include social assistance, the registry office, some roads and communication systems, territorial planning and building permits, environmental protection, primary schools, sports and parts of health care.

For their part, the newly created self-governing regions are to gain responsibility for regional development, territorial planning, secondary schools, social assistance, health care, cultural events and the protection of monuments, road transport and communications, civil protection, and some international cooperation functions. For the most part, these responsibilities are currently discharged by the national government's district and regional offices. The latter currently spend about 5.8 percent of GDP (see Tables 5.3 and 5.4).

In parallel, the national government's regional and district offices would disappear. Placed under the authority of the Ministry of Interior, regional offices are the deconcentrated bodies of the central government at the regional level; they manage separate budgetary chapters, regrouping the spending items delegated to them. They also supervise 79 district offices, the lowest level of national government administration, which administer the national services placed closest to the citizen, and, most important support and oversee the activities of municipalities. The transition was supposed to take place in 2002, but since neither regional nor district office functions have yet been replaced, the latter are continuing to operate "by default."

Initially, newly transferred responsibilities would be funded by itemized "decentralization subsidies" from the national government. Over time it is envisaged that the said subsidies would be increasingly untied and would become a more residual source of finance, as self-governing bodies develop their own sources of revenues.

---

197. Act on the Transfer of Some Competencies From Public Administration Bodies to Municipalities and Higher Territorial Units (Act no.416/2001).

TABLE 5.3: REGIONAL OFFICES EXPENDITURES (SKK billions)				
	1999	2000	2001	2002
Regional Offices	47.6	46.5	50.5	57.8
% of General Govt. Expenditure	14.7	13.8	12.9	13.9
% of Central Govt. Expenditure	24.4	23.0	23.2	22.4

Source: Ministry of Finance

TABLE 5.4: BUDGETS OF MUNICIPALITIES, 1999–2000 (SKK millions)		
	1999	2000
Total Revenues	24,181	27,355
Tax	11,609	12,799
Non-Tax	9,117	10,692
Transfers	3,362	3,739
Borrowing	93	124
Total Expenditure	23,918	26,458
Current	16,777	18,748
Capital	7,020	7,366
Balance	262	897

Sources: Actual figures, Ministry of Finance.

Clarification of Responsibilities

A first order of business is to clarify the roles and responsibilities of each of the layers of national and local/regional government. As things currently stand, there is confusion regarding the following issues:

(a) *The ownership of public assets.* Assets affected by the decentralization were supposed to be transferred to regional and municipal governments by July 1, 2002. In the absence of a comprehensive up-front inventory, considerable uncertainty remains as to exactly what assets are to be transferred, including the associated land holdings and utility connections. Furthermore, confronted with new responsibilities for which they feel unprepared, many local governments have resisted the transfer of a number of hospitals and other health care facilities.

(b) *The liabilities attached to public assets.* While the law provides that assets would be transferred free of debt, considerable debt has arisen during the transfer period, apparently in the expectation of an ultimate national government bailout. The fate of that new debt is now being debated.

(c) *The exact nature and distribution of the responsibilities being transferred.* The law has left many aspects of the new division of labor among public administrations vague (see Box 5.1) Given the untested nature of the proposed arrangement, this lack of specificity may have been unavoidable and perhaps even welcome, as it leaves room for adjustment in line with the practical circumstances encountered. After a period of experimentation, the final arrangements might be defined in subsequent legislation to be adopted in, perhaps, a year or two.

BOX 5.1: DEFINITION OF RESPONSIBILITIES IN THE DECENTRALIZED SYSTEM OF PRIMARY AND SECONDARY EDUCATION

"Decentralization gives rise to many issues concerning education policy. Among other things, we wish to point out the key issues—that of responsibilities. Relations between mayors and municipal authorities, and the heads of regional and district offices and regional authorities, school boards, headmasters, students, and parents are very complicated, and thus may disguise who is actually responsible for a particular school's results.

This general observation is of particular importance as far as headmasters are concerned. The headmaster of a school has been and remains a powerful element—being in charge of personnel and financial management for the school and acting as a state administration body in other important areas.

On the other hand, it is not clear to whom the headmaster as the highest manager of the school will be accountable. The division of appointment and removal powers among school boards and regional self-governing authorities (municipal and regional) renders actual responsibilities ambiguous and creates room for the headmaster to misuse this condition and points to the need for agreement between both parties for decreasing the headmaster's real responsibility. In addition, the process of school board election is not sufficiently regulated and these elections are usually organized by headmasters themselves. There are several decisions that the headmaster can make only after consultations with the school board, the pedagogical board, or a social partner, but the consequence of their non-agreement is not specified. Schools are founded and closed down by municipalities and higher territorial units, but only the Slovak Republic's MoE can remove them from the school network, and the procedure for this is not defined. The problems mentioned above may seem trivial, yet we have to realize that primary and secondary schools are entering a period in which a high number of autonomous players will begin to operate in this complex environment and the present hierarchy, from the ministry to the district offices, will cease to be in force. Moreover, most of the relevant participants will act in a political environment, and professional representatives in charge of education will be undergoing the process of transition from regional and district offices to self-governing authorities. This transition will include a huge amount of property administered to date by schools, school facilities, and state administration. In such an environment, any obscurities regarding responsibilities will lead to many serious problems, as has been witnessed in the past."

Source: National Report on Education Policy of the Slovak Governance Institute (SGI) and the Institute for Economic and Social Reforms (INEKO).

An Integrated Regional Administration

What is more troubling is that essential pieces of the institutional framework exist only on paper. This is the case with the self-governing regional administrations. When devising ways to fill this gap, it will be useful to keep in mind that the emergence of self-government at the regional level should not necessarily lead to a duplication of administrative structures between the new self-government administration on one hand and the remnants of the remaining regional office of the national government (from which it was created), on the other.

It would be preferable for regional administrations to remain integrated. This would avoid administrative duplications, facilitate coordination across services, and simplify their interactions with the citizens. In addition, an integrated administrative structure would allow for a seamless transfer of personnel as the scope of regional autonomy expanded over time. It is easy to envision that activities financed by tied "decentralization subsidies" would continue to be performed by national government personnel placed under the administrative authority of the regional head, but remaining under the technical jurisdiction of their national administrations. Conversely, the regions could rely on their own personnel to discharge the gradually expanding set of responsibilities funded by the regions' own resources or by general grants. The transfer of personnel would be made smoother if regions employed their own personnel, if not under a "unified" civil service regime,[198] at least under one that is closely "integrated" with the national government scheme.[199]

Fragmentation of Municipalities and Role of Districts

Another obstacle that will need to be overcome in the implementation of decentralization is the weak capacity of municipalities. This weakness is hardly surprising, given the atomization of municipalities: there are currently 2,886 municipalities for a population of 5.4 million inhabitants (an average of less than 2,000 persons per municipality). At that size, it would be unreasonable to expect municipalities to have either the fiscal or the human resource capacity to carry out more that basic "proximity" functions (such as street lightening, parks, public hygiene, population rolls), or to be able to reap the economies of scale involved in more elaborate public services.

Several options have been used by European countries to resolve this kind of problem. One option is *to abolish and/or consolidate small sub national units,* as many EU countries have done since 1960. In Sweden the number of localities was reduced from 2,500 to 278. Denmark merged 1,388 into 275 localities, Germany moved from 24,512 to 8,500 localities by 1980 and Belgium, from 2,663 to 589 localities between 1961 and 1980. Britain went even further, and has no local authorities in its villages; the basic unit is the district with an average population of 120,000.[200] Similarly, Latvia is seeking to lower the number of its municipalities from 580 to 102.

An alternative is for the central government to *provide incentives for inter-municipal cooperation* in local service delivery. This has enabled France to operate 36,000 municipalities of an even smaller average size than the Slovak municipalities. The new legal framework for decentralization allows municipalities to cooperate in service delivery as a means of taking advantage of economies of scale and of acquiring the potential to offer more diverse services—most notably, public utilities. It is important that the financing system encourages such cooperative efforts and does not encourage more fragmentation. Further, the grant system must not provide greater funds to smaller municipalities. For example, a grant that provides a constant amount to each municipality encourages fragmentation because the per capita amount is higher in small municipalities. Also, a grant that gives a larger percentage to smaller places (say a higher proportion of shared taxes) encourages fragmentation. Indeed, the grant system can be designed to encourage cooperation by providing more funds to municipalities that work together in delivering services (as is done in Hungary). Whatever option is chosen, there will be a need to develop the capacity of local governments to generate and to manage a larger volume of resources.

As long as the problems linked with fragmentation persist, however, it will make sense to retain the district levels of national administration in their role of: (i) encouraging such inter-municipal cooperation; (ii) operating, where needed, inter-municipal services and infrastructures; (iii) back-stopping weak municipalities, where they are unable to provide mandated services or to satisfacto-

---

198. Under a unified regime (e.g., Ireland, Jamaica, Sri Lanka), local governments employ their own personnel under statutory rules for all local civil servants defined at the national level. The advantage of this system is the harmonization of employment and salary systems, which makes it possible to organize careers and mobility across local governments, while limiting the risk of cronyism. The disadvantage of the system is that it necessitates a central management of staff rules and possibly cumbersome coordination procedures among local governments.

199. Under an integrated regime (e.g., the Netherlands), local governments employ their own personnel under specific provisions of single statutory rules for all civil servants, national or local. The advantage of the system is that it facilitates the mobility of staff between the state and local governments. The disadvantage is a lower level of loyalty of local personnel and more complex civil service management at the state level.

200. Ebel, R., I. Varfalvi, and S. Varga, "Sorting Out intergovernmental Roles and Responsibilities," in Bokros, Lajos, and Jean-Jacques Dethier, editors, *Public Finance Reform during the Transition: The Experience of Hungary,* World Bank: Washington, DC, 1998.

rily perform mandated tasks (such as maintaining proper accounts); and (iv) more generally, overseeing their financial and administrative operations.

Funding Local and Regional Self-Government

The arrangement whereby newly transferred responsibilities would be initially financed by itemized, tied grants is appropriate to a situation in which administrative capacities are either weak (municipalities) or, at best, untested (regions). Beyond being more secure, such an arrangement leaves to the national government the necessary leadership to (re)deploy public resources as needed for the overall fiscal consolidation effort. Certainly, the implementation of the proposed financing of education on a strict per capita basis would be made much easier, as would the related painful decisions to close down, downsize, or merge facilities (or, conversely, to avoid "beggar thy neighbor" policies among territorial jurisdictions).

Although limited at the beginning, the role of elected, municipal and regional assemblies could expand gradually over time as the revamped expenditure arrangements become the norm. This expansion may take the form of untying parts of the decentralization subsidies, or of providing greater leeway for local taxation. The property tax, a PIT surcharge, and the business tax could gradually become the major sources of local revenues. This would increase the ratio of revenues subject to local discretion, and hence would also increase local accountability. As in other OECD countries, however, transfers will continue to be the principal source of funds for current expenditures. The annual level of untied transfers could be linked to macroeconomic benchmarks such as inflation and GDP growth (as in France) or determined as a fixed percentage of taxes (as in Japan). Over time, the system for allocating current grants could gradually be simplified and consolidated into a single equalization fund designed to compensate imbalances across municipalities and regions.

Conclusion

In the immediate future however, the priority is to consolidate the present phase of decentralization by taking the following steps:

  (a) Clarifying the roles and responsibilities of old and new players
  (b) Creating integrated regional administrations
  (c) Funding newly transferred responsibilities through itemized, tied decentralization subsidies
  (d) Stimulating inter-municipal cooperation, with district offices continuing to oversee and backstop weaker and smaller municipalities.

Judiciary Reform

Modernizing the justice sector is critical for accelerating and maintaining economic growth, addressing the critical needs of the vulnerable groups, and increasing social cohesion and stability. Despite the reform measures implemented over the last decade, the justice sector has earned a reputation for being slow, overly expensive, corrupt, and unresponsive to the market and social needs. In diagnostic surveys of perceived corruption, courts come second only to health care in terms of the frequency of bribes and the first in terms of the average size of the bribes. Legal services are not accessible to the majority of citizens and serve predominantly to the corporate clientele. While the Government failed to establish effective supervision over the legal profession that could protect the interest of the clients, lawyers have acquired considerable economic and political power and are believed to be intimately involved in judicial corruption. Chapter 2 notes the crippling problems these issues pose for debt resolution, as well as the collateral damages for the economy.

The challenge faced by the incoming government is to translate the growing political urgency for justice sector reform into sound public policy focused on the needs of those affected by the justice sector's performance: its clients. This can be achieved via a set of well-targeted reforms aimed at: (i) strengthening the court performance and image; and (ii) improving the provision of non-court legal services.

Court Reform

Achieving prompter resolution of cases and increased quality of courts' decisions and outcomes should be the two major objectives of the Slovak Government. At present, *court congestion and poor quality of decisions* appear to be the most visible problems of the Slovak judiciary. In debt resolution cases, such delays give unfair advantages to the debtors as the value of the underlying assets dissipate over time. Combined with poor service quality, delays foster *corruption,* reduce *predictability of outcomes,* undermine *the public confidence in the justice system.*

The causes of court underperformance are complex. A brief analysis of the court system conducted by the Bank suggests that the underperformance is closely associated with *bad management practices* in litigation and in administering the judicial system at the court and system levels. More specifically, bad management practices extend to the vertical and horizontal allocation of management functions; inadequate capacity of the organizations concerned to carry out their mandates including the lack of proper management tools and procedures both legal and operational; suboptimal distribution of jurisdiction among different levels of the courts; ineffective resource and information management.

During the 1990s, the Government tried to improve court performance mainly through allocating additional resources and making judges work more intensively. As a result, the number of judges increased from 16 to 23 per 100,000 population and the judges' productivity more than doubled. However, these measures proved inadequate to compensate for the rapidly growing quantity and complexity of cases and the clearance rate actually decreased. The worst delays are concentrated in the Supreme Court. Although it has grown to become one of the biggest in the world (it employs 90 judges), its clearance rate has dropped from 100 to 60 percent. In the late 90s the Government attempted to carry out structural reforms, but they were not well planned and did not enjoy a censuses of stakeholders. Under these reforms the Government streamlined civil and criminal procedures, optimized court jurisdiction, strengthened alternative dispute resolution mechanisms, introduced automated file management, and improved the provision of legal information to judges.

The justice sector reforms of the 1990s did not produce the anticipated results. Some of them were not well targeted; others will take more time to produce results. Overall, that reform period highlighted the need for: greater prioritization; building consensus; better analytical and coordination capacity; and strong leadership. This period of reform also clearly demonstrated that without professionalization of justice sector management, improvements in performance are very difficult to achieve.

Professionalization of the justice sector management will first of all require strengthening the management capacity in the Ministry of Justice (MOJ), which is the key institution in developing and implementing justice sector reform. The MOJ should undertake a review of its organizational structure, operating procedures, cadres and budget and, if necessary, regulatory framework in order to develop and implement a strategy aimed at becoming a more effective court manager. Creating a specialized court management unit should be a part of such strategy. Judicial independence should be given the attention it deserves but should not be used as an excuse for not proceeding with strengthening the MOJ's court management capacity.

Courts, on the other hand, are in need of professional administrators who would support the judges in resolving those tasks for which they do not have monopoly. The workload can be distributed more effectively if the number of judges be reduced while the number of administrative staff increased. Judicial training should be institutionalized and its focus should be expanded from the texts of the laws to critical reasoning, trial management, and economic and business knowledge. The Government needs to sustain its commitment to the automation of file management and expand this program geographically and technically, for example by rolling out the automated document management and recording of the court hearings. It should also continue its work on streamlining the civil and criminal procedures.

Corruption in the courts is a very serious issue and requires immediate attention. Systemic changes in court management should promote transparency of the process and accountability of judges while protecting their impartiality. However, systemic changes must be accompanied by exposing and disciplining corrupt and under-performing individuals. This requires a transparent performance monitoring system and capacity for internal investigation.

Strengthening Professional Regulations and Client Protection

Improving court performance is not enough to ensure justice. Legal services are too costly, their quality is uneven, and, for the last decade, their supply has been lagging behind demand. The Government has allowed legal service providers i.e., lawyers, notaries, and executors to retain their professional monopoly. The bars of lawyers used their self-regulation power to restrict entry into the profession, suppress competition, and maintain information asymmetry for example through prohibition of specialization and advertisement. The regulatory framework for the lawyers emphasizes loyalty to the profession, but is largely ineffective in protecting the interest of the clients.

The regulatory framework for the provision of legal services is, in principle, not very different from such in Western Europe. However, in the Slovak conditions the regulation is much less effective in controlling for market failures. The price for the legal services is monopolistic and depends not on the marginal costs of the suppliers, but on the consumers' ability to pay. It is not unusual for a Slovak privately practicing lawyer to earn as much as his/her US counterpart, while the cost of living is Slovakia is many times lower. The information asymmetry between the lawyers and their clients is amplified by unstable legislative and institutional environment, low public awareness, and reluctance to challenge lawyers that is rooted in the post-socialist culture.

While legal service provision was privatized, the mechanisms for ensuring the access to legal services for underprivileged groups have remained unchanged. Although the courts assign lawyers to those who cannot afford one, the regulated fees are not high enough to attract good lawyers. The discrepancy between official and actual legal fees makes it difficult to recover the actual legal expenses by the wining party as they cannot recover what they actually paid for their representation. The recently introduced amendment to the official fee schedule raises the regulated fees to a more realistic level, but does little to facilitate access to legal services for the underprivileged groups.

The Government needs to develop a capacity to monitor the legal service market and design policy interventions consistent with broader economic and social objectives. These policy interventions should be aimed, among other things, at increasing the competition among the legal service providers, protecting the client, introducing disclosures by providers and self-regulatory bodies, strengthening disciplinary mechanisms and ensuring a minimum level of access to the legal services by underprivileged groups such as the Roma.

Conclusions

The recent EU regular report on progress toward Accession underscores the need for the Slovak Republic to strengthen its governance framework. The discussion above has highlighted some of the priorities involved. In responding to this challenge, it will be important for the country to eschew the temptation of paper solutions. Not only are such solutions pointless, they are potentially dangerous, as they create the illusion that problems are being addressed at the same time they force actual practices into a legal vacuum.

In the areas of *public expenditure management,* the most important challenges over the next few years are: (i) to give institutional authority to the multi-year fiscal framework as a basis for budgeting; (ii) to ensure that program budgeting is well understood and fully adopted by all involved; (iii) to develop a realistic implementation schedule for the Treasury system and ensure that the needs of all clients (line ministries, Ministry of Finance) for improved budget execution information receive priority attention; and (iv) to enhance the security and probity of budget execution systems.

As regards *decentralization,* the order of the day is to consolidate the recent advances before planning (or executing) new ones. Immediate priorities involve: (i) clarifying the roles and responsibilities of each of the layers of national and local/regional government; (ii) creating integrated regional administrations; (iii) funding newly transferred responsibilities through itemized, tied decentralization subsidies; and (iv) stimulating inter-municipal cooperation, with district offices continuing to oversee and backstop weaker and smaller municipalities.

Finally, priority for judiciary reform involves: (i) refocusing the Supreme Court on its core mandate; (ii) strengthening the management and policy capacity in the Ministry of Justice; (iii) creating a body of professional court administrators; (iv) rolling out the modernized case management system throughout the judiciary; (iv) stepping up the investigation and prosecution of corrupt judges; (v) strengthening the regulatory bodies of legal profession and separating this role from that of advocacy; and (vi) enhancing client protection.

ANNEX

TABLE 1: KEY DEMOGRAPHIC ASSUMPTIONS FOR PENSION PROJECTIONS

	2001	2005	2010	2020	2030	2040	2050	2060	2070	2080
Average Lifetime Men										
Pessimistic	69.6	69.9	70.5	73.5	74.8	76.1	77.4	77.6	77.8	78.0
Base	69.6	69.9	70.5	72.5	73.8	75.1	76.4	76.6	76.8	77.0
Optimistic	69.6	69.9	70.5	71.5	72.5	73.5	74.4	74.4	74.4	74.4
Average Lifetime Women										
Pessimistic	76.6	76.9	77.5	79.5	80.4	81.4	82.4	82.6	82.8	83.0
Base	76.6	76.9	77.5	78.5	79.5	80.4	81.4	81.6	81.8	82.0
Optimistic	76.6	76.9	77.5	77.5	78.2	78.8	79.5	79.5	79.5	79.5
Total Fertility Rate										
Pessimistic	1.35	1.40	1.45	1.70	1.72	1.74	1.75	1.75	1.75	1.75
Base	1.35	1.42	1.50	1.80	1.90	2.00	2.10	2.10	2.10	2.10
Optimistic	1.35	1.42	1.50	1.80	1.90	2.00	2.10	2.10	2.10	2.10

Source: World Bank calculations.

STATISTICAL APPENDIX

TABLE 1: SLOVAK REPUBLIC—GROSS DOMESTIC EXPENDITURE AND PRODUCT
(shares based on current price data)

	1995	1996	1997	1998	1999	2000	2001	2002 proj.
A. Shares of gross domestic expenditure at market prices								
1. Final consumption	71.8	75.6	74.3	75.9	76.1	76.0	76.6	76.9
a) General government	21.3	23.3	22.2	22.5	20.7	20.7	20.8	20.7
b) Private	50.5	52.3	52.2	53.4	55.4	55.3	55.8	56.2
2. Gross capital formation	26.5	35.6	35.2	34.7	28.2	26.4	31.9	31.0
a) Gross fixed capital formation	25.2	32.4	34.3	36.2	30.3	29.5	31.3	25.7
b) Change in inventories	1.4	3.2	1.0	−1.5	−2.0	−3.1	0.6	5.3
3. Total Absorption (1+2)	98.3	111.2	109.6	110.6	104.3	102.4	108.5	107.9
4. Resource balance	1.7	−11.2	−9.6	−10.6	−4.3	−2.4	−8.5	−7.9
a) Exports of goods & services	57.4	53.2	56.1	59.2	61.0	71.8	74.0	73.3
b) Imports of goods & services	55.7	64.4	65.6	69.9	65.4	74.2	82.5	81.2
5. Gross domestic product (3+4)	100	100	100	100	100	100	100	100
6. Net income from abroad	−0.1	−0.2	−0.6	−0.7	−1.5	−1.8	−1.5	−1.6
7. Gross national income (5+6)	99.9	99.8	99.4	99.3	98.5	98.2	98.5	98.4
8. Net current transfers from abroad	0.5	1.0	0.8	1.7	1.0	0.6	1.0	0.8
9. Gross national disposable income (7+8)	100.4	100.8	100.3	101.0	99.5	98.8	99.5	99.3
10. National savings (9-1)	28.6	25.2	25.9	25.1	23.4	22.8	22.9	22.3
B. Shares of GDP by Industrial Origin								
1. Agriculture	5.5	5.1	5.2	4.9	4.2	4.3	4.1	..
2. Industry	35.4	35.5	32.0	31.1	31.4	30.0	29.0	..
Construction	4.7	6.9	6.6	6.5	5.0	4.9	4.6	..
Gas, electricity, water	4.6	4.2	3.6	3.1	4.0	3.6	2.4	..
Mining and quarrying	1.0	0.9	0.8	0.8	0.8	0.8	0.7	..
Manufacturing	25.1	23.5	20.9	20.7	21.7	20.7	21.3	..
3. Services	51.6	51.3	55.3	55.1	55.0	56.8	58.2	..
4. Total value added at basic prices	92.5	92.0	92.6	91.1	90.7	91.0	91.3	..
5. Taxes less subsidies on products	7.5	8.0	7.4	8.9	9.3	9.0	8.7	..
6. GDP at market prices	100	100	100	100	100	100	100	..
Memo Item (billions koruny)								
Gross domestic product at market prices	568.9	628.6	708.6	775.0	835.7	908.8	989.3	1066.

Source: LDB.

TABLE IA: SLOVAK REPUBLIC—GROSS DOMESTIC EXPENDITURE AND PRODUCT (CURRENT PRICES)
(billions of koruny)

	1995	1996	1997	1998	1999	2000	2001	2002 proj.
A. GDP by Expenditure								
1. Final consumption	408.4	475.1	526.7	588.2	636.1	691.0	757.8	820.3
a) General government	121.3	146.5	157.1	174.3	173.3	188.5	205.8	221.0
b) Private	287.1	328.6	369.6	413.9	462.8	502.5	552.0	599.3
2. Gross capital formation	150.8	223.6	249.7	269.2	235.8	239.8	315.2	330.5
a) Gross fixed capital formation	143.1	203.4	242.9	280.9	252.9	267.9	309.6	273.9
b) Change in inventories	7.7	20.2	6.8	−11.7	−17.1	−28.1	5.6	56.6
3. Total Absorption (1+2)	559.2	698.7	776.4	857.4	871.9	930.8	1,073.0	1,150.8
4. Resource balance	9.7	−70.1	−67.7	−82.4	−36.2	−22.1	−83.7	−84.7
a) Exports of goods & services	326.4	334.7	397.4	459.1	510.0	652.4	732.3	781.1
b) Imports of goods & services	316.7	404.8	465.1	541.5	546.2	674.5	816.0	865.8
5. Gross domestic product (3+4)	568.9	628.6	708.7	775.0	835.7	908.7	989.3	1,066.1
6. Net income from abroad	−0.4	−1.4	−4.1	−5.5	−12.5	−16.3	−15.1	−16.7
7. Gross national income (5+6)	568.5	627.2	704.6	769.5	823.2	892.4	974.2	1,049.4
8. Net current transfers from abroad	2.7	6.2	5.9	12.9	8.1	5.4	10.3	9.0
9. Gross national disposable income (7+8)	571.2	633.4	710.5	782.4	831.3	897.8	984.5	1,058.4
10. National savings (9-1)	162.8	158.3	183.8	194.2	195.2	206.8	226.7	238.1
B. GDP by Industrial Origin								
1. Agriculture	31.3	32.3	36.8	37.6	35.4	39.0	40.6	..
2. Industry	201.3	223.2	226.9	241.2	262.7	272.5	286.9	..
Construction	26.7	43.3	46.9	50.2	41.8	44.3	45.6	..
Gas, electricity, water	26.0	26.3	25.8	24.4	33.3	32.9	23.9	..
Mining and quarrying	5.5	5.6	6.0	6.2	6.5	7.0	6.9	..
Manufacturing	143.0	147.9	148.2	160.4	181.1	188.3	210.6	..
3. Services	293.8	322.8	392.2	427.4	459.6	515.9	576.0	..
o.w. Transportation	43.4	47.8	53.1	56.7	61.6	66.5	83.3	..
Trade	75.5	77.5	101.1	112.6	121.5	138.2	150.6	..
4. Total value added at basic prices	526.4	578.2	655.9	706.2	757.7	827.3	903.5	..
5. Taxes less subsidies on products	42.5	50.4	52.8	68.8	78.0	81.5	85.8	..
6. GDP at market prices	568.9	628.6	708.6	775.0	835.7	908.8	989.3	1,066.1

Source: LDB.

TABLE 2: SLOVAK REPUBLIC—ANNUAL GROWTH RATES OF NATIONAL INCOME AND PRODUCT AT CONSTANT PRICES
(percentages)

	1996	1997	1998	1999	2000	2001	2002 proj.
A. GDP by Expenditure and Income							
1. Final consumption	11.3	2.6	7.8	0.1	−1.0	4.2	4.0
a) General government	16.5	−4.7	12.7	−6.3	1.1	4.7	2.3
b) Private	9.1	5.9	5.8	2.9	−1.8	4.0	4.6
2. Gross capital formation	36.1	6.3	5.1	−20.2	2.7	15.2	2.9
a) Gross fixed capital formation	30.9	14.3	11.0	−18.5	1.2	9.5	..
b) Change in inventories	132.5	−76.5	−297.6	28.9	−24.3	−122.2	..
3. Total Absorption	18.0	3.8	6.9	−6.2	0.0	7.2	3.6
4. Exports of goods & services	−1.3	19.0	13.2	5.2	13.8	6.5	5.9
5. Imports of goods & services	19.8	13.8	16.8	−6.3	10.2	11.7	5.3
6. Capacity to Import[1]	−3.9	17.6	15.9	3.2	14.2	3.6	5.8
7. Real GDI at market prices	4.4	4.7	5.4	0.0	2.2	1.1	..
8. Real gross national income	4.3	4.3	5.2	−0.8	1.9	1.3	..
9. Real gross national disposable income	..	..	6.1	−1.5	1.5	1.8	..
10. Real gross national savings	..	..	1.1	−6.7	9.9	−5.7	..
B. GDP by Industrial origin							
1. Agriculture	−2.1	9.7	5.4	0.3	−0.2	−5.0	..
2. Industry	11.2	−4.7	−0.3	−0.4	−4.5	3.0	..
Construction	51.6	−1.5	−15.6	−29.9	2.7	−1.5	..
Gas, electricity, water	19.0	−21.9	−10.7	22.2	−24.5	−43.1	..
Manufacturing	2.2	−2.5	5.2	2.9	−2.0	10.2	..
3. Services	2.0	13.1	4.6	1.2	7.6	4.6	..
4. Total value added at basic prices	5.3	5.7	2.9	0.6	2.9	3.5	..
5. GDP at market prices	5.8	5.6	4.0	1.3	2.2	3.3	4.0

Notes: 1/ Exports deflated by import price index.
Source: LDB.

TABLE 2A: SLOVAK REPUBLIC—GROSS DOMESTIC PRODUCT BY EXPENDITURE, NATIONAL INCOME AND SAVINGS
(billions of 1995 koruny)

	1995	1996	1997	1998	1999	2000	2001	2002 proj.
A. GDP by Expenditure and Income								
1. Final consumption	408.4	454.5	466.4	502.6	503.3	498.3	519.4	540.0
a) General government	121.3	141.3	134.6	151.7	142.1	143.7	150.5	154.0
b) Private	287.1	313.2	331.8	350.9	361.2	354.6	368.9	386.0
2. Gross capital formation	150.8	205.2	218.2	229.3	183.0	188.0	216.6	222.9
a) Gross fixed capital formation	143.1	187.3	214.0	237.6	193.7	196.1	214.8	..
b) Change in inventories	7.7	17.9	4.2	−8.3	−10.7	−8.1	1.8	..
3. Total Absorption (1+2)	559.2	659.7	684.6	731.9	686.3	686.3	736.0	762.8
4. Resource balance	9.7	−57.4	−48.5	−70.6	−16.2	−1.6	−28.7	−26.9
a) Exports of goods & services	326.4	322.0	383.2	433.8	456.3	519.2	552.8	585.4
b) Imports of goods & services	316.7	379.4	431.7	504.4	472.5	520.8	581.5	612.3
5. Gross domestic product (3+4)	568.9	602.3	636.1	661.3	670.1	684.7	707.3	735.9
6. Trading gains or losses	0.0	−8.3	−14.3	−6.2	−15.1	−15.5	−30.9	..
7. Real gross domestic income (5+6)	568.9	594.0	621.8	655.1	655.0	669.2	676.4	..
8. Net income from abroad	−0.4	−1.3	−3.7	−4.7	−10.0	−12.2	−10.8	..
9. Real gross national income (7+8)	568.5	592.7	618.1	650.4	645.0	657.0	665.6	..
10. Net current transfers from abroad	..	..	5.3	11.0	6.5	4.1	7.3	..
11. Real gross national disp. inc. (9+10)	..	..	623.4	661.4	651.5	661.1	672.9	..
12. Gross national savings (11−1)	..	..	157.0	158.8	148.2	162.8	153.5	..
Memo Item:								
Capacity to import	326.4	313.7	368.9	427.6	441.2	503.7	521.9	552.4
B. GDP by Industrial origin								
1. Agriculture	31.3	30.7	33.7	35.5	35.6	35.5	33.7	..
2. Industry	201.2	223.7	213.1	212.5	211.5	201.9	208.0	..
Construction	26.7	40.5	39.9	33.7	23.6	24.3	23.9	..
Gas, electricity, water	26.0	30.9	24.1	21.6	26.3	19.9	11.3	..
Mining and quarrying	5.5	6.1	6.5	7.2	7.1	6.4	5.9	..
Manufacturing	143.0	146.2	142.6	150.0	154.4	151.4	166.9	..
3. Services	293.8	299.7	339.1	354.7	359.1	386.5	404.3	..
5. Total value added at basic prices	526.4	554.1	585.9	602.7	606.2	624.0	646.0	..
6. Taxes less subsidies on products	42.5	48.0	50.2	58.6	63.8	60.8	61.4	..
7. GDP at market prices (5+6)	568.9	602.1	636.1	661.3	670.0	684.8	707.3	735.9

Source: LDB.

TABLE 3: SLOVAK REPUBLIC—PRICES

	1995	1996	1997	1998	1999	2000	2001	2002 proj.
Exchange Rates (koruny per US$)								
Nominal official avg. exchange rate (rf)	29.7	30.7	33.6	35.2	41.4	46.0	48.4	47.1
Real effective exchange rate (1995=100)[1]	100.0	99.7	104.6	102.3	99.9	109.3	107.8	..
Price Indices								
Wholesale price index (1995=100)	100.0	104.1	108.8	112.3	116.6	128.0	..	..
Consumer Price Index (1995=100)	100.0	105.8	112.3	119.8	132.5	148.4	159.3	166.0
CPI (% change Dec-Dec)	7.2	5.4	6.4	5.6	14.2	8.4	6.5	4.0
CPI (% change in period average)	9.8	5.8	6.1	6.7	10.6	12.0	7.3	4.2
Real growth of avg. monthly wages (%)	4.1	7.1	6.6	1.6	−3.0	−4.9	0.8	..
Manuf. Exp. Unit Val. Index (% change)	6.1	−4.9	−7.8	−3.7	0.0	−1.9	−1.0	..
Implicit Deflators (1995=100)								
Gross domestic product	100.0	104.4	111.4	117.2	124.7	132.7	139.9	144.9
Exports of goods and services[2]	100.0	103.9	103.7	105.8	111.8	125.7	132.5	133.4
Imports of goods and services[2]	100.0	106.7	107.7	107.4	115.6	129.5	140.3	141.4
Terms of trade Index	100.0	97.4	96.3	98.6	96.7	97.0	94.4	94.4

Notes: 1/ Source: IMF—IFS May, 2002.
2/ Calculated based on SNA data.
Source: LDB and IMF, IFS May 2002.

TABLE 4: SLOVAK REPUBLIC—CONSOLIDATED PUBLIC SECTOR FINANCE
(in percent of GDP)

	1996	1997	1998	1999	2000	2001
Overall balance includ. grants	−3.2	−4.8	−5.1	−4.3	−9.1	−8.5
Total Revenues, incl. current Grants	43.5	40.1	37.8	39.8	37.9	35.7
Expenditures and Net Lending	46.7	45.0	42.9	44.0	47.0	44.2
Overall balance excl. current Grants[1/]	−3.2	−4.9	−5.1	−4.2	−9.1	−8.5
Current Revenue/Expenditure						
Current Budget Balance, incl. current Grants	3.6	1.9	0.5	2.8	−0.2	−1.5
Total Current Revenues, incl. current Grants	42.6	39.1	37.1	39.3	37.3	35.1
Current revenue, excluding grants	42.6	39.0	37.1	39.2	37.3	35.1
Direct Taxes	24.8	22.3	21.9	20.8	20.5	19.8
Indirect Taxes	13.2	13.0	12.0	11.9	12.7	11.0
On domestic goods & services	11.6	11.2	10.4	10.4	11.2	10.6
On international trade	1.6	1.8	1.5	1.5	1.5	0.4
Nontax Receipts	4.7	3.8	3.2	6.6	4.1	4.3
Grants, current	0.0	0.0	0.0	0.0	0.0	0.0
Total Current Expenditures	39.0	37.2	36.6	36.4	37.5	36.6
Interest payments	2.1	1.9	2.8	3.2	3.2	4.0
Interest on Bank Restructuring Bonds	0.0	0.0	0.0	0.0	0.3	0.8
Other Current Transfers	21.8	20.0	19.7	20.0	19.5	19.5
Subsidies and contributions	3.3	2.8	2.5	2.2	3.8	2.0
Consumption	11.9	12.4	11.6	11.0	11.0	11.1
Wages and Salaries	6.8	6.8	6.8	6.4	6.2	6.0
Capital Receipts/Payments						
Total Capital Revenues	0.8	1.1	0.7	0.5	0.6	0.6
Total Capital Expenditures and Net Lending	7.7	7.8	6.3	7.3	9.5	7.6
Capital Transfers and Net Lending	3.3	2.4	2.3	4.5	6.3	4.4
Budgetary Investment	4.4	5.4	3.9	3.2	3.2	3.2
Debt (at end year)						
Total Government Debt[2/]	26.4	28.8	28.8	40.1	44.1	43.0
External Debt	..	8.3	11.4	13.9	17.2	17.4
Domestic Debt	..	20.5	17.4	26.2	26.9	25.6
Other Series						
Primary balance, excluding interest	−1.2	−2.9	−2.3	−1.1	−5.8	−4.5
Memo Items:						
Privatization Proceeds	1.8	0.6	0.7	0.3	4.4	3.7
GDP at market prices (billions of koruny)	628.6	708.7	775.0	835.7	908.7	989.

Notes: 1/ Excludes privatization receipts, includes called off guarantees and interests on bank restructuring bonds.
        2/ Includes debts assumed by the bank restructuring agencies in 1999–2000, and Sk 100 billion (11 percent
        of GDP) in bank restructuring bonds issued in the first quarter of 2001.
Source: Slovak Ministry of Finance and Staff Calculations.

TABLE 5: SLOVAK REPUBLIC—MONETARY SURVEY AND INTEREST RATES
(billions of koruny)

	1995	1996	1997	1998	1999	2000	Nov. 2001
I. Monetary Survey							
A) Billions of koruny-stock end year							
Net foreign assets	91.7	88.5	131.2	121.5	177.8	268.5	282.8
Domestic credit	270.8	349.2	469.4	483.9	490.8	531.0	600.4
Claims on public sector	118.9	152.2	165.5	153.9	186.7	255.6	362.2
Claims on private sector	143.4	184.4	289.1	329.3	303.7	275.0	237.9
Claims on Other Financial Institutions	8.5	12.5	14.8	0.7	0.4	0.4	0.3
Total assets (= total liabilities)	362.5	437.7	600.6	605.4	668.7	799.5	883.2
Liquid liabilities[1]	353.0	410.1	445.8	467.8	522.2	601.4	646.8
Bonds	4.4	12.0	13.3	12.0	8.7	7.1	5.5
Long term foreign liabilities	15.4	14.8	14.2	12.9	5.5	1.9	4.8
All other net	−10.4	0.7	127.4	112.8	132.3	189.0	227.0
B) Shares of GDP (%)							
Net foreign assets	16.1	14.1	18.5	15.7	21.3	29.5	28.6
Domestic credit	47.6	55.5	66.2	62.4	58.7	58.4	60.7
to public sector	20.9	24.2	23.4	19.9	22.3	28.1	36.6
to private sector	25.2	29.3	40.8	42.5	36.3	30.3	24.1
Liquid liabilities	62.1	65.2	62.9	60.4	62.5	66.2	65.4
Long term foreign liabilities	2.7	2.4	2.0	1.7	0.7	0.2	0.5
C) Real annual growth rates (%)							
Net foreign assets	..	−8.8	39.7	−13.2	32.3	34.8	−1.8
Domestic credit	..	21.8	26.7	−3.4	−8.3	−3.4	5.4
to public sector	..	21.0	2.5	−12.8	9.7	22.2	32.1
to private sector	..	21.5	47.8	6.7	−16.6	−19.1	−19.4
Liquid liabilities	..	9.8	2.4	−1.6	0.9	2.8	0.2
Long term foreign liabilities	..	−9.2	−9.7	−15.1	−61.1	−69.5	135.7
II. Interest rates (%)							
Money market rate	..	..	..	..	..	8.1	7.8
Central Bank Discount Rate (end period %)	..	8.8	8.8	8.8	8.8	8.8	8.8
Treasury bill rate	..	..	..	..	..	8.3	7.8
Deposit rate[2]	9.0	9.3	13.4	16.3	14.4	8.5	6.4
Lending rate[3]	16.9	13.9	18.7	21.2	21.1	14.9	11.2
Real deposit rate[4]		3.3	6.9	9.0	3.4	−3.2	−0.8
Real lending rate[4]		7.7	11.8	13.6	9.5	2.6	3.7

Notes: 1/ Includes Money and Quasimoney only.
2/ Beginning in January 1996, weighted average interest rate offered on short-term deposits of the private sector during the reference period; 1995 weighted average rate offered by commercial banks on all accepted deposits.
3/ Beginning in January 1995, weighted average interest rate on short-term loans granted to the private corporate sector during the reference period.
4/ CPI based.
Source: IMF, IFS May 2002.

TABLE 6: SLOVAK REPUBLIC—BALANCE OF PAYMENTS
(US$ millions)

	1995	1996	1997	1998	1999	2000	2001	2002 proj.
Current Account								
Exports of goods & services	10,955	10,899	11,809	13,015	12,292	14,161	15,122	16,490
Exports of goods	8,579	8,831	9,639	10,720	10,229	11,914	12,632	13,812
Exports of services	2,376	2,068	2,170	2,295	2,063	2,247	2,490	2,678
Imports of goods & services	10,643	13,156	13,816	15,349	13,167	14,619	16,776	18,281
Imports of goods, f.o.b.	8,807	11,124	11,720	13,074	11,322	12,812	14,766	16,055
Imports of services	1,836	2,032	2,096	2,275	1,845	1,807	2,010	2,226
Net trade in goods & services	312	−2,257	−2,007	−2,334	−875	−458	−1,654	−1,791
Income receipts	..	..	316	437	300	269	322	333
Income payments	..	..	438	594	601	622	635	688
Net income from abroad	−14	−45	−122	−157	−301	−353	−313	−355
Private current transfer receipts	..	..	543	646	465	345	500	..
Private current transfer payments	..	..	368	279	270	227	288	..
Net private current transfers	92	203	175	367	196	118	212	190
Net official current transfers	..	..	..	−1	0	−3	−9	0
Current Account Balance	390	−2,099	−1,954	−2,124	−980	−693	−1,755	−1,956
Capital & Financial Account								
Net official capital grants	46	30	0	71	160	91	78	105
Net total private investment inflows	380	295	121	1,107	1,379	2,751	1,243	4,914
Net direct investment inflows	134	199	95	314	756	1,914	1,460	4,168
Net portfolio investment inflows	246	96	26	793	623	837	−217	746
Net LT borrowing	395	985	1,146	796	301	−345	−46	−166
Disbursements	1,052	2,033	2,226	1,843	1,511	1,543	1,119	1,307
Repayments due	726	1,184	1,187	1,214	1,226	1,804	1,127	1,508
Other LT inflows, net	69	136	107	167	16	−84	−38	35
Other capital flows, net	559	1,150	549	−145	−306	−1,025	593	945
Net short-term capital	91	882	581	27	84	−1,099	619	261
Capital flows n.e.i.								
Errors and omissions	468	268	−32	−172	−390	74	−26	684
Reserves, net change (negative sign indicates increase)	−1,771	−362	137	295	−555	−779	−112	−3,842
Other Series								
Net reserves (end of period, incl. gold)	3,449	3,498	3,302	2,937	3,430	4,075	4,186	..
Reserves as months of imports GS	..	3.2	2.9	2.3	3.1	3.4	3.0	5.3
GDP (millions of US$)	19,147	20,506	21,079	21,996	20,204	19,742	20,459	22,62

Source: LDB and IMF Art. IV Consultation June 2002.

TABLE 7: SLOVAK REPUBLIC—TRADE
(millions of US$)

	1995	1996	1997	1998	1999	2000	2001
A. Exports (fob, US$)							
Food and live animals (0)	431.3	331.3	332.1	343.4	306.9	300.1	346.7
Beverages and tobacco (1)	75.0	63.6	65.7	56.9	51.1	51.0	55.3
Crude materials (2)	437.2	393.4	409.4	382.6	388.7	385.3	418.5
Fuels and related products (3)	362.5	434.3	444.6	375.4	491.0	830.6	836.2
Animal and vegetable oils and fats (4)	9.2	12.1	14.8	19.8	15.3	14.4	18.1
Chemicals and related products (5)	1,132.1	1,096.8	1,039.5	949.7	808.1	941.7	926.3
Intermediate manufactured products (6)	3,469.1	3,379.5	3,272.6	3,201.4	2,792.5	3,172.7	3,472.8
Machinery and transport equipment (7)	1,614.7	2,047.0	2,737.3	3,982.7	4,040.5	4,690.7	4,887.9
Miscellaneous manufactured articles (8)	1,045.5	1,065.8	1,318.2	1,350.7	1,319.5	1,519.9	1,718.7
Other (9)	2.3	7.3	4.7	4.1	15.3	7.6	10.5
Total	8,578.9	8,831.1	9,638.9	10,666.7	10,228.9	11,914.0	12,691.0
B. Imports (fob, US$)							
Food and live animals (0)	604.7	670.9	659.2	686.3	583.0	572.8	671.7
Beverages and tobacco (1)	96.1	120.3	122.4	116.3	130.2	106.1	117.2
Crude materials (2)	525.6	543.7	516.0	500.2	430.2	495.7	539.3
Fuels and related products (3)	1,535.1	1,861.4	1,826.9	1,534.0	1,460.4	2,236.4	2,234.6
Animal and vegetable oils and fats (4)	17.6	19.4	21.5	27.3	22.6	30.1	41.7
Chemicals and related products (5)	1,189.2	1,282.1	1,354.0	1,382.1	1,279.3	1,399.1	1,514.4
Intermediate manufactured products (6)	1,560.8	1,700.5	1,929.3	2,343.5	2,071.7	2,266.6	2,713.8
Machinery and transport equipment (7)	2,534.9	3,917.6	4,190.6	5,184.2	4,268.0	4,556.3	5,524.4
Miscellaneous manufactured articles (8)	698.0	995.6	1,046.5	1,294.4	1,075.5	1,148.9	1,325.2
Other (9)	8.5	11.9	5.5	6.3	0.0	1.8	2.7
Total	8,770.5	11,123.4	11,671.9	13,074.6	1,320.9	12,813.8	14,685.0

Source: IMF Statistical Appendix Art. IV Consultation, July 2002.

TABLE 8: SLOVAK REPUBLIC—EXTERNAL DEBT AND DEBT SERVICE

	1997	1998	1999	2000	2001
I. (millions of US dollars)					
A. Debt Outstanding and Disbursed (DOD)					
Total long term	5,443.6	7,347.6	7,874.4	8,573.1	8,570.6
Public	1,526.3	2,560.9	2,876.1	3,567.9	3,709.3
Private	3,917.3	4,786.7	4,998.3	5,005.2	4,861.3
Short term	4,290.0	4,604.5	2,706.0	2,415.1	2,943.9
IMF	258.2	188.5	136.2	0.0	0.0
Total DOD	9,991.8	12,140.6	10,716.6	10,988.2	11,514.5
B. Debt Service					
Interest	274.4	524.7	567.9	557.8	584.1
Amortizations	1,154.4	1,274.5	1,391.8	1,837.7	1,087.1
IMF repurchases	67.7	80.3	60.0	132.8	0.0
Total	1,496.5	1,879.5	2,019.7	2,528.3	1,671.2
II. Ratios (%)					
Total DOD to GDP	47.4	55.2	53.0	55.7	56.3
Total DOD to Xgsict[1/]	..	86.1	82.1	74.4	72.3
Debt service to Xgsict[1/]	..	13.3	15.5	17.1	10.5

Notes: 1/ Xgsict—exports of goods, services, income and current transfers.
Source: LDB.

TABLE 9: SLOVAK REPUBLIC—FINANCIAL SECTOR INDICATORS

	1999	2000	2001
A. Banking System			
1. Depth and Structure			
Total domestic credit (% of GDP)	58.7	58.4	60.7
of which private credit (% of GDP)	36.3	30.3	24.1
Number of deposit money banks	26	23	21
Number of banks with foreign participation to capital (%)	14	16	15
2. Efficiency and Strength			
Domestic interest spread (%)[1/]	6.7	6.4	4.8
Spread of (5-y benchmark) bond (basis points)[2/]	248.0	181.0	56.0
Non-performing loans as % of total	23.7	15.3	14.0
Return on equity	−36.5	25.2	25.3
B. Stock Market			
Capitalization (% of GDP)[3/]	23.3	23.7	23.6
Trading Turnovers (% of GDP) Bratislava Stock Exchange (BSE)	22.5	28.1	39.8
No. of listed companies on the stock exchanges[4/]	1,014	926	906
Share price index (1996=100)	43.3	51.7	68.0

Notes: 1/ Calculated as difference between short-term lending and deposit rates as per Table 5.
    2/ Five-year euro-denominated eurobond, over German five-year bond.
    3/ Market capitalization of registered companies on the Slovak Stock Exchange and on BSE.
    4/ Includes number of listed companies on BSE and registered companies on Slovak Stock Exchange.
Source: LDB, SNB, Bratislava Stock Exchange, DataStream and WB Survey of Bank Regulation and Supervision.

TABLE 10: SLOVAK REPUBLIC—VULNERABILITY INDICATORS

	1999	2000	2001
A. Market Indicators			
Annual percent change in average exchange rate (SKK/USD)	17.4	11.3	5.0
Annual change in T-Bill rates on the primary market (%)	−17.0	−51.9	5.4
Spread of (5-y benchmark) bond (basis points)[1/]	248	181	56
Annual change in stock market index (%)	−18.0	19.5	31.5
B. Risk Ratings			
Foreign currency sovereign rating (Moody's)[2/]	Ba1	Ba1	Baa3
Foreign currency sovereign rating (Standard & Poor's)	BB+	BB+	BBB−
C. Financial			
Annual growth in real domestic credit (%)	−8.3	−3.4	5.4
Foreign currency deposits to total deposits e.o.y. (%)	15.9	16.4	16.6
Non-perfm. loans of commercial banks (% of total)	23.7	15.3	14.0
D. Reserve Cover Indicators			
Reserve cover of imports (months of imports)	3.1	3.4	3.0
Reserves to short term debt	126.8	168.7	142.2
Reserves/M2	27.5	31.8	29.9
E. Prices			
Annual change in terms of trade (%)	−2.1	−0.2	−2.2
Annual appreciation REER (%)	2.2	−9.8	−0.1
F. External			
Current account balance (% of GDP)	−4.9	−3.6	−8.6
External Debt (% of GDP)	53.0	55.7	56.3
G. Fiscal sustainability indicators			
Total Government Debt (% of GDP)[3/]	40.1	44.1	43.0
Overall public sector balance (% of GDP)	−4.2	−9.1	−8.5
Primary balance (Overall bal.-interest; % of GDP)	−1.1	−5.8	−4.5

Notes: 1/ Five-year euro-denominated eurobond, over German five-year bond.
2/ Since November 2001 stable outlook; in 2002—Baa3 positive outlook (change in outlook in October).
3/ Includes debts assumed by the bank restructuring agencies in 1999–2000, and Sk 105 billion (11% GDP) in bank restructuring bonds issued in the first quarter of 2001.
Sources: IMF, IFS May 2002, NBS and LDB.

TABLE 11: SLOVAK REPUBLIC—INVESTMENT CLIMATE

	Year	Slovak Republic	Income Group Average	High-Income Average
Private Investment Environment				
Private Investment/Gross Domestic Fixed Investment (%)	1995–1999	..	77.9	79.0
Domestic Credit to Private Sector (stock, % GDP)	2000	30.3	48.4	136.3
Real lending Rate[1]	2001	3.7	..	..
Highest Marginal Corporate Tax Rate (%)	2000	25	..	..
Euromoney Credit Rating	Sep-01	..	57.2	90.2
ICRG Composite Risk Rating	Mar-02	73.5	73.8	83.7
Institutional Investor Risk Rating	Sep-01	..	49.5	85.3
Governance				
ICRG Corruption Rating (1–6, bad to good)	Oct-01	4		
ICRG Bureaucratic Quality Rating (1–6)	Oct-01	3		
ICRG Law and Order (1–6)	Oct-01	4		
Openness				
Trade (imports+exports)/GDP (%)	2001	133.8	56.7	44.0
FDI inflows (net, % GDP)	2001	7.1	3.3	4.1
WTO member?	1995	Y		
Infrastructure				
Paved Roads, % of total	1999	86.7	47.3	92.9
Vehicles (per 1000 persons)	2000	260	191	..
Cost of Calls to US (US$ per 3 min)	2000	1.1	2.4	1.8
Internet Users (per 10,000 people)	1999	39	763	2,988
Electricity consumption (kwh per capita)	1999	4,216.2	2,427	8,496
GDP per unit energy use (PPP $ per Kg oil equivalent)	1999	3.2	4.7	4.8
Wages and Productivity				
Minimum Wage (US$ per year)	1995–99	1,063.5	..	..
Labor Cost Per Worker in Manufacturing (US$ per year)	1995–99	3,829.4	..	..
Value Added Per Worker in Manufacturing (US$ per year)	1995–99	11,066.7	..	..
Labor Force with Secondary Education (% of total)[2]	1998	91.1	..	..
R&D Expenditure (% of GNI)	1995	1.0	1.0	2.3

Notes: 1/ CPI based.
 2/ Includes unfinished secondary education.
Source: WDI.

TABLE 12: SLOVAK REPUBLIC—MILLENNIUM DEVELOPMENT GOALS INDICATORS

	1990	1995	1999	2000
1 Eradicate extreme poverty and hunger 2015 target = halve 1990 $1 a day poverty and malnutrition rates				
Population below $1 a day (%)	2.0	..	..	..
Poverty gap at $1 a day (%)	0.5	..	..	..
Percentage share of income or consumption held by poorest 20%	11.9	..	..	..
Prevalence of child malnutrition (% of children under 5)	..	..	..	..
Population below minimum level of dietary energy consumption (%)	..	..	..	..
2 Achieve universal primary education 2015 target = net enrollment to 100				
Net primary enrollment ratio (% of relevant age group)	..	..	..	..
Gross primary enrollment ratio (% of relevant age group)[1/]	..	..	102.9	..
Percentage of cohort reaching grade 5 (%)	..	..	..	..
Youth literacy rate (% ages 15–24)	..	..	..	..
3 Promote gender equality 2005 target = education ratio to 100				
Ratio of girls to boys in primary and secondary education (%)	98.1	95.2	96.8	..
Ratio of young literate females to males (% ages 15–24)	..	..	..	..
Share of women employed in the nonagricultural sector (%)	30.7	45.8	46.7	..
Proportion of seats held by women in national parliament (%)	10.0	..	21.0	..
4 Reduce child mortality 2015 target = reduce 1990 under 5 mortality by two-thirds				
Under 5 mortality rate (per 1,000)	14.1	13.1	..	9.7
Infant mortality rate (per 1,000 live births)	12.0	11.0	8.3	8.3
Immunization, measles (% of children under 12 months)	..	99.0	99.0	..
5 Improve maternal health 2015 target = reduce 1990 maternal mortality by three-fourths				
Maternal mortality ratio (modeled estimate, per 100,000 live births)	..	14.0	..	..
Births attended by skilled health staff (% of total)	..	..	..	..
6 Combat HIV/AIDS, malaria and other diseases 2015 target = halt, and begin to reverse, AIDS				
Prevalence of HIV, female (% ages 15–24)	..	..	0.2	..
Contraceptive prevalence rate (% of women ages 15–49)	..	..	..	..
Number of children orphaned by HIV/AIDS	..	..	..	..
Incidence of tuberculosis (per 100,000 people)	..	..	28.0	..
Tuberculosis cases detected under DOTS (%)	..	..	36.0	..

TABLE 12: SLOVAK REPUBLIC—MILLENNIUM DEVELOPMENT GOALS INDICATORS (CONTINUED)

7 Ensure environmental sustainability 2015 target				
Forest area (% of total land area)	41.1	..	..	42.5
Nationally protected areas (% of total land area)	..	21.8	22.6	..
GDP per unit of energy use (PPP $ per kg oil equivalent)	2.2	2.7	3.2	..
CO2 emissions (metric tons per capita)	8.1	7.6	7.1	..
Access to an improved water source (% of population)	..	..	..	100.0
Access to improved sanitation (% of population)	..	..	..	100.0
8 Develop a Global Partnership for Development 2015 target				
Youth unemployment rate (% of total labor force ages 15–24)[2]	..	24.8	32.2	35.2
Fixed line and mobile telephones (per 1,000 people)	135.2	210.7	429.6	519.4
Personal computers (per 1,000 people)	..	41.0	109.3	136.9

Notes: 1/ Enrollment ratio for 1999-2000 according to UNESCO Statistics.

2/ Source for 2000: Slovak Statistical Office - Social Trends in the Slovak Republic 2001.

Source: World Development Indicators and Statistical Office of the Slovak Republic.

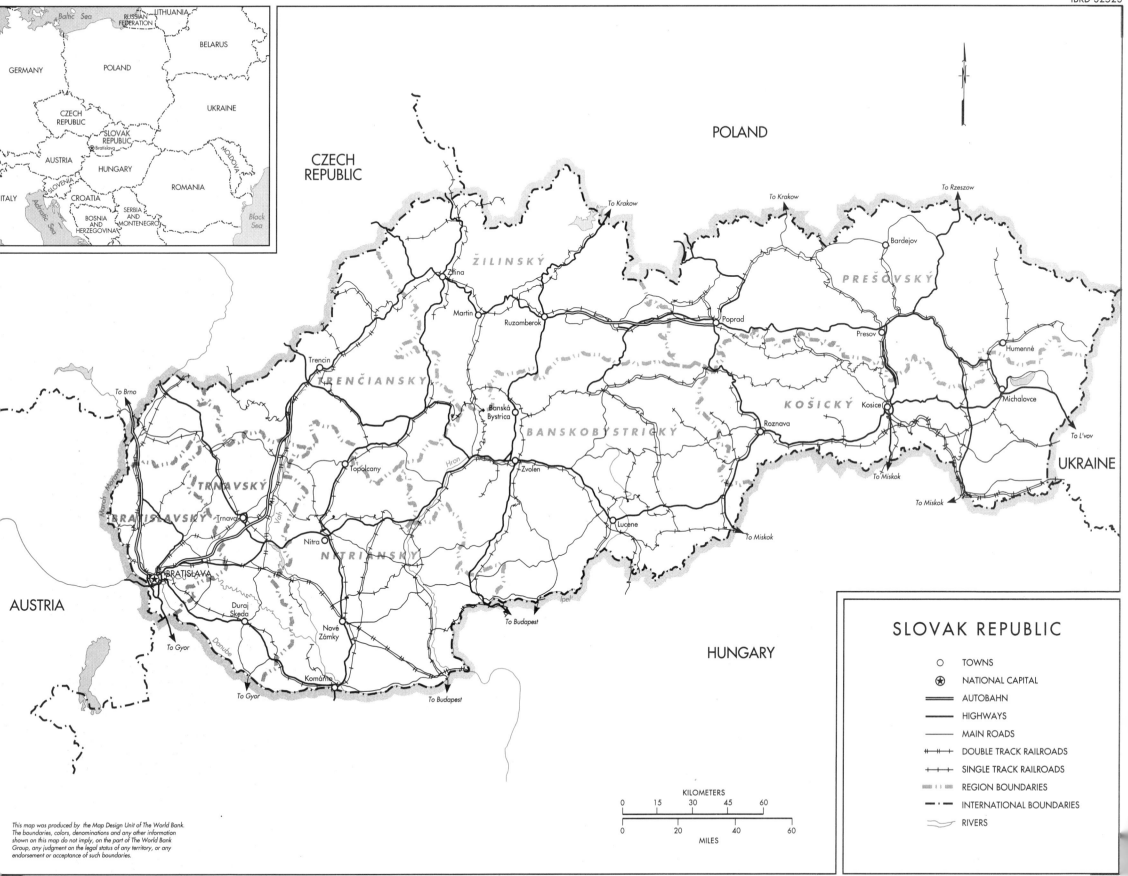

IBRD 32523

SLOVAK REPUBLIC

LITHUANIA
RUSSIAN FEDERATION
BELARUS
GERMANY
POLAND
UKRAINE
CZECH REPUBLIC
SLOVAK REPUBLIC
Bratislava
AUSTRIA
HUNGARY
MOLDOVA
SLOVENIA
CROATIA
ROMANIA
ITALY
SERBIA AND MONTENEGRO
BOSNIA AND HERZEGOVINA
Baltic Sea
Black Sea
Adriatic Sea

POLAND

CZECH REPUBLIC

To Krakow
To Krakow
To Rzeszow

ŽILINSKÝ
Zilina
Bardejov
PREŠOVSKÝ

Martin
Ruzomberok
Poprad
Presov
Humenné

Trencin

TRENČIANSKY

Banská Bystrica
KOŠICKÝ
Kosice
Michalovce

To Brno

BANSKOBYSTRICKÝ
Roznava

Topolcany
Zvolen
To L'vov

UKRAINE

TRNAVSKÝ
Hron
To Miskok

Vah

Nitra
Trnava
Lucene
To Miskok

BRATISLAVSKY

NITRIANSKY
To Miskok

BRATISLAVA

Moroe

AUSTRIA

Duraj Skeda

Nové Zámky
Ipel
To Budapest

To Gyor
Danube

HUNGARY

Komárno
To Gyor
To Budapest

SLOVAK REPUBLIC

○ TOWNS
⊛ NATIONAL CAPITAL
AUTOBAHN
HIGHWAYS
MAIN ROADS
DOUBLE TRACK RAILROADS
SINGLE TRACK RAILROADS
REGION BOUNDARIES
INTERNATIONAL BOUNDARIES
RIVERS

KILOMETERS
0   15   30   45   60

0   20   40   60
MILES

This map was produced by the Map Design Unit of The World Bank.
The boundaries, colors, denominations and any other information
shown on this map do not imply, on the part of The World Bank
Group, any judgment on the legal status of any territory, or any
endorsement or acceptance of such boundaries.

JUNE 2003